Last Man Standing

Last Man Standing

'Pick up Christy O'Connor's book *Last Man Standing*.
You won't regret it.' *Irish Examiner*

'Features a series of brutally honest interviews with several of the best
hurling goalkeepers in the game, and should be made mandatory
reading for every GAA fan in the country. Not just because of its
style and content, both of which are top-class, but because
of what it reveals.' *Irish Examiner*

'One of the best GAA publications ever released.
A perfect book for GAA fans.' *Irish Daily Star*

'As good as it gets in the GAA genre.' *Munster Express*

'O'Connor offers the reader unrivalled insight into the lives of people
such as Fitzgerald, Donal Óg Cusack, Damien Fitzhenry and James
McGarry. Carries some fascinating accounts about what it takes
to become the best in your field and what it's like to win
and lose in the Championship.' *Irish News*

'It doesn't come as a huge surprise to learn that [Seán Óg Ó hAilpín]
is close to Donal Óg Cusack, a highly-motivated figure like himself.
Insights into Cusack's obsessive nature are contained in Christy
O'Connor's excellent book, *Last Man Standing*, revealing long
and lonely hours spent preparing for the hurling season.'
Sunday Independent

Last Man Standing

CHRISTY O'CONNOR

THE O'BRIEN PRESS
DUBLIN

First published 2005 by The O'Brien Press Ltd,
20 Victoria Road, Dublin 6, Ireland.
Tel: +353 1 4923333; Fax: +353 1 4922777
E-mail: books@obrien.ie
Website: www.obrien.ie
Reprinted 2005.

ISBN: 0-86278-922-2

British Library Cataloguing-in-Publication Data
Last Man Standing : hurling goalkeepers
1.Hurling players 2.Hurling (Game)
I.Title
796.3'5

2 3 4 5 6 7 8 9
05 06 07 08 09 10

Editing, typesetting, layout and design: The O'Brien Press Ltd
Printing: Creative Print and Design, Wales

DEDICATED TO MY PARENTS

TOM AND JOAN

ACKNOWLEDGEMENTS

It would not have been possible to write this book without the assistance and access granted to me by the twelve hurling championship goalkeepers. Every single one of them could not have been more helpful and giving of their time and their loyalty and honesty is more appreciated than they will ever know. Some of them are friends who I have known for a long time, while others are people who I have got to know really well, but all of them are players I have always admired and respected.

I also owe a huge debt of gratitude to all the other people who agreed to be interviewed for this book. Due to restrictions, some people who were very generous with their time have not appeared in this book, but I would like to thank everyone who spoke to me.

This book was definitely the most rewarding and enjoyable project of my career but it was made even more enjoyable by the fact that my fiancée, Olivia, was there to accompany me during most of the matches and to share the experiences. She was the one constant for me and it is great to be able to look back and remember the special times we had on the terraces all summer.

Kieran Shannon has been a great friend to me, both as a journalist and as a person. He is someone I have learned a lot from as a journalist and he has always been very helpful during my career. Damian Lawlor, Aoife de Paor and Michael Foley are three other journalists who have always been very supportive to me as well and I would like to take this opportunity to thank them too.

I would also like to extend my gratitude to Sportsfile, and especially to Damien Eagers, to Gearóid in The O'Brien Press and to Liam Griffin. I would also like to thank Seán, Donal, Joe, Lorcan, Patsy and Claire for their friendship and to extend my thanks in particular to Eoin and Fran for all their support during the writing of this book. I would also like to say a big thanks to Derek, for helping me to come up with the title.

The final word goes to my family. My brother James has brought great pride and honour to our family: he and my younger brother John and my two sisters, Sheila and Claire, have always been very special people in my life. Finally, this book is dedicated to my parents, Tom and Joan, the two people in this world who have had the greatest influence on me as a person.

Christy O'Connor, Ennis, July 2005

CONTENTS

FOREWORD

When Christy O'Connor first asked me to read this book, I didn't really know what to expect from it. I knew it would be a good read but I didn't expect to be blown away like I was. This is one hell of a sports book.

I think anyone who reads this book will have their views on goalkeeping and goalkeepers altered forever. Only a goalkeeper could have written this book but he had to be a particular kind of keeper. He had to have lived, not at the very top, but within touching distance of it. He had to have lived there to really understand.

Christy O'Connor lived for many years in the shadow of Clare's Davy Fitzgerald, one of the greatest and most driven goalkeepers the game of hurling has ever known.

Christy has a broad, deep and genuine passion for the game of hurling that very few people possess. The trust, understanding and respect he has earned from his fellow goalkeepers has enabled him to breach the inner sanctum of the GAA world for the first time ever. It offers a fascinating insight into that world.

It is a fantastic read because Christy also has the combined gift that the goalkeepers, whose stories he tells, do not have: the gift of the writer and the storyteller.

This book is of great value and it will help rid some men of their demons. It should also teach us to stop demonising these exceptional, courageous and often lonely souls, who have the guts to be the 'Last Man Standing'.

Liam Griffin, Wexford, June 2005

JUST DO IT

Monday morning 5 January 2004, it's cold and dank and you can almost feel the gloom of depression hanging in the air as people head back to work after the Christmas break. At 6.01am, Donal Óg Cusack's alarm goes off in his house in Cloyne. He knows what's ahead of him so he has already prepared the night before. His gear is laid out across a chair in the corner of the room and his work clothes are already packed away in his bag. At 6.15am, he's out the door. Time to purge the guilt.

He heads off for work in De Puy Johnson and Johnson in Ringaskiddy. It takes him forty minutes to get there and when he arrives, he heads straight to the gym, already suited up and ready for action. He works in the facilities department of the plant and looks after the company gym, so he lets himself in. There's rarely anyone ever there at that hour of the morning and there certainly isn't anybody present this morning. He likes the silence of working alone and he goes about his business for an hour before he starts work.

Cusack begins with a run, then some stretching before concentrating on core exercises. It's not easy this morning but he banishes any thoughts of neglect and punishes his muscles until they threaten to desert him. He completed this routine every day for six weeks before Christmas before he took a break. It's time to deposit more fuel in the tank now before the Cork panel heads off to Vietnam for their team holiday on Thursday. After that, this is a ritual he's determined not to break.

Even now, with over six weeks of hard work behind him, which was only briefly punctuated by some mild Christmas excess, Cusack doesn't feel that fit. The rest of the Cork panel, especially Timmy McCarthy, are always taking the piss out of him about his bowlegs that are always hopping off one another. The only response he has for them is that if he had Seán Óg Ó hAilpín's gazelle-type limbs, or if he didn't have that dragging, consistent pain inside his right knee all the way up through his groin, he'd leave them all for dust in his vapour trail.

Cusack probably does that bit extra, not because he has to, but because of who he is. He is a goalkeeper. A hurling goalkeeper. Although nearly all players train on their own at one stage or another, goalkeepers do it more often than most others because they have to get accustomed to being alone when it matters. Of course they train with the team but they do more training, specific to their needs, alone. They can work and work on the technicalities they need to master, and they do, but no amount of training can prepare you to be alone at the death. Or to learn how to take the blame. Goalkeepers learn to be lone-minded and are familiar with such a frame of mind. They have to be because of the position they play in. Disappointment is one of the most fundamental emotions in sport and goalkeepers are the natural focus for it because they walk a tightrope between triumph and disaster. In Cusack's position, calmness is the only means of survival and he has depended on it plenty of times in the past. Especially in the last year and a half.

On the night after Cork beat Wexford in the previous year's All-Ireland semi-final replay, Cusack got a taxi home to Cloyne after a night's drinking with the squad in Cork city.

Before long, the talk drifted to hurling and that day's other All-Ireland semi-final between Kilkenny and Tipperary. The taxi-driver honed in on Brendan Cummins' outstanding display, and without knowing who his passenger was, used it as a stick to beat Cusack with. He told him that if Cork had a keeper half as good as Cummins, they wouldn't have needed a replay to beat Wexford. Cusack agreed with him, and let him continue with his stream of invective.

The vitriol rolled off his tongue for nearly twenty minutes. Cusack urged him on, agreeing with everything he said about how poor the Cork keeper was in an attempt to see how much poison he could extract. By the time they got to Cloyne, the air was septic with it. Cusack paid him, got out and then spotted a friend across the road who was locking his car. 'What's my name, Jamesie?' he asked his friend. 'Donal Óg,' his friend replied with a bemused look. 'Donal Óg who?' 'Donal Óg Cusack.' The Cork hurling goalkeeper just turned to the taxi-driver and introduced himself. He left it at that and walked in home.

He knows the knives are out for him. A lot of people in the county blame him for losing the 2003 All-Ireland final against Kilkenny. Martin Comerford's goal with five minutes to go plunged a dagger into Cork's hearts and most of the public felt it was a ball that should have been stopped. Even though Comerford was inside the 14-metre line, Cusack was still beaten at his near post.

Comerford didn't strike it well, but there was plenty of deception concealed in the shot. It hopped off the ground and spun past Cusack. It was one of those balls that a keeper almost watches going past him in slow motion. Every keeper feels a shot like that should be saved, but it's extremely difficult to judge the flight of the ball when it kicks off the turf. Especially with the new sliotar on that Croke Park sod that's like concrete. Everyone might blame him, but he doesn't blame himself. He firmly believes that but he's standing up for himself because nobody else will.

He has to be big now because there is a chasing pack on his tail. Paul Morrissey has been playing well with Newtownshandrum while Martin Coleman was solid last season with the Under-21s. All summer the public had been building a case against Cusack, but after the All-Ireland they didn't have to look too far for hard evidence to corroborate their view that he wasn't good enough to play for Cork anymore.

He was captain of Cloyne last year and they reached the semi-final of the Cork championship for the first time in their history. Even though they were facing the champions, Blackrock, they felt their time had come. They trained like US Navy Seals and Cusack became the focal point for that fanatical ambition. Before the quarter-final, seven of the panel announced their plans to take a sun holiday. They would be home in time for the match but Cusack told them he didn't want them to go. A few home truths were spelled out. In the end, six cancelled the holiday and the guy who did go came home on the Thursday before the game.

On the night before the semi-final, Cusack got nailed with a job at work. It had been scheduled for three months in advance, he had committed himself to it and he wasn't going to break his word. He would still be in bed early and focussed for the game the following day.

On the night, the job consisted of closing 2.500 amp circuit breakers that feed the power into the Johnson and Johnson plant. It involved more hand movement than he anticipated but he still thought nothing of it. He went home, got a good night's sleep and got up ready the next morning to lead his team into history.

Out on the pitch beforehand, he did a full half an hour warm-up with the rest of the squad. He had worn a tracksuit in the warm-up but he took it off just before the game began. He was wearing a short-sleeved jersey and his hands began getting cold and stiff as the sweat was cooling off his body. Ten minutes into the game, he called Seán Motherway, the Cloyne subkeeper, and instructed him to go to the corner-flag and drop a few balls into him. He wanted to check if it was just the cold or whether it was the effects from the previous evening's toil. Cloyne were facing into a stiff breeze and he wanted his handling to be spot-on.

A couple of minutes later, a ball was launched from the Blackrock half-back line and it carried in the breeze. In an instant, it was dropping down on top of Cusack.

Bodies were gathering around him, he should have batted it away, but instinct took over. He tried to grab it, the ball broke off his hand and sneaked inside the far post. Cloyne lost by two points.

If they'd won, they felt they would have rattled Newtownshandrum in the final. A Munster club title could possibly have been bagged and Cusack would have been nominated Cork captain this season. If you thought his head was wrecked before, it felt ten times worse after that incident.

'There still isn't a day that goes by that I don't think about those two games,' said Cusack. 'When I think of those two goals, it's like pure torture for me. Even now, it just rips me apart thinking about it. That Kilkenny goal still constantly flashes into my mind but it's not as bad now as what it was. It only comes into my mind now about once a day. It just breaks my heart and you'd wonder about packing it all in. But I'm after deciding now to go hell for leather and do my best again this year. And after that, I'll think about it again.'

On Thursday 8 January, the Cork squad flew to Vietnam for their holiday. When they arrived in Ho Chi Minh City, Donal O'Grady left Cusack, Seán Óg Ó hAilpín and Joe Deane in charge of organising collective training. On their first day out there, Cusack and Ó hAilpín went off looking for a field for thirty guys to train in. Tom Kenny, Paul Tierney and Adrian Coughlan joined them.

Just one hundred metres down the road from their own hotel in the centre of Saigon, they spotted a field adjacent to another hotel that looked perfect for their requirements. They asked security in the hotel about the possibility of using the field, but the request wasn't even entertained. So they set off in search of another training facility. The heat was savage and the humidity was a killer but the five of them walked roughly ten miles in their pursuit of a piece of green grass. It was torture but they never relented.

They checked out every backwater and hick piece of territory around the town but nothing materialised. At one stage they ran into a group of English guys who wondered were they looking for some crowd to take them on in a five-a-side soccer match. In the end, they failed to find something suitable and decided to take their chances with the first field. They weighed up their options and reckoned that they'd only need it for forty minutes before anyone would cop it. After half an hour of shuttle runs the following evening, the security personnel from the hotel arrived out and cleared them. The field had served its purpose.

After the training session thirty white bodies crawled up the street suffering from near exhaustion. Some venerable old locals that were sitting out in the street looked on in amazement. Some of them had that stare, that perplexed look on their faces that suggested that perhaps time had just played a trick on their minds and a batch of US marines were returning from a training camp without their armoury!

When the squad flew east to China Beach a week later, it was like landing in paradise for Cusack and the commando wing of the panel. Their hotel backed right onto the beach so their training ground was in their back yard. On the first day there they decided to go for a three-mile run in the sand. They mapped it out but they didn't know what they were letting themselves in for. The heat was ridiculous and the sand was sticky but the competition was even worse. They all dogged it out.

After that, if they didn't train they played soccer amongst themselves almost every day, picking the teams on the basis of the country lads versus the city boys. The games were never less than ultra-competitive. At one stage, Sean Óg Ó hAilpín called the city fellas into a huddle after getting a hiding. The country lads were sewing it into them, telling them they couldn't win a game unless it was down in Páirc Uí Chaoímh. It was like a red rag to a bull with Ó hAilpín. 'Have ye any pride in Cork city?' he asked them. Thousands of miles from home and O hAilpin couldn't let it go.

When they drank, they drank, but Cusack never wanted the holiday to be an alcoholic haze. One morning, Ó hAilpín called for him at 6.55am. They went down to the gym and did an hour and a half session, before heading to the beach for an hour's hurling. When Cusack went on his first holiday with the Cork seniors after they won the 1998 National League title, Brian Corcoran told him that the fellas who didn't bring their hurleys would spend the week asking the fellas that did for a loan of them. Cusack has often quoted him since and most fellas brought their sticks.

After the hurling session, Cusack and Ó hAilpín went to the pool for a dip, had their breakfast and then went for a lie-down. By 11am they were back on the beach again for another soccer game. On the beach that day, Cusack really felt that the bond between the players had cemented even more since the holiday began. Their bond has been made tighter from the hurt of last year. They're all still hurting. Badly.

They had Kilkenny on the ropes during the second half of the 2003 All-Ireland final but they just couldn't land the punch to knock them on the canvas. Comerford's goal was the sucker punch that flattened them instead and they couldn't recover. Thousands of miles from home, the memory of that loss and the mental inquisitions over the goal are still eating Cusack up. Eating him.

'Every day of the holidays, I thought about the last two games I played last year,' said Cusack. 'I just didn't feel right. Personally I didn't know whether to go drinking or training and I got caught between the two of them. Between training with Seán Óg in the morning and then going drinking with some of the other lads, I nearly fucking killed myself.'

The rest of them are still trying to rid themselves of the bad memories, the missed chances, and the lost opportunity. They're being positive about it all though. A couple of nights after the final, the squad was drinking in a lock-in at a city bar when a card game started up. John Gardiner was at the bar and one of the card players asked him if he wanted to join the game. Gardiner inquired what they were playing when someone said it was a game of 45. Gardiner told him that he didn't play 45, and he hardly had the words out of his mouth when some wisecrack told him that he couldn't hit 45s either. The painful memories of Gardiner's missed frees in the final were washed away momentarily by the laughter.

'Even though we're still fairly young, we're after seeing a lot of shit,' said Cusack. 'I don't think any other group gets on as well as we do, there's no fighting or anything and we all stick up for one another.'

Even though he's still only twenty six, this year is Cusack's eighth year on the panel, and he hopes it will be his sixth season as first choice keeper. He isn't the oldest member on the panel, or the team captain, or the best player, but in the Cork squad there is no influence greater than his. Brian Corcoran, Mark Landers, Fergal Ryan and Kevin Murray have all drifted away in the last couple of years and Cusack's presence has filled the vacuum.

He is one of their chief leaders now. Even though he had just lost an All-Ireland final and had conceded a goal as a result of which most people blamed him for losing the match the previous September, when the Cork players gathered in a huddle after the presentation, one voice dominated the discussion. Cusack could be spotted in the middle of the huddle, waving his finger and still laying down the law.

'I just remember the stadium being practically empty. Even though the presentation was just over, the place was deserted. I remember Mickey *(O'Connell)* with his nose bust and it was all just pure misery. I remember being so sad for the boys and saying that whatever we have to do over the winter, we have to get back here. Whatever had to be done, whatever cost it would be to ourselves.'

Everyone within the squad knows this guy has serious balls anyway. When the Cork hurlers went on strike two years before, Cusack was their leader and their median point. He was the player who went on Cork's 96FM and claimed that the County Board was being run by a crowd of yes men who were totally oblivious to the needs of the players. The players put their necks on the line with their subsequent strike but the guillotine was always perilously dangling over his head.

He knew he had set himself up but he did it for the good of the Cork players, with no thought of the potential damage it could do to himself. He didn't get that fanaticism from just anywhere. Eighty-three years ago, Christy Ring was born in a house which used to be two doors up from where Cusack grew up in the middle of Cloyne village. That house is levelled now, its site occupied by a statue of the greatest hurler that ever lived.

When Cusack was buying a house last year, there was only one place he had in mind. Ring's father and Cusack's great grandfather were brothers and the gable end of Cusack's new house is just ten yards from the Ring statue created by the Breton sculptor Yann Goulet. Just behind that is the Cloyne field where Ring's genius was forged and where the young goalkeeper went about perfecting his game as a child in the crucible of practice.

Home.

The holiday party flew back into Cork on 24 January and four days later they realized the holiday was really over. When they gathered in

Carrigtwohill for training, it was minus 2 degrees. They knew it was freezing because they could see the frost settling on top of the training cones. Cusack normally spends part of every training session with the other keepers but Morrissey and Coleman weren't there tonight so he ground his teeth and dogged it out. He has to dig in because he knows the knives are being sharpened for him around the county.

Over Christmas, he was in town with Diarmuid O'Sullivan and O'Sullivan's girlfriend Gráinne. They were in Reardons' and Cusack was afraid of losing his jacket so he got the keys of Gráinne's car and went out to deposit the jacket. Just a few yards outside the pub, he met a gang of seven fellas coming against him. They recognised him straightaway and, with force of numbers, rounded on him.

'You're fucking useless Cusack!' they roared at him. 'You bollocks, you cost us the All-Ireland!'

It saddened him that people he didn't know could be so callous but he'll always be ready for that type of abuse. He's had plenty of time to condition himself for it. Just as long as he is ready for the fight to hold onto his place.

'It's a big year for Donal Óg and he knows himself now that he's going to come under pressure,' said Ger Cunningham, who Cusack took over from in 1999 after eighteen years as Cork's first-choice keeper. 'I know that the selectors are going to give people chances this year and maybe the test will really come if they give Martin Coleman, Paul Morrissey or Anthony Nash a chance. If that happens, how will he react in that situation? These things kind of go in cycles and if he gets over this period and gets established again, he'll be fine.

'For now he knows the pressure is there and sometimes that can be a good thing or a bad thing. People buckle under pressure or they react to it. But he certainly won't be doing any less training than what he was doing because he's such a driven goalkeeper. He's so focussed and is so attentive to detail. That won't change but I'd maybe look at some of his training methods. That's just a personal opinion but Ogie will know how he's going. He's very independent. He's his own man.'

In January 2003, Cusack wrote down his three goals for the year ahead on a piece of paper. When he looked at them again a couple of weeks ago, he didn't change any of them because he hadn't met his targets or achieved those goals. He wanted to be as fit as he possibly could and he doesn't think he reached that standard. He had hoped to become the best goalkeeper in the country and he knows he fell a long way short of that target. And he wanted to do everything possible to help Cork win an All-Ireland. That is what's driving him on now.

At 9.30pm after training, Cusack sat into his car and drove home to Cloyne. The pain has returned in his leg, as it does after every hard training session. That dragging pain that crucifies him when he gets into the car. When he arrived in Cloyne, he hauled himself out of the vehicle and went in home. He laid out his gear again across the chair and packed his work clothes into his gearbag. The morning will soon be here and the gym will be calling him. This is it now. This is what lies ahead of him.

'I don't know if you get immune to this thing at all. I don't even know how to describe my motivation for playing or going back training. I was asking myself going down in the car "why am I doing this now and why am I going to go through all this again?" There's no description for it. It's like as if I have to do it. It's like as if it's something that I just have to do.'

He's just going to do it.

HOLE IN MY SOUL

Donal Óg Cusack may have his worries in the first week in February but at least he's still raging against the machine. Over in Limerick, Timmy Houlihan is gone. Mowed down, like roadkill, more like. At present, he's so far out in the wilderness that he can see the tumbleweed sweeping by him. And it hurts like nothing else.

In any other county with three All-Ireland Under-21 titles in four years, there would be no need to forensically trawl for two hundred players and herd them into practice games for six weeks before Christmas. It was a statement more than anything else from the new management that any amount of Under-21 medals didn't give you any special rank. Houlihan appreciated that the status of being one of only six players in the county to have played in all three wins wouldn't cut too much ice with the new management. But he didn't expect to get axed.

He lives just seven doors down from Ollie Moran in Castletroy and they were chatting one evening in December and they both decided if they couldn't make the first fifty, they'd pack it in. The word on the street around that time was that the management wasn't happy with Houlihan. About a week later the axe fell on his head

The new management came up with fifty names and four goalkeepers and Houlihan's name wasn't amongst them. What's more, Joe Quaid was also asked back but declined the offer. Houlihan doesn't know that and at this stage, he's better off. He doesn't need any more salt rubbed into the wound.

He was heading down to Waterford to see his girlfriend Tina the Saturday before Christmas when he found out. The rest of the drive was a bit of a haze and when he arrived at Tina's house in Lismore, he went straight upstairs. He couldn't face her family.

'I was speaking to Tina one day in January and she was fairly upset with Timmy because she couldn't get through to him,' said Ollie Moran. 'She didn't know what to say to him. It's Timmy's whole life. His life revolved around hurling and playing for Limerick. When something like that is taken from you, you don't know what to do.'

Christmas was a bit of blur for Houlihan. The week afterwards, there was an intensive weekend of training for the fifty players in the University of Limerick. Houlihan lives just down the road from the college and every night he was tearing himself up inside, wondering what the players were doing and what was being said. He felt embarrassed that he wasn't there but he didn't take the easy option and sink into a morass of self-pity.

'By all accounts he's training like mad and some people were saying that he went down to Ger Cunningham in Cork for training,' said Joe Quaid, the keeper Houlihan took over from in 2001. 'I'd say he's fair pissed off but he definitely deserves to be on the panel.'

Houlihan rang Cunningham in Cork just after Christmas for a chat because he knew him from his days with the Under-21s. He tried to arrange a coaching session with him in January but Cunningham couldn't fit him in. He's coming to Limerick on 26 February though, and a session is planned for that afternoon.

It's going to be tough on Houlihan to make up some of the ground that he's lost. Especially after last summer. In the drawn Munster semi-final, Houlihan's mistake for Paul Flynn's third goal nearly buried Limerick. Dave Bennett drove a ball in from about forty yards, Houlihan tried to control it on his hurley but it spun off his stick and Flynn pounced on it. His mistake for Flynn's goal in the replay was worse. Flynn angled away from three Limerick defenders and when a point seemed to be the limit of the opportunity, he drove the ball across Houlihan. It wasn't a hard shot but Houlihan went to ground and it squirmed in under his body. Waterford won by two points.

Although a lot of people have lost faith in him, Houlihan is a far better keeper than he's been given credit for. Although there is a kind of freemasonry of goalkeeping, where it is taken for granted that non-goalkeepers will not understand, Houlihan is regarded and rated within the inner sanctum of hurling goalkeepers.

'If you were to go through all the goalkeepers now, I'd say Timmy Houlihan from Limerick is the most natural of them all,' said Seamus Durack, the former Clare goalkeeper who won three All-Stars. 'I like his style but I don't know what's gone wrong with him. Providing he hasn't a major attitude problem, I think if he's worked on he has an awful lot to offer.'

Ger Cunningham isn't in total agreement with Durack just yet. 'I think he's got a lot of work ahead of him. Timmy is very strong on one side and if he's honest, he'd tell you his weakness is on his left side. He may not say that to me but I'd expect him to. Still, it's a brave call to drop him. You'd wonder why they're doing it but they obviously must have doubts about Timmy.'

Donal Óg Cusack reckons he has an idea where the real problem lies. 'Timmy has something, he has it as a keeper but his nerve could be gone. That's what it looks like to me anyway. And the poor old devil, I know what it's like, it's a terrible situation to be in.'

Houlihan admits his confidence is on the floor but he doesn't think he's lost that edge, that concrete belief that he needs as a base to survive as a goalkeeper.

'I wouldn't say my nerve is gone. After the Wexford game (*All-Ireland quarter-final 2001*), my confidence was totally gone. That was the nail in my coffin and that affected me for ages. Ages. My confidence in general was gone. I suppose my confidence was low after last year as well and it affected me. But I wouldn't say my nerve is gone. It's probably not what it should be but it's not gone.'

He has no option now but to go back to basics and re-evaluate where he stands as a goalkeeper. The hard questions have to be asked. Did he work hard enough? Did it go to his head? Has he been coached properly and if he hasn't, what's he going to do about it?

'To be totally honest about it, I definitely didn't work on my game over the last few years as much as I should have. I know I can't be making excuses but maybe a bit more guidance wouldn't have gone astray either. I never did any specialist training and maybe that affected my attitude, in that I got a bit casual by not concentrating more on what I should have been doing. It's a specialist position and you have to be coached. I haven't been coached since I started hurling at eight years of age but it's something I aim to rectify this year.'

When he first emerged on the scene as a minor on the senior team for the 2000 League campaign, Houlihan looked like the complete keeper. Solid, good shot-stopper, cocky and a diamond puckout to boot. When the Clare hurler David Forde played with him in UL, he used to say that Houlihan was so accurate with his puckout that 'he'd put it into your eye'.

He had everything and when Joe Quaid packed up after the 2000 campaign, it seemed that Houlihan would be Limerick keeper for as long as he wanted.

When Joe Quaid was the same age as Timmy Houlihan is in February 2004, he had yet to make his championship debut or even get a decent run in the League. He did his time but that time has passed now. Although he was asked back at Christmas, Quaid had made his mind up to quit inter-county hurling after damaging his shoulder last February.

'I'm a great keeper since I gave it up,' he said. 'All it takes is your man in goals to play a few bad games and you become a hero again.'

Although Quaid returned to play championship in 2002, his edge was gone two years earlier. By that stage, shots were passing him that he would have stopped between his teeth years earlier. When he was in his prime between 1994 and 1997, Quaid was one of the greatest shot-stopping goalkeepers in the history of hurling. He fell down in other departments of his game that meant he didn't deserve to be rated amongst the Greats. Nor did he have the longevity associated with his career that grants that status. But in terms of classic shot-stopping, Quaid was that good.

He always had trouble with his flexibility and as his career progressed, that slowed his reactions down. He always had dodgy groins and he ended up having two knee operations. A few extra pounds began to cling to his hips with every passing year too and that did for him as well. His body fat ratio in 1994 was 9.6%. In 2003 it was 20.4%.

In the latter years of his career, he was only a shell of the goalkeeper he once was. He'd still pull off the odd outstanding save but his reactions were slower, his clearances terrible and his puckout was gone to the dogs.

It is easy though, to pinpoint the exact moment when his career hit the downward curve. When Limerick played Laois in a League game in Kilmallock in 1997, Quaid hit a wall that buried him. Physically he knew it but he never realised that he was also deeply affected psychologically by the events of that day.

It all began when David Cuddy struck a rocket of a penalty that bounced off the ground and Quaid got his body behind it. He knew it had hit him but he didn't know where. The ball spilled loose and as he was trying to scramble it away, the pain kicked in and he collapsed in a heap. He knew then that the ball had struck him in the testicles. He played on but when the pain got worse fifteen minutes into the second half, he signalled to the management to take him off. They refused to do so.

He was almost afraid to look inside his togs after the game because the swelling had expanded his underpants. The minute the team-doctor saw his testicles, he was ordered to go straight to Limerick Regional Hospital. The swelling had become so enlarged at that stage that Quaid couldn't close up his jeans. His girlfriend Majella drove him to hospital but on the way back into the city, hunger got the better of him and he stopped off at Supermacs. The minute he was attended to by a doctor they wanted to operate straightaway. But Quaid had scuppered that plan with a Big Mac, fries and a milkshake.

Quaid had no option but to sit it out and wait for the operation. When he got to the theatre late that night, a nurse recognised him and just as he was about to get knocked out with an anaesthetic, he signed an autograph for her son.

'After it happened, I said to someone that I looked out over the back wall in Kilmallock to see if the two of them were gone, but I was hoping it wasn't that bad. Just before I was put out for the operation, I asked the nurse what the story was. She said "I don't know." But I knew well from her reaction and I said to myself "there's one of them gone anyway."'

His right testicle had exploded on impact from the force of the ball and the surgeon had to remove half of Quaid's testicle. When the doctor arrived down to talk to him the following morning, Quaid was stuck into a newspaper reading the match report from the previous day. The doctor asked him if he wanted counselling but all Quaid was worried about was getting his head and his body right for the Waterford game in six weeks time.

He wasn't able to return to training for four weeks and then on his first night back, it appeared that someone had put a contract out on his crotch. During a training game, TJ Ryan came through and unleashed a rocket of a shot which hit Quaid straight between the legs. Everyone threw their eyes up to heaven but Quaid was wearing a jockstrap with a guard and the ball flew thirty yards back out the field.

'I just got up and said to Ryan "Jaysus, that implant is some yoke."'

He wasn't fit enough to line out against Waterford in the Munster quarter-final in May but he was back for the semi-final against Tipp in mid-June. The match weighed heavily on his mind for a few days beforehand but it wasn't the only thing that occupied his thoughts. 'At that stage I had the most famous testicle in the country.' He knew what was coming.

As he made his way down to the Killinan end goal in Thurles for the second half, he could sense the storm brewing on the terrace. Ten minutes into the half, a cluster of Tipp fans started into a chorus of a song they had made up that went to the tune of the *Go West* number from *Village People*. 'JOE QUAID, ONLY HAS ONE BALL, JOE QUAID, ONLY HAS ONE BALL!' Ten minutes later when another break came in play, the songwriters had managed to teach the rest of the terrace their new song and the whole crowd were belting it out at the top of their voices.

The umpires looked at Quaid sympathetically but he all he could do was laugh. The game was gone from Limerick and there was no point throwing more petrol on the flames behind him. Quaid decided to play his party piece. He turned around to the terrace, jumped up like Batman and grabbed his crotch on the way down. Immediately the singing stopped, the crowd universally clapped him and that was the end of it. Respect.

'While the match was going on I was actually whistling the tune of it to myself but I knew if I turned around and gave them the finger, they'd have been enough songs made up about me to enter the Eurovision. I could hear the bastards up the back trying to start it up again a few minutes later but I could hear guys down the front roaring back telling them to leave me alone.'

Although Limerick went on to win the League in October, that was effectively the end of the road for that Limerick team that had been to two All-Ireland finals in the previous three years. Cork blew them away in the following year's championship and then Eamonn Cregan took a wrecking ball to the side that Tom Ryan built. The reconstruction was slow and painful but Quaid's form had already begun to fall in tandem with the team's fortunes.

'I never played a good game for Limerick after that incident. To be honest about it, I probably never had the same confidence again afterwards. When I was at the top of my game, I used to have lumps taken out of me and some of my best saves were made with my body from throwing myself at the ball. When we played Waterford in 1999, Paul Flynn came in with a ball and I turned my arse to it. The ball ended up in the net. Before I'd have thrown myself at it and probably kept it out.'

Even though he played senior hurling for Limerick for eight years, he only had four years at the top of his game. He has two Munster SHC medals and two All-Stars to show for that timespan but no All-Ireland medal. And what's worse, he knows he is still seen by the a great deal of the hurling public as the fall-guy for costing Limerick one All-Ireland and playing a big part in wrecking the second attempt as well.

'A lot of people around Limerick still blame me for losing the two

All-Irelands and fellas have said that to me. Sure I've heard all the jokes that were out about me, especially after '94. "What's the difference between Cinderella and Joe Quaid? Cinderella got to the ball." "What's the difference between Joe Quaid and a turnstile? A turnstile only lets in one at a time." You just have to laugh at some of that stuff.'

In the 1994 All-Ireland final, Limerick were five points up with five minutes to play when Johnny Dooley stood over a 20-metre free. There were six players on the Limerick goal-line, Dooley didn't strike it as well as he'd hoped to but it still went in. That was the score that started an avalanche but many people believe that it was Quaid who rolled the snowball off the top of the hill.

He picked the ball out of the back of the net, walked behind the goals and spotted Ger Hegarty on his own near the sideline halfway out the field. He landed the ball into Hegarty's hand, but he turned into a shoulder charge and the ball slipped from his grasp. Johnny Pilkington drove it in behind the Limerick full-back line and Pat O'Connor stole in and let fly. Bang! Game effectively over.

'The one thing I took responsibility for that day was the lining of the goals for Johnny Dooley's free,' said Quaid. 'There were six inside instead of five and I had my angles wrong. The puckout theory for the next goal is complete rubbish. I've looked at it again and I've timed it and that puckout was hit out the same amount of time I took to take every other puckout. You had apes saying that I should have pucked it out over the Hogan Stand but these were obviously guys who were playing in the 1930s when there was only one sliotar in Croke Park.

'They were looking for someone to hang and I was the one who was hung for it.'

Two years later, in 1996, the rope was still dangling. Even though Quaid made two of the best saves ever seen in an All-Ireland final, Ger Loughnane opened the debate on the merits of his performance a week later in a newspaper interview. He said that after Wexford were reduced to fourteen men, Quaid was the one player who had time on the ball to find the loose man. But by going for length instead of accuracy, Quaid handed Wexford a 50/50 chance of winning possession.

'That's easy to say but you don't realise what was going on inside my head,' said Quaid. 'After all the shit that had gone on in 1994 with the puckout, no way was I going to risk it again. When I saw Mark Foley calling for a ball in the second half, I thought about it for a split second and I just said to myself: "No way, it's a hurley I have, not a scud missile launcher."'

Quaid had to wrongly live with the blame again for losing another All-Ireland final and he knew that no matter what he did for the rest of his career, there would be no redemption from the past. No matter the hundreds of goals he had prevented, he would be cruelly remembered for two matches.

The blame was just deposited with him, without his sanction or control. He knew it would always affect his reputation and it did, but he still did his best to project the image that he was indestructible. He tried to always look in control and his demeanour gave off an aura of someone with ice in his veins. But it was really only blood.

'People often said to me that I was one of the cockiest keepers they ever saw but if they only knew what was going on inside my head,' said Quaid. 'I used to be planking it. My routine in the morning before any big match was a newspaper, twenty Carrolls, into the jacks, sit down, smoke and get sick. Every morning, I'd get sick with nerves. On the Saturday before the '94 All-Ireland, I got as sick as a dog. My routine then before the match was to get a cigarette and a lighter and go to the jacks for a crap and a smoke.

'You ask me what made me tick, well I was thick enough for it. I remember marching behind the band on my debut against Cork in Limerick in 1994 and saying to myself "what am I doing here?" I was just absolutely shitting it and after fifteen minutes when two goals had gone past me I was saying to myself "Ah, I'm not able for this craic". I remember leaning up against the post and looking out and it was misting and miserable and saying to myself "Ah, I want to go home".

'It was a complete nightmare at times. I loved the impossible situation because that was a no loss situation but I used to hate high balls dropping in. I was never standing under them thinking I was going to catch this and drive it down the field. I was thinking to myself "Holy Shit, don't drop it." I often wondered what went through other keepers' heads when balls were dropping in because I know what was going through my head. *(Brendan)* Cummins is the best I've seen under a dropping ball but I was never like that. If I saw a ball going over the crossbar, I'd be saying to myself "thanks be to God that's not dropping in here."

'It was tough going. It takes a certain type of individual to play in goals and you'd always wonder why you put yourself through some of the hardship. It is hard to look back and think that I should have an All-Ireland medal, but what can you do now? Maybe if we'd won the All-Ireland in '94, I'd have gone stone mad, turned into an alcoholic and I'd have no wife and family now.'

Inter-county hurlers often get labelled, even though nobody outside their family and friends knows anything about them. Everyone thinks they know them and what their problem is. Now that Timmy Houlihan has been mowed down, most of the opinion feels that he walked right out in front of the oncoming traffic. That he became full of shit and that it all went to his head.

'He's a good keeper but I heard that he doesn't give a shite about hurling,' said Kilkenny goalkeeper James McGarry. 'I don't know if it's true but that's what I heard.'

It's easy to hear and make assertions in a small hurling community. When he was in UL, Houlihan's status was legendary. Every so often his new nickname would be posted up on the college's hurling website and another bushfire of gossip on Houlihan would rage. Some of the players reckoned that he was bringing women along to watch him training. It was complete trash but it all added to his cult status within the hurling club.

The UL players reckoned he was so image-conscious that he was going to sign a contract with the Barbie Doll brand-name and begin bringing out his own range of 'Timmy' dolls. The nickname 'Timmy Hilfiger' did the rounds for a while after he wouldn't wear anything only 'Tommy Hilfiger' clothing. Then it was 'Timmy Text-message' because he was always on the phone. The one that stuck though, was 'Timmy Toiletries', because of his post-match grooming routine.

'He's a perfectionist by nature and that's where all of that came from,' said Ollie Moran, who coached the UL Fitzgibbon Cup winning team that Houlihan was part of in 2002. 'He'd have his boots waxed and cleaned, his gear all laid out and after the match he'd step into the Calvin Klein boxers. He had every kind of deodorant, after-shave and face cream under the sun, but that wasn't him trying to make an impression. That was just Timmy by nature and he was the same in the way he used to prepare for matches. He was just methodical.

'When I hear people say that he deserved to be dropped because he's arrogant, I see red. If every guy had the attitude and approach to preparation that Timmy had, Limerick would be doing a lot better than they are. Timmy must be the most misperceived and misunderstood guy you ever saw in your life. He took a fair hammering when he was dropped two years ago and he battled back. To pick four goalkeepers ahead of him now, you'd wonder was there something else to it.

'He's never the fifth best goalie in Limerick. All Timmy needs is reassurance. Tell him he's a fine keeper that just needed to clean up a few things. No one could tell him that, so rather than do that they just dropped him. I was angry in a way and I think someone could have been big enough to tell him where he stood. He's a very hard guy to get into and to get seriously talking to. I'd know him well but I'd say I've only hit that level with him three or four times ever, where he's really opened up to me. He must be going through torture inside his head.'

Cusack looks at Houlihan now and tries to imagine himself in his position. The thought is unbearable but Cusack knows that he wouldn't be put through it in Cork.

'You'd just wonder if a fella that good has been managed properly, but the GAA falls down desperately in the department anyway. There's no structure in a lot of places. In fairness Cork have that at the moment. Donal O'Grady has that idea of developing guys, training them and educating them. It doesn't sound right that such a talented guy has been let go like that and just left there.'

When Moran was training UL two years ago, he knew what Houlihan needed more than anything else. Someone to put a hand around his shoulder and tell him how good he was. Reassure him, relax him and calm his nerves. Moran brought in Eamonn Meskell from his own club in Ahane and he was brilliant for Houlihan. He kept telling him he was the best keeper in Limerick and he responded to it. He was excellent in UL's run to the title.

'If Timmy was to ever relax, he'd be a much better keeper,' said Moran. 'I always felt he was playing within himself. It was almost like a burden on him sometimes and it definitely affects his performance. When you're nervous you start going through all the negative permutations in your head and he's so conscious of all of that.

'His biggest fault as a goalkeeper is when he loses concentration, that manifests itself in a match when he tends to go to ground too early. *(Paul)* Flynn's goal last year highlighted that, but that's something that can be corrected very easily. It's a small kink in his game but it's manifesting itself in a very big way. Timmy needs very little to correct his game because he has all the natural ability in the world. Image, my arse, it's nothing to do with that. Some people just love to slate and cut other people.

'You see *(Brendan)* Cummins, Davy Fitz, *(Damien)* Fitzhenry, they're all nice guys who aren't arrogant but who are really confident fellas. They're not obnoxious but they all know that they have it. You see Timmy then who's equally as good as them and he's nearly made feel ashamed that he's talented.

'It's his mental game that he just has to work on. There would be nothing wrong with bringing a sports psychologist in to see him to address the problems he has. If he had a fella to do that and it worked on him, he'd be doing cartwheels inside in goals. That's something that just has to be developed. He's too good not to be helped out because the big danger is that he could end up on the scrapheap.'

Within the squad, the experienced players feel that they need him. 'I think he just has to be brought back,' said Steve McDonagh. 'Timmy's biggest attribute is his puckout. Hurling isn't as much about stopping shots anymore, it's about being able to place your puckouts. I feel we're really missing that at the moment and he would be a big addition to our system.'

All Houlihan can do for the moment is keep on keeping on. No matter what he does anyway, he can't change opinions and what people really think of him. And if he's to be really honest about it, he may have given some critics a rod a few years ago that they are leathering off his back now.

'I won't say that it totally went to my head, but definitely the second year I was on the panel, it affected me. I remember talking to my brother Tony one night and he said that he even found it hard to talk to me. I was living in Limerick and wasn't going home that often and I suppose I didn't even notice it myself. That statement really opened my eyes.

'People were saying that I was arrogant. I was always confident but you have to be when you're playing in goals. I find it hard to put a finger on it now but it affected me and definitely affected my approach to the game. When that happens with your family, you have to take a step back and say to yourself that there's something seriously wrong here. I had to take myself down a peg or two and realise that when things do go wrong, your family are always there for you. But that was the big turning point for me and definitely, I'm after changing in the last two years.'

It's not as if he hasn't been down this road before. Houlihan was dropped off the squad altogether in 2002 after Quaid returned from a year in the wilderness. It sobered him up and forced him into deep introspection.

'I felt my attitude had changed last year. I never put in so much effort into training in the last year and a half. I was never the fittest player but maybe I'd taken the easy option at times in the past. I thought I'd turned a corner when I came back last year, but this is definitely a bigger kick in the teeth. I knew I had to improve and play better and I was going back this year to try and prove a point to everyone else. And to myself, that I was better than I had been showing. I still think I can compete with the best of them. I'm not going to say that I'm as good as Brendan Cummins because he's just outstanding, but I definitely think I could hold my own with a lot of keepers.

'People can think what they want of me now but I'm not going to throw in the towel and if anything this has made me stronger and more determined. I made some big mistakes in the last couple of years, but I can correct them. Without a shadow of a doubt I know I can. I just have to prove myself again, but it probably won't happen this year. I just haven't got that chance now.'

For now, he just has to grin and bear it and wait for that chance, if it ever comes. And, in the meantime, live with the perception people have of him. Last week he was out at one of his work-sites and was walking past student accommodation when someone roared out of a window at him that he was a clown of a keeper and would be better off in the circus. If it happened two years ago, Houlihan would probably have gone after your man and anything could have transpired. He just let it go.

He's had to grow up quickly. By the time Houlihan was twenty he had three All-Ireland Under-21 medals in his pocket and had been captain of one of those winning teams when he was under nineteen. By the time he was twenty one, he'd been on a roller-coaster spin that a lot of players couldn't cram into a full career. He played National League as a minor, made his championship debut at nineteen, was dropped at twenty, called back at twenty one and dropped again before he was twenty two. Recently Stephen Larkham, the Australian rugby fly-half, said that even though the French rugby poster boy Frédéric Michalak was still only twenty one, it felt like he'd been around for years. Houlihan can empathise with that scenario.

'I feel like the oldest twenty-one year old alive. It's crazy, like. I was playing senior hurling with the club at fifteen so I kind of grew up with fellas who were a lot older than me. I had to mature a bit more quickly because of that. I've been dropped twice off an inter-county panel before I was twenty two and that's not easy to deal with. Not too many players have had to try and deal with that.'

At the moment, there's a hole in his soul that's reflected in his face. But how he deals with his situation will be the making or breaking of Timmy Houlihan.

RUSSIAN ROULETTE

On February 25 2004, three days after the National Hurling League began, Bayern Munich and Real Madrid squared up to one another in Munich in one of the most compelling games of the second phase of the Champions League. Bayern should have won the game, but instead they travel to Spain in a couple of weeks only level at 1-1. They would have been taking a 1-0 lead there and travelling with a lot more confidence against the most talented side in Europe if Oliver Kahn, the goalkeeper and Bayern and German captain, hadn't made an absolute mess of a Roberto Carlos free-kick.

Afterwards Kahn was shell-shocked and wanted to run away. He dropped his gloves on the pitch and stormed off. He was gone from the stadium before most of his team-mates were out of the showers, unable to fathom how he had let Carlos's free-kick to squirm horribly under his body. 'It was one you could stop without arms and legs,' he cursed.

Kahn was panned, mocked, insulted. Twelve hours after the blunder, braving a media inquisition, he laid his demons bare. 'I need to look inside myself, ask questions and find out what it all means. Maybe you have to ask yourself if it's actually worth it. Something's not quite right. It's an area where I've simply got to find out the reason for myself.'

The bottom line is that Kahn's world has been rocky for twenty months now. It all dates back to a defining moment in the 2002 World Cup final. On the ultimate stage, Kahn messed up, and that destroyed something at the core of his belief system which it took years of super-competitive work to develop. As Brazil celebrated with the trophy, he sat paralysed against the goalpost, painfully alone, sending out a crystal-clear signal that there was an exclusion zone around him. The Do Not Disturb sign was up. 'Dangerous animal within'.

Having played like a goalkeeping god for the entire tournament, having committed himself intensely to following every tiny detail he believed would make him the best on the planet, Kahn was exposed. Even though he was playing with a badly damaged finger, he spilled a Rivaldo shot, which Ronaldo poked home. It showed he was as fallible as the next man, but it was a shocking revelation to a man whose obsession with goalkeeping supremacy gripped him like a madness.

Away from football he went off the rails afterwards and his private life plummeted into well-publicised chaos. An extra-marital affair with a Munich barmaid, while his wife was pregnant, kept the headline writers in overdrive. Kahn considered leaving Germany, but after a while endeavoured to change, to become a better person. He admitted that maybe the pressure he routinely put himself under was a little excessive. He is trying now to find a better balance, to maintain the deep concentration he needs without being so uptight.

So far it hasn't really worked. *Kicker* magazine, whose marks for all Bundesliga players are a respectable gauge, rates him fifth in the goalkeeper rankings at the moment – four below the only number that means anything to him. And now this. At the moment, Kahn appears so strung out that he looks like he'd bite a striker's head off as soon as look at him.

Aside from the vast sums of money he earns though, Kahn only has to wait a couple of weeks to try and put things right. Donal Óg Cusack, who is a big fan of Kahn, had to wait over five months to get back into competitive action and he has to wait another three months, if he's even there at that stage, to right some wrongs in the championship. That's the reality of hurling goalkeeping at championship level.

Cusack, who is nearly as obsessed with goalkeeping supremacy as Kahn is, isn't going to go off the rails either and live in Havana Brown's nightclub for a week before going off with some married barmaid. At least he is in possession for the number one spot and that's the most important thing at inter-county level. But over the border in Waterford, Stevie Brenner has lost pole position and he doesn't know if he'll even get back into the driving seat.

Before the League began, Waterford played five challenge games in January and February and Brenner only lined out once, against Offaly. Ian O'Regan from Mount Sion played against Kilkenny in the opening round of the League on February 22 and did well. He's been chosen to play against Laois at the weekend as well and Brenner is concerned that a trend that Justin McCarthy set when he took over as Waterford manager two years ago is returning.

When McCarthy came in, Brendan Landers had been first-choice goalkeeper with the county since 1998. He had plenty of big-time experience and had generally done well during his previous four seasons. That still cut no ice with the manager. He liked the look of Brenner and favoured his puckout over Landers'. Brenner got in and by the time Waterford won their first Munster title in thirty nine years that July, Landers was long gone off the panel. He had walked himself.

Although Landers had made his debut in the 1997 championship, Brenner was in line for the number one spot the following year. He had impressed in challenge games and was picked to play the first League match against Tipperary in February. He made one bad mistake for a goal and Landers got back in. Brenner never saw action again for a second afterwards as Waterford reached the League final, the Munster decider and lost the All-Ireland semi-final to Kilkenny by a point.

He had to wait for four more years to get a second chance and he would have had every right in the meantime to jack it all in. Landers was four years younger than him and had twice as much experience. Brenner had never even played underage for the county but the thought of opting out never crossed his mind.

'Never. I couldn't. I just wouldn't let it defeat me. All that was going through my mind was the fear of being on the panel for so long and never even get a game. I wanted to prove that I was good enough to play. I knew I was. When the chance did come around I said I was going to grab it with both hands and bring it on.'

Since he made his debut in May 2002, Brenner has probably been the most low-profile and inconspicuous keeper amongst the top strata of hurling counties. He hasn't made any spectacular saves, he hasn't done anything out of the ordinary but he has been consistent and his past two seasons have ended in credit.

The only goal which he had a case to answer for was Setanta Ó hAilpín's opener in the Munster final last year. Brenner came off his line to collect a ball from a Niall McCarthy centre but he misjudged Ó hAilpín's lanky stride and the ball was in the net before he knew it. He was unlucky but maybe that's in the back of McCarthy's mind now and in any case, the manager likes the look of O'Regan.

'He *(Brenner)* is going to have a battle on his hands to hold onto the spot,' said McCarthy. 'Your man *(O'Regan)* is definitely up to scratch. He's very cocky, really quick, a good shot-stopper and a very plucky lad. The next few games will tell a lot and he has to get his chance. But experience will come down to it at the end of the day and Stevie has a lot of experience.

'He reminds me a lot of Ger Cunningham when he was starting off. He's a big man with a huge puckout. Ger put a huge amount into his game to improve and that was the key to his development. But that was back in the 1980s and this is 2004 and I'm not sure if Stevie has that amount of time to put into his game now. He got married last year and he moved into a new house and it will be difficult for him to make the time to get his game right. He will be under pressure to stay number one.'

The other side of that coin is that perhaps McCarthy is reading a bit more between the lines and is trying to shake Brenner up a bit. 'When Landers was there, I was under pressure because he was pushing me. But last year, it was the opposite. He *(Landers)* was gone and I was thinking that I had established myself here now and I was sitting back a small bit. I was getting married and moving into a new house and I wasn't putting in as much an effort as I should have been. I wasn't getting the benefits out of it so I am determined to give it a right lash this year.'

It's going to be difficult now though.

'He *(McCarthy)* could be playing mind-games with me, I just don't know,' said Brenner. 'After I got the game against Offaly *(challenge game)*, I thought I was back in again but I didn't play against Tipperary and that was a week before the first round of the League. I was thinking was I going to be thrown out or what was the story?

'I don't think he will give him *(O'Regan)* all the games like he did with me two years ago. If he does, it will add more fuel to my fire and push me on that bit more. I'm not a quitter, but I'm not a begrudger either. I want this badly because I hung in there so long to get there. This is just going to make me work harder. I was happy he came onto the panel, because he is a good goalkeeper and he is one for the future. I knew he would put me under pressure. If he's playing well during the League I can't crib with that but I'll still be pushing hard for the number one spot.

'Still, I'm a bit pissed off at the moment. McCarthy said to me the other day not to be disappointed that I wasn't playing. If I don't play, I'm disappointed. That's what killed me. Of course I'm going to be disappointed if I'm not playing. I want to play and it's a pure nightmare at the moment. I'm just not able to watch matches. Even club matches or challenge matches, I just can't do it. I don't know what it is. I have to be playing and I have to be involved.'

In the minds of some people, Ray 'Laylay' Barry is still regarded as the best keeper in Waterford. The flipside to that coin is that everyone knows Barry is capable of anything. When Justin McCarthy took over in October 2001 he called Barry back into the squad for the first time since January 1997. Waterford took on Clare in a challenge in Walsh Park and the first ball that came into Barry, he collected it before drawing a Clare forward. Then he flicked the ball over the Clare player's head before catching it and driving it down the field.

'Justin McCarthy came into me at half-time and said "don't ever do that again",' recalled Barry. 'The first ball I got in the second half, I did exactly the same thing. I just couldn't help myself.'

Barry was just like a cheeky little skinhead from a bratpack, who had a brazen attitude and who would cut you in two with his caustic tongue.

Most of the time he played in goal, he'd get up the wick of the forwards so much that they'd want to go in and slap him around the place, but that was part of the plan too. Some of the stunts he tried on the pitch defied logic and mental stability and he often gave the impression that he was just stone mad. But being the Waterford goalkeeper was his big stage and he wanted to play the only part he knew how.

Barry was the goalkeeper on the Waterford Under-21 team that won the 1992 All-Ireland and he had nailed down the number one spot on the senior team by 1995. He'd got runs during the League in the previous two seasons but when the successful All-Ireland Under-21 management took over the senior team in late 1994, Barry got his chance for real.

The day before the first round of the League against Offaly, Passage East were beaten in the county final by Mount Sion and Barry went on the tear afterwards. None of the Mount Sion players showed, but Barry turned up hung-over and was sent off before the game was over.

Waterford were in Division Two that season and began gobbling up the points but at one stage, Barry went AWOL. He was fond of the horses and before he knew it, he was in the red after betting away money he didn't have.

Rumour had it that he was on the duck from some Mafia-type figure and that he was hiding out in the dressing rooms of the Passage clubhouse. That was the theory but no one could catch a glimpse of him up there to prove it. He was nowhere to be found.

'I went to Dublin for a couple of weeks. No one knew where I was gone but I was above in Artane with first cousins. I was into the horses big-time. I just liked the bet, like, but I was backing money that wasn't mine. I owed some lad money and I just disappeared. I told no one but I got my head together, made a couple of calls and sorted it out. And that was it then.'

When he returned to Waterford, he rang one of the selectors, Peter Power, who he was friendly with. Power just told him to come back to training, put the head back down and go again. Barry was still first-choice keeper and Waterford were on their way to winning the

Division Two League title. When they thrashed Galway in the League quarter-final in April, they really looked to be heading places.

From the very outset of their semi-final clash with Clare, Barry instigated a running battle with Jim McInerney, the Clare corner-forward. Barry kept on roaring out to the veteran Clare player to 'give it up old man' and McInerney was giving it back just as good. The game was still in the balance early in the second half when Barry came out for a ball behind Tom Feeney and got caught in no-man's land. He spilled it and McInerney was on hand to drive it into the net. The ball had no sooner gone past the line when McInerney danced a jig around Barry.

Waterford collapsed after that goal and Clare went on to beat them by twelve points. Tipperary took a mental note of Barry's mistake and weren't long reminding him of the error when the sides met in the championship a few weeks later.

'The very first ball that came in that day, Tommy Dunne got a point and (John) Leahy ran across me and said "you're only a cowardly fucker and we're going to pump high balls down on your head all day and you won't get under them",' said Barry. 'The next high ball that came in, I caught it and cleared it and just went out and grinned at Leahy. After that I was fine. They bombarded me with high balls afterwards but I dealt with them.'

He couldn't have any complaints about Leahy having a go at him because Barry took slagging players to a new level when he played inter-county hurling. He rarely punched below the belt but he'd keep verbally hammering away all through a game to throw them off or to try and get someone to crack. It didn't matter who they were; nobody was spared.

'I'd be talking and intimidating forwards the whole time. If a young fella was playing I'd be telling him that he was only playing in the League because this fella or that fella wasn't there. If an auld lad was playing I'd be telling him he was gone past it.

'We were playing Galway one day below in Dungarvan and when I came out for the second-half, I ran past Joe Cooney. I said "you're still here boy, Jesus ye must have nothing on the bench". He just grinned at me as if to say "who the fuck are you?". It was my first year on the panel and he was a legend but I didn't care who anyone was. It was all the same to me.'

His attitude reflected his goalkeeping: 'I used be wicked nervous before games but if I got my first touch right, I'd be liable for anything then. I was carefree and it wouldn't bother me what I'd do in a match. I wouldn't have been your normal goalkeeper. I was an entertainer more than anything.'

Trying to be a hurling goalkeeping entertainer was, and is, unheard off at inter-county level. It is like trying to juggle five sticks of fire in one hand while holding the hurley in the other. Eventually you'll get scorched but Barry still went out and performed, hoping that his risk-theory would prove a brilliant counterpoint to the safety mantle that forms the cornerstone of goalkeeping. His favourite trick was flicking the ball over a forward's head and then lashing it down the field.

'I used to love doing that and taking the mickey out of fellas. I used to get a ball and wait on purpose for a fella to come to me and then flick it over his head. And then I'd give him a little grin on the way back. Winding fellas up more than anything.'

He's always tried that stunt at underage level and with the club and he could see no reason why he should stop when he began playing for Waterford. It was like a dare to himself too because he wanted to prove to himself that he could try it and get away with it.

He was only on the panel a year when Waterford took on Tipperary in a tournament game in Clonmel. Tipp rolled out their big guns of Pat Fox and Nicky English in the full-forward line and the challenge was immediately laid down before Barry. He wasn't thinking about keeping a clean sheet or staking a claim for a championship place at that moment. He just wanted to play a game of Russian Roulette.

The chance presented itself midway through the first half when Barry picked up a loose ball and waited for English to come to him. He went to strike and when English moved in to block him down, Barry dinked the ball over his head. Just as he did, Fox intercepted it and flicked the ball back over Barry's head and into the empty net.

'He *(Fox)* said to me "don't ever try that again, little boy." Eamonn Cullinane from Passage was corner-back and he was going to go back in and kill him for calling me a little boy.'

Even though he'd been advised by one of the best forwards in the game, Barry took no heed. When Tipperary met Waterford in the 1996 championship in Walsh Park, Barry chanced another quick game of Russian Roulette, except this time he knew that more than one chamber had a bullet. It was only his second championship match and he was really risking losing his head but he just had to try it.

'I got the ball and waited for English to come to me. I flicked it over his head and caught it again and drove it down the field. I was running back into the goal and I said to him "I got you this time". He just smiled.'

It was lunatic asylum stuff but it was all governed by the paradoxical nature of Barry's character. Like most goalkeepers, he'd be as cranky as hell if a goal went past him, but the little voice inside his head kept telling him to chance it. If he were in the circus, he'd have been a daredevil star.

'If I let in a goal, I'd crack up. I wouldn't like it at all, even in a challenge game. But I'd still be liable for anything. Even if I messed up, I'd still try it again the next time. I just wanted to prove to myself that I could do it. I had the confidence in myself that I knew I wouldn't get caught.'

He was a lethal cocktail of a goalkeeper. He wasn't just keen on the daredevil stuff and the horses either. 'I would have been fond of the liquor when I was playing. I would, yeah. I'd always have one or two pints a couple of nights before a game. I wouldn't go mad on it but after the game I'd go a bit mad all right. I'd still have my few pints. My attitude was that it didn't matter what I got up to during the week as long as I went out and performed on Sunday.

'If it was affecting my game on Sunday, I'd have said something but it wasn't. *(Johnny)* Pilkington came out there a few years ago when Babs Keating was above in Offaly and he said that even if he was smoking forty fags and drinking ten pints a week, once he performed on Sunday, he did what he wanted. He wasn't getting paid for it and that's the attitude that I took.'

Barry was first choice for two seasons and was still the man in possession until a training weekend in Clonea in January 1997. The squad trained on Clonea strand on Saturday before booking into a hotel that night. There wasn't a drink ban but Waterford were following the template of physical preparation set by Clare, Limerick and Wexford and manager Gerald McCarthy was instituting a rigorously policed level of discipline. It was known that night though, that Barry and Seán 'Growler' Daly had spent a good deal of the night in the residents' bar.

When the squad convened again on the strand early the following morning, Barry showed but Daly didn't. By the time the squad had moved onto Cappoquin for a hurling session at midday, however, both Barry and Daly had absconded, having got a tip for a horse that was running at a point-to-point in Dungarvan. Waterford needed both players at the time but the new regime was short on allowances and the two were shown the door.

Although Seán Daly was called back to the Waterford panel in May 1998, Barry didn't get a recall until October 2001. He remained on the Waterford panel until February 2002 when work commitments forced him to pack it in. He was working seven nights a week in a taxi firm at the time and while Justin McCarthy wanted him to remain on the squad, Barry didn't have the time or the energy. When he could have given the commitment five years earlier, he blew it. All for a few pints and a horse he can't remember the name of now.

'I think myself and Growler thought we could do it and get away with it at that time. If I could turn back the clock, there's no way I'd have done it. Gerald McCarthy just wasn't taking that kind of craic no more.'

The horse came in at 20-1 and secured the two lads a nice little bounty in the short-term. But in the long-term, the money wasn't worth a damn.

'The money from the horse is long gone now, but the boys will always have their Munster medals.'

Brenner might have his Munster medal but that's the last thing on his mind right now. As Round Three of the League rolled around and February segued into March, Ian O'Regan is still between the posts and doing well. When the team was announced for the game against Dublin, two of the full-back line - Tom Feeney and David O'Brien - paid the price for the concession of three goals against Laois the previous Sunday but O'Regan is still number one. It's not getting any easier for Brenner.

'I told him to ask Justin straight out where he stood because Stevie is the type of guy who would just keep working away hard and not ask what the story is,' said his club-mate Joey Carton, who was a selector on the Waterford Under-21 team in 1992 and the senior side in 1995.

Brenner slightly dislodged the joint in one of his hips at training last weekend and he went for physiotherapy to a local physio because Shay Fitzpatrick was away at the Fitzgibbon Cup with Waterford IT. He rang Justin McCarthy to clear it with him, but he also used it an excuse to find where he stands at the moment.

'I said to him "look, if Ian is playing well, he deserves his place and there's no sour grapes or bitterness from me". I said that I'll keep poking away, keep doing my thing and put pressure on him. He said "that's the attitude to have." He told me that I was flying and that I was fitter than I ever was. He said that it was still early days and the jury was still out on your man.

'He said to me that I was still there or thereabouts and not to be getting worried. I thought: "For fuck's sake like, don't be getting worried!". What are they waiting for, are they waiting for him to play a really good game so he can really establish himself? I said I'd let it slide and he told me that he'd talk to me on Thursday night. But he never did.'

Two days later in Parnell Park, O'Regan had a blinder as Dublin pelted him with shots. His diving save from Ronan Fallon was the pick of the bunch and Brenner was the first to congratulate O'Regan afterwards. But the questions are beginning to circle inside his head. He's worried that the trend McCarthy set with Landers two years ago has come full circle now.

'That's on my mind now, yeah. I'm just trying to put it to the back of my mind, you know that sort of way. I know I am good enough to be there at the moment but as I was saying to Joey *(Carton)* the other day, it could be reverse psychology that he's playing with my mind because I slackened off a bit last year. But it would be nice to get an indication of what he's thinking.

'I don't think I deserved to be dropped in the first place to give him a chance. I've played one game so far this year and we're in March now. Before I could have seven or eight games behind me at this stage.

'The championship is coming fast. I've April to prove myself, if I get a chance. It's not the best time to be proving yourself. If I don't get a chance in the next few weeks, well then that's it. I'm keeping myself motivated by telling myself that I am getting in, like. Other people might throw their hat at it but I don't think I could do that.

'I'm in the situation now that if I do get my chance I'll be able to take it because I have the work done. I'm playing in training like I'd play in a match. I'm focussed in on everything and I'm trying to stop everything. It's shit or bust now because I have to try and make an impression.

'The way I have to look at it now is I don't have much time left to play at this level so I have to make the best of the time I have and keep pushing myself harder and harder. I can't afford to relax. Otherwise I'm going to be gone.'

For now, it's hard for Brenner to see even a pinprick of light in the distance.

COMMANDO REGIME

On the night of Friday March 14 2004, before Clare took on Galway in Round 3 of the National League, a serious sense of anxiety was permeating the Clare camp. They've been keeping it quiet all week but they're afraid of their lives that Davy Fitzgerald is going to get a heavy suspension tomorrow for verbally abusing the referee Pat Horan. Fitzgerald is coach to Limerick Institute of Technology (LIT) and after they were beaten by UCC in the Fitzgibbon Cup semi-final the previous weekend, he lost the head.

Fitzgerald rang Horan on the Monday to apologise but the referee's report had already been submitted and the last five days have been a sweat for the Clare management. Using abusive or threatening language towards a referee is a category A offence which carries a minimum of eight weeks' suspension and the Games Administration Committee (GAC) showed no mercy to Fitzgerald on Saturday afternoon. He was sent down for two months but the sentencing hasn't put him on the road to perdition; his suspension is up a week before Clare play Waterford in the first round of the championship.

Before Clare played Galway on Sunday, Fitzgerald togged off and completed the warm-up with the rest of the squad in the Galway Mayo Institute of Technology (GMIT) grounds in Renmore on the far side of the city. He kept to his normal routine, completed the warm-up and said a few words to the squad before togging back in. When the bus arrived at Pearse Stadium, he took his place in the stand. The referee for the game was Pat Horan.

'I felt I was right in what I said to him *(Horan)* because I felt he did us,' stated Fitzgerald.'I make no apologies for it. We trained hard for months and decisions that went against us were not right. The whole thing has pissed me off and it's fierce disappointing. It's a killer having to watch these games in the stand now. I find it very hard to do it but I've made my mind up that I'm not going to start sulking. I'm going to do the best I can for the team.'

Unless Clare get to the final, Fitzgerald is going to miss the entire League campaign. He will have to rely on training games for sustenance. However, he'll manage, because in terms of the time he puts into his game, Fitzgerald is the most professional hurler to ever play the game. He has earned that status because of the huge emphasis he puts into his preparation. Some professional athletes couldn't match it.

A month before the championship, he will take two weeks off work to train twice, sometimes three times, every single day. In the six weeks before the championship, he will still continue to train twice during most days. He is surely the first hurler in the country to pay a personal trainer to assist him with his training and preparation and he is still toying with the idea of taking on a second personal trainer to help him reach an unprecedented standard of goalkeeping.

Fitzgerald recruited Darren Ward two years ago and they work together three times a week. Ward is a former boxing coach, who worked with Chris Eubank in England, and most of their sessions take place in the Shannon Shamrock Hotel in Bunratty, where Ward is now leisure manager. Fitzgerald's training programme is designed to cater for his game but he also uses Ward's techniques to toughen up his mind; the two will regularly go sparring with no holds barred.

Fitzgerald works on flexibility, core development, aqua-strengthening, plyometrics and power training in the gym while he plays badminton and squash whenever he can to keep his eye in. That's all before he even touches a hurley. Outside of Clare training, he religiously goes to the handball alleys and he has had his own personal goalkeeping advisor with him for the last fifteen years.

Fitzgerald always referred to him as the 'mystery man' but Kevin 'Trixie' Toomey has been fine-tuning Fitzgerald's game since he handed him the Clare minor jersey at sixteen. Toomey won a batch of county medals as a goalkeeper with Newmarket-on-Fergus before taking

Fitzgerald under his wing after getting involved with Sixmilebridge. Ever since Fitzgerald made it to the top with Clare, Toomey has been his silent executive consultant.

'If I have any little weakness in my game, he'll spot it and I'll go away and work like hell on it,' said Fitzgerald. 'I believe in absolutely everything he tells me. One hundred per cent.'

In the weeks leading up to the championship, Fitzgerald will round up three or four hurlers to machine gun him with over sixty sliotars and Toomey will stand behind the goal to observe him. He studies his feet movement, timing, sharpness and how he's covering his angles. They'll also work on puckouts, handling and delivery and Toomey will verbally deliver his report card to Fitzgerald afterwards. Fitzgerald will then go away to work further on his game and he trains the way he plays: with a fanaticism that borders on an extreme edge.

'Maybe I go a bit overboard but I'm so happy then when I go out on a field that I know I have everything covered and the only thing that could be wrong is my head,' said Fitzgerald. 'That's up to myself to get right. I feel the strongest part of my goalkeeping is my head. A lot of people feel I'm over the top at certain times on the field but I can guarantee you that 99% of the time, I know exactly what I'm doing.

'Even when I do get hyper and start roaring, I know exactly why I'm doing it and what effect it has. Most of the time it will be to piss off the opposition and to encourage my own lads and to show that we're not going to lie down to nothing. Players will call me a hothead who can't keep his mouth closed and that's the way they think. They hate me and that's fine. If that means they're going to throw the ball over the bar, I'm happier again.'

He is one of the best shot-stoppers the game has ever seen but ultimate preparation has always been Fitzgerald's cornerstone. When he takes part in the All-Ireland Poc Fada competition in the Cooley Mountains every year, he'll travel up the day before to practise on the course. He brings his own masseur and an entourage of individuals who he has coached in marking out the best way around the course.

Fitzgerald never does things at half-pace, either on or off the field. Two years ago he coached the Antrim Under-21s and after Clare beat Galway in the All-Ireland quarter-final, he drove straight from Dublin to Antrim to take them for a training session. He drove home later that night, arriving back at his house at 5.am. Despite his hectic training and playing schedule, he has always found more time to train teams. This year he's coaching LIT, the Clare Under-21s and the Ennistymon Junior side.

Everything he does at sport is driven by an elemental instinct to win and to be number one. When he was first breaking onto the Clare senior team, he was in competition with Leo Doyle from Bodyke. Doyle worked in Shannon and he used to drive the same route to work each morning, so Fitzgerald would regularly rise out of his bed, cycle a few miles down the road and begin pucking the ball off a wall on the side of the road. After Doyle's car would pass, he'd cycle back home. He just wanted to psyche out Doyle by letting him know that whatever training he was doing, it would never compare to Fitzgerald's commando regime.

Fitzgerald could never accept being second at anything. Even if a subkeeper beat him in a game of goal-to-goal in Clare training, he might not talk to him for the rest of the session. He's a near-scratch golfer who works religiously at his game, and in 2001 he played in the South of Ireland championship in Lahinch.

Before the previous Christmas, the former Clare trainer Louis Mulqueen beat Fitzgerald in a game of squash and it cut him to the bone. At 9.am on St Stephen's Day, Mulqueen got a phonecall looking for a rematch. It's that edge that has kept him at the top for fifteen years but perfection is not achieved when there is nothing more to add. But when there is nothing left to take away. Physically or mentally.

'I believe in myself and I believe I'm the best goalkeeper in the country,' said Fitzgerald. 'Brendan Cummins and Damien Fitzhenry are absolutely super keepers but I still think I'm better than them. I set myself a standard and I want to be better again than I have been. No one can ever take away what I've done but I still want more.

'People ask me how I have that desire. I have it because I know that in two or three years' time, I'll never, ever put on the Clare jersey again. I will find it hard to walk away from it and I won't do it until I feel I'm not at my best. But if I feel I can keep going and I have the desire at forty, I'll keep going. I know that it has to end sometime but that's why I have all these new training methods. I want to get more out of myself but I know that nobody else is doing the training I'm doing.

'That's the way I feel it has to be done, otherwise I'm not going to stay at the top. You have to have a drive and an ambition to be number one and that's my ambition. I don't want to be number two in the country, I want to be number one. I work so hard because I want to have the edge on everyone else. I don't want to leave anything to chance. It's fucking dog eat dog out there and you have to be ready for everything.'

Fitzgerald made his championship debut in 1990 against Limerick on a day that Clare were wiped out by fourteen points. Fitzgerald played well but it was a disaster for the Clare fans to have to stomach such a hiding from their neighbours in Cusack Park. The only positive aspect of the whole day was that the junior team had managed to beat Limerick in the curtain-raiser.

At that stage, it was those crumbs of comfort that Clare hurling supporters had to live on. Just two weeks earlier, Kerry had beaten the senior team in a National League play-off and the All-Ireland success five years down the road was an impossible dream. Supporters viewed the junior and underage teams as their best chance of success and even that was a struggle at the best of times. The main reason the juniors had managed to beat Limerick was because of an inspired performance from their goalkeeper.

'Jesus, that lad is some keeper,' remarked one gentleman at the back of the stand during the junior game. 'Who is he?', he enquired of his friend. 'Eoin McMahon,' responded the man. 'Yer man who turned his arse below in Killarney? Sure that lad isn't worth a shite!'

When young goalkeepers were growing up in Clare in the late 1980s they always received one fundamental piece of advice from their coaches. 'Whatever you do, don't do an Eoin McMahon on it.' In Clare, the name Eoin McMahon became a by-word for goalkeeping disaster after June 21 1987.

Although Clare had been unlucky to lose the 1986 Munster final to Cork, it took them until 1991 to recover from the twenty-one points' hammering Tipperary dished out in the 1987 Munster semi-final replay. Although they scraped past Waterford in the 1988 Munster quarter-final, their average losing margin in the championship between 1988 and 1990 was fourteen points.

People struggled to believe that matters could spiral so out of control after a young team had nearly won a Munster title in 1986. The manager and a host of the players were shafted in the aftermath of the '87 debacle but when people were looking for a patsy to lay the blame on, the majority of them looked no further than Eoin McMahon.

If he'd jumped off Mount Everest, McMahon couldn't have fallen any lower than he did in the space of one season. In 1986, he was an All-Star nominee and was chosen on the Rest of Ireland team that played Cork in the annual Goal challenge three days after the All-Ireland final. He had been excellent in Clare's run to the 1987 League final and in the drawn first round of the championship a month later, he was just pipped by Nicky English for the man-of-the-match award.

Clare were lucky to get out of Killarney with a draw the first day but no one saw what was coming in the replay. A Tipperary machine that would win four Munster titles and two All-Irelands within five seasons mowed them down.

'No one remembers that we were beaten so badly that day,' said McMahon. 'They just remember the incident involving me.'

The incident happened in the first half when a high ball dropped in between the late John Moroney and Bobby Ryan.

'Ryan had got past John and was veering a little bit to the right of the goal so I instinctively went towards my right because the natural thing for him was to hit the ball to the far corner,' said McMahon. 'I instinctively turned my body to that side to try and save it but in the meantime, John Moroney had hooked him. It looked like I was turning away from the ball but if Bobby Ryan had hit it the way he wanted to, and the way I anticipated him to, I may have saved it. I was gone to my right and the ball trickled in to my left and dribbled over the line. And that's what actually did happen.'

The official line from the mob was that McMahon had turned his arse to the ball, he was yellow and should never be allowed wear a Clare jersey again. Some people wanted him burned at the stake for treason against his county.

'I had to live with that tag for years and I always will but I still refute that theory that I turned away from the ball. Big time, because I would never, ever do that. Ever. I never did up to that and I never would do it. No-one has ever really asked me what happened because they all think they know what did.'

Everyone had their mind made up in Clare as to what really happened. Including the new management team, which took over for the first League game that October. It was still logical for McMahon to assume that he would be the goalkeeper but Seán Hehir approached him and told him that he would no longer be required in goal. McMahon asked him why and Hehir 'mentioned to me something about Killarney'. That's when the penny dropped. 'That was when it really hit me how big this thing was and what people really thought of me.'

Pat Collins from Sixmilebridge played the first five League games before Christmas and when the New Year dawned, so did the realisation that McMahon was wasting his time and that he wasn't going to get a chance to prove himself. It all ended with an abrupt phone call between himself and Hehir.

'You can't change what happened but I've learned in life that you cannot change what people want to think of you,' said McMahon. 'You can try as hard as you can, but if people have their mind made up, you're not going to change it.'

Ever since that day, a lot of people in Clare still unfairly regard Eoin McMahon as a coward.

'It would always be thrown at me jokingly that I turned my arse to the ball, and remarks like that,' he said. 'In the beginning I used to take it very seriously and try and explain myself and explain my version of events. I soon found out that people weren't even listening to me; they didn't even care because they had their minds made up.

'I realised that the only way to knock it on the head was to face it straight up and say "yeah you're right, I did turn away from it." I had to do that because if people saw that they weren't getting to you, it was one way of shutting them up. It was a defence mechanism in a way. Everyone has their opinion but as far as I'm concerned, they're all 100% wrong and I'm 100% right. Because only I know what happened. And that's all that really matters to me.'

McMahon had served his apprenticeship in Eire Óg under the legendary Seamus Durack but he always had an excellent pedigree. His three first-cousins (Seán and Diarmuid McMahon and Alan Markham) still hurl for Clare while the former Clare captain and present manager, Anthony Daly always claimed that Eoin's father, Jim, had a massive influence on his hurling outlook, when he trained the Clare Under-21 team in 1988.

Eoin had that fire in him too but it was slowly being extinguished after 1987. He departed from the Clare panel in early 1988 and although Clare were going through a goalkeeping crisis in 1989, he still received no call. At that time, James Seymour from Garrykennedy in Tipperary had transferred to the Eire Óg club. Seymour was a keeper who had played underage with Tipp and who had won the 'save of the year' award in 1983 for a stop he made in that year's All-Ireland minor semi-final against Galway. McMahon was in goal and Seymour was playing wing-forward for Eire Óg but the Clare management decided to draft Seymour into the team for the first round of the championship against Waterford. He had a nightmare match and five goals went past him.

When Len Gaynor took over in 1990, McMahon was drafted back into the squad but Fitzgerald had arrived at that stage and the battle lines were drawn. McMahon was undergoing a difficult period in his personal life and he walked away from Clare after playing a challenge game against Tipperary the following April. After Clarecastle beat Eire Óg in the championship semi-final in September, McMahon announced his retirement that evening. He was still only twenty seven and hitting his best ever form. He never hurled again.

Looking back on his hurling career now, McMahon can run his eyes over the contours of it as easily as he can run his finger along the line of a scar. In his own mind, he achieved a great deal but the general perception of Eoin McMahon in Clare is that he only ever played one game. The 1987 replay was the starting and finishing point of his hurling career in the eyes of the mob. And in his own eyes too, that was really where the line was drawn underneath it all.

'I always thought that some people were very narrow-minded to make an opinion on my hurling because of one incident,' said McMahon. 'It affected me big time. I just felt so bad that people would actually think that of me. I probably would have been a shy individual and that made it harder to take. I didn't want to think too much of it, but I often look back and wonder if that didn't happen, and if people hadn't reacted like the way they did, would I have played on for Clare for another six or seven years? I just got a burning from people and it did affect me. I'm not saying that it did make up my mind to give up the game but it probably went a long way towards it.'

Then he pauses and thinks before changing his plea before his submission to the court is off the ground.

'Yeah, it probably did force me to pack it all in early all right. I knew there was more in me but I was a sensitive soul at the time and I just had enough of it. There's only so much you can take when people brand you something that you know yourself that you're not.'

Clare decided their gameplan against Galway when the bus pulled up outside Pearse Stadium and they all saw how strong the breeze was drifting in from the Atlantic Ocean just over the road. The war paint was immediately daubed across their cheeks and if they could win the toss, an early raid was going to be swift and decisive.

Although they only scored once in the second half, Clare won by three points because they largely outfought and outmanoeuvred the home side all day. They led by eleven points at the interval and while the pattern of the second half became a mess, Clare created that texture to suit themselves. When a game descends into the trenches and the inches have to be fought for, Clare know they will grind it out.

It was a huge win and there was a really positive vibe in the squad afterwards. Fitzgerald was delighted and the result has reinforced his steely determination to come out on top.

'It's going to be tough not having any games before the championship but I have to look at the positive and maybe this suspension might be the best thing to happen to me because it will give me an awful buzz for training. I'll be right, I know I'll be right for that game. The most important thing now is that my suspension will have no effect because the team comes first. That's the way I'm going to approach it. I have to row in and do my bit but I'm confident that I'll handle myself properly. I have to deal with it but I'm just anxious that Clare do well. All I want is to see Clare doing well.'

WHAT DRIVES YOU ON CAN DRIVE YOU MAD

Stevie Brenner is back. After Galway rifled five goals past Ian O'Regan and the Waterford defence on March 21 in the League, the management took a sledgehammer to the back seven and reconstructed a new model for the crunch game with Clare in Cusack Park on Sunday. Waterford can't really afford to lose and even if they do, they have to keep the margin tight to deny Kilkenny sneaking into their spot. Kilkenny are expected to demolish Dublin in Nowlan Park.

The following Tuesday night, Brenner went straight up to Justin McCarthy and told him that he felt he'd earned a chance to play. McCarthy told him that he was playing well and to hang in there. Then when the team was announced after training on the Thursday night, Brenner heard his name called out for the first time all year. After that, fourteen names from the Waterford Under-12 side could have been announced and he wouldn't have noticed. It's sweet because all he wanted was a chance and now he's got it. The minute he had togged in afterwards, he rang his wife Helena and then phoned his mother with the good news.

'It was more relief than anything else,' said Brenner. 'It reminded me of the first time I got picked to play for Waterford, I was wicked excited. It's a big weight off my shoulders because I was just wondering was all the hard work ever going to pay off. I was finding it impossible to watch the games and it was getting tougher every week. I'd sit there and watch the match but I'd have to be talking to someone to keep my mind occupied. It was wicked tough.'

When the jersey was handed to Brenner on Sunday, he took one look at it and made a promise to himself that he would keep it for the rest of the year. He knew he always wanted it to be his but it took the last couple of months for him to really appreciate how badly he did want it. There was pressure on him but he didn't let it smother him. Although Waterford lost by two points, they still secured their passage through to the next phase of the League and Brenner played well.

'There was a little bit of pressure there alright but I knew that was going to be the case. The pressure doesn't really affect my game the majority of the time. I don't go out and have a stinker because I'm wicked nervous. I didn't feel that much pressure on me, even if there seemed to be. I'd have felt a lot more pressure if it was a home game and I was delighted that it was on in Clare. Down here, you're expected to win and there would have been a lot more focus on me.'

Brenner felt sharp but maybe the edge to his game has come from a pop psychology experiment from Justin McCarthy.

'That could have been the case, yeah. It probably wasn't a major mind game thing but there was probably a certain bit of it there. He came to me before the game and said that if I played like I was capable of, there would be no fear of me. He was delighted afterwards when I played well. He's happy now that he took the risk with me and I think the whole thing has made me a better keeper.

'I really think it's after giving me the kick up the arse that you sometimes need. Even if you're playing well, you need to be brought down to earth sometimes and that's what it did for me. After two championships in a row, you kinda think you're invincible and that probably catches up on everyone at some stage.

'That caught up with me a bit last year and that's why I was so determined to put that right this year. That's why the last few months were such a worry, I was just afraid that I wouldn't get that chance. This could be my last year, next year could be my last year, I could have five years left. You wouldn't know but I just had to get back in this year. I had to live for the day and for the moment and keep pushing on.'

The following Wednesday night, young Gary Mullan travelled over to Portaferry in the Ards Peninsula in Down, with senior hurling selector

Hugh Pat McCosker. Down were training and Mullan had only one thing on his mind. He is only sixteen but he is the Down minor keeper and is expected to be the junior keeper later in the summer and all he did for the evening was stand behind the goalmouth and observe Graham Clarke. When Clarke told him afterwards that he'd take him for a training session anytime he wanted, Mullan nearly collapsed.

He doesn't get the chance to meet Clarke too often. He is from Ballela, near Banbridge, which is over an hour away from Portaferry. Even though the hurling heartland in the county is concentrated in a tiny area at the tip of the peninsula that is shared between three clubs – Portaferry, Ballygalget and Ballycran – there are tiny oases like Ballela spread out over the vast Down hurling desert. But only very few because half of the county's hurling clubs have disappeared off the map in the last fifteen years. The real extent of the decline was highlighted two years ago when an internal review of Down hurling estimated that the game was facing near extinction.

The County Board have tried to rectify that situation but hurling in the county is in a vastly different state now to what it was when Clarke first joined the senior panel twelve years ago. Back then Down were just after winning their first Ulster senior hurling title in fifty one years and were much more than just a handy target for the big boys. In 1993 they travelled to Nowlan Park and beat a Kilkenny side with twelve of their All-Ireland winning team on board. The result steered them into a National League quarter-final and consigned Kilkenny to Division Two in the process.

They had a good senior team but nevertheless the writing was on the wall. Minimal underage success meant that Down went into decline after winning further Ulster senior titles in 1995 and '97. They haven't won an Ulster title since and most of the big names have drifted away in the last few years. Clarke is the most senior player in the squad now and in many ways now, he is the silent face of a near anonymous Down hurling team.

In Ulster, everyone knows he's an outstanding goalkeeper. Down south, they hardly know he exists. Against Antrim in last summer's Ulster semi-final, he gave the third best individual display in the hurling championship. There may have only been a handful of supporters at the game, the stakes might not have been as high and the opposition not as pumped up, but Clarke's display was almost as impressive as Brendan Cummins' five-star showing against Kilkenny in the All-Ireland semi-final.

You had to be in Croke Park and have sampled the crowd's reaction to fully appreciate Cummins' magic performance, but technically, Clarke's was every bit as impressive. Antrim were ten points a better team but when Down drew level with two minutes remaining, it was Clarke who had thrown them that lifeline.

After that game, his name never resurfaced for the remainder of the year. Cummins rightly got his All-Star award in November but afterwards the Kilkenny county secretary, Pat Dunphy, launched a verbal hand grenade when he made veiled suggestions about Cummins in his annual report because James McGarry didn't get the All-Star. If Dunphy had stopped for a second to even consider Clarke in the whole debate, he might have altered his tone.

Clarke didn't get a second game, never mind the faintest consideration for even an All-Star nomination, because the beaten Ulster semi-finalists don't get a second chance in the championship. Antrim may be part of the poor relations brigade in hurling, but there would have been uproar if Clarke's heroics had torpedoed their season in one fell swoop. In his world, talk of even an All-Star nomination exists in a parallel universe. McGarry might not have won his All-Star but he has an opportunity to do something every year that Clarke would give his right arm for. And it's not the chance to win All-Stars or All-Ireland medals.

When Clarke was fifteen, he played on a Down minor team that ran Offaly to three points in an All-Ireland semi-final. That was his first and last time playing in Croke Park. He was there as a sub with Down for the 1995 All-Ireland semi-final and he got a few pucks in during the half-time of a couple of Railway Cup games but that's all he's seen of the hallowed sward since he played there half his lifetime ago.

He thought his chance had arrived seven years ago when Down defeated Antrim in the Ulster final. Then they realised a showcase American football game was being staged in Croke Park that weekend and their All-Ireland quarter-final against Tipperary was moved to Clones on a Saturday evening before a handful of people.

'That knocked the heart out of me for ages,' said Clarke. 'You hear counties complaining about this and that and then us boys earned the right, as we thought, to play in Croke Park and then you see American footballers running about the place. I waited all my life for a day like that and then you see that shit. I don't think the authorities realise how much something like that can really destroy a hurler from Down.

'I'm always listening to DD *(DD Quinn, the Antrim goalkeeper)* telling me "I want back there." He's always telling me about the atmosphere and the echoes around the place and I'd give anything to play in Croke Park. Anything. I'd swap all my medals to play there in a League final or whatever. Just that once would do me, that's how badly I want it. John Crossey *(manager)* says to me the other night "you'll get your game in Croke Park yet son." He knows how badly I want it too because that's the only reason I'm still playing hurling at county level.'

When Clarke turned up early for training in Ballygalget a couple of nights later, the detritus of the previous evening's club training session was still strewn across the floor. He got out the brush and swept the dirt out the door before his county team-mates arrived.

'I wonder does Davy Fitz do this before a Clare training session?' he wrote in his diary that night.

Welcome to life on the hurling breadline. There have been so many spellbinding and moist-eyed hurling days over the last ten years that it is easy now to forget the bigger picture. May will be here in less than a month and the Munster championship will ignite on a short fuse and the carnival will begin. The spring will be soon forgotten about but just now as the League has reached the point of dividing into winners and losers, no one bats an eyelid as to what's happening further below the waterline in Divisions Two and Three. The managers of Derry and Carlow have already walked away, citing a lack of commitment from their players, but that has been the only thing worth talking about in Division Two.

Try telling that to the Down and Kerry hurlers who meet in a huge game on Sunday April 11 in Portaferry. Down lost their Division One status in 1994 and then lost a play-off to get it back in 1995. They spent one season in Division One in 1999 when the League was restructured, but got hammered in every match. The prospect of Division One hasn't appeared on the radar again until now. Even though Kerry lost last year's Division Two League final to Antrim, that match was the making of them. They got a run-out in Croke Park and the confidence garnered from their early season exploits was a big factor in them frightening the daylights out of Limerick in the first round of the championship qualifiers.

Down saw the benefits Kerry accrued from it and took a mental note. With Antrim up in Division One and Derry in total disarray, this is their chance to get close to the big-time. With Westmeath having to travel to Kerry for their last game, Down will hold all the aces if they can win on Sunday. Furthermore, this could be Clarke's last opportunity to get to Croke Park.

'It's a massive game for us boy, it really is,' said Clarke. 'Promotion probably means more to us than the championship, it does. Promotion is the thing that could bring Down hurling on. A lot of people might ask if it would help Down hurling to go up and get stuffed by Kilkenny. Well, it would help Down hurling if DJ Carey was standing above in Ballygalget pitch. You might not win a whole load of matches but you have to have something like that to aim for.

'(Brendan) Cummins is a great goalkeeper who is far better than I'll ever be, but I'm sure if he was in my position, he'd be the same. He'd want to be playing against the best and at the end of the day, you want to be playing in the big games and making saves as good as Cummins or Davy Fitz can. We may not be at the same standard up here but as far as I'm concerned Liam Watson can hit the ball just as hard as Eddie Brennan can. That's not being bigheaded but you have to be confident in your own ability that you can stop anyone's shots.

'That's what I want and we all want it and every game from now on is like championship for us. We've done nothing this week in preparation for Sunday. Crossey said to us last night that "if the wife says that you need coal on the fire, tell her to go and get it." It's total focus now and we're going to pull out all the stops to win. It starts here on Sunday.'

They pulled out all the stops and an eleven-point victory was achieved as Down produced their best performance in seven years. They hit 2-28 - 2-20 from play - and three goals in the last four minutes from Kerry put a false complexion on the scoreboard. Even with the win, Clarke is still disappointed.

'I wasn't great now, to be honest. I'm telling you boy, I don't know what the hell is wrong with me. I'm trying to do absolutely everything at the moment and I'm getting absolutely nowhere. On my day, I'd have stopped two of those four shots. It's a long time since I let in four goals and it's kinda playing on my mind a wee bit; am I slipping a bit or whatever? But it's all confidence, I know it is. I just need to be doing more than I'm doing and that confidence will come back in, like.

'Their first goal was hit from the 21-yard line and it's all coming back to this whole sliotar thing again. I've been training with Gaelic Gear balls all year. I stopped the shot, it bounced off my hurley and the forward just came in and knocked it. I just looked at the ball after I picked it out of the net and went "you bastard!" It was an O'Neills ball and I drove the fucking thing out over the road.'

Almost a year on from the sliotar, which caused a raft of recrimination during last year's championship, the dreaded ball is still haunting keepers. That ball is still available to buy because O'Neills had so much stock to clear. Given that so many of them are still at large, they have been showing up at venues all over the country during the National League. Clarke found that out on Sunday.

For all the debate the sliotar caused last summer, it was the keepers who had to endure the real hardship. It was like trying to catch a rock, control a golfball and stop a bullet. Tests are continuing in search of a new core that can be imposed as the standard for all sliotars and all the main suppliers were invited to submit sliotars to Dublin City University (DCU) in January for a series of tests.

Only sliotars that meet specific criteria will be approved for the inter-county roster in the 2004 season. The testing in DCU is being overseen by an English bio-mechanist, Kieran Moran, who has a background in tennis ball research, and at a later stage this year, players will be included in the testing process before any final decisions are made.

In the context of last year's disquiet, the bounce of the balls submitted for approval will be closely watched. Last year's O'Neills ball, with a polyurethane core, used to bounce like a golfball. O'Neills have been experimenting with new cores, changing the polyurethane mix to moderate the bounce and they have submitted a couple of new prototypes for the DCU tests. Croke Park are still driving towards a position where all sliotars will be made containing the same core but in the meantime, not every sliotar will play ball.

'I'm just cracking up with these sliotars,' said Clarke. 'I was hitting out our heavy balls against the wind in the first half but every ball that hit the net after that was an O'Neills ball. You can't be making excuses and they probably would have hit the net anyway, but my striking was perfect every time I pucked out a Gaelic Gear ball. That's what I'm used to and it's a totally different ball game, control-wise, everything, with a ball you're not used to. And we're not used to those yokes up here.'

The whole-complicated ballistics of the flight and bounce of the ball is their normal business, but it has been a nightmare for goalkeepers over the last few years. Clarke was like an Antichrist when the goals were flying in past him and he took it out on the sliotars as if belting the hell out of them was some kind of cathartic payback. When he spoke to former Down keeper, Hugh Dorrian, after the game, Dorrian read him.

'He said "as soon as those balls went in the net, you drove them up the field with pure temper, that won't win you nothing." I just said "I know, I know, I just don't like letting in goals." He said "I'm telling you now, if a ball goes in that net, count to ten because you've an awful temper on you."'

Clarke had plenty of time to cool down because when the game was over, he turned the car south with his wife Mary and five-month old baby daughter Lauren to head for Killarney for a week's holidays. They stopped outside Naas for a bit to eat before arriving in Killarney just after 11pm.

When Clarke first met Mary Doolan in Galway in the summer of 1993, she knew nothing about hurling and when they first started going out, her late father Seán wondered if Clarke was just filling his daughter's head of notions because he didn't know they even hurled in Down. Nearly three hundred miles separated them but they were married in July 2000 and by that stage, Mary didn't have a choice about hurling. She just accepted that it was who her husband was.

'When I first started going to matches I hadn't a clue what was going on,' said Mary Clarke. 'I'd see a bird flying overhead and I'd think it was the ball.'

For a while, her family thought that Clarke was a complete basketcase. He'd often get up at six o clock on a Sunday morning in Killarney and drive straight to north Antrim for an Antrim League game. If you were to pick the furthest spot on the map away from Killarney, Ballycastle near the north Antrim coast would be it. Yet Clarke has made the journey a couple of times in the last few years and played a match after it. On another occasion, he'd nearly broken the land-speed record to get from Killarney to Ballycran for a match. He got to Portaferry in time but there was fog over Strangford Lough and the ferry was off. He hit the road for the one-hour journey around the peninsula and eventually ran from the car straight to the pitch.

Sunday wasn't the first marathon trip of the season either. When Down played Derry in the opening round of the League at the end of February, the Clarkes drove two hours to Banagher in south Derry before heading south for Killarney. The car pulled into Kerry that night just before midnight.

'That was the longest day of my life,' said Clarke. 'I didn't play that well but I don't think it was great preparation beforehand when you knew you had to face an eight hour trip afterwards. It was absolute madness but I said to Mary afterwards that some day it might be worth it. If it gets me a game in Croke Park, I don't care.'

The journey last Sunday was made shorter too for Clarke with the knowledge that he had somebody to train with during the week. After the game, Clarke spoke to Kerry forward Shane Brick coming off the field and informed him of his plans. Brick told him that he could come training with his club Kilmoyley and they exchanged phone numbers. On Thursday evening, Brick rang Clarke to tell him that a training session planned for that night was called off but that he was more than welcome to come along to Kerry training on Friday night. Clarke didn't even think for a second about feeling awkward. He jumped at the offer.

'I'd talk away to most of those boys anyway after any match but those boys are dead-on. I was just there as one of them, if you know what I mean. They treated me like royalty. They were asking me questions about my striking and all of that and they got me to show their wee keeper what way I was striking the ball to try and get him get a few extra yards onto his puckout. And I got a few drills off him as well. It was great and I enjoyed it. I've been going down there for nearly ten years now and it's nice to have a few contacts down there, where you can go for a few pucks with boys over the summer. Shane Brick is as good a hurler as there is in Ireland. There's no airs or graces about them boys down there.'

On Sunday morning at 8am, the Clarke family were back on the road again, heading to Arklow for Down's crucial league game. Mary had the map out while Lauren slept in the back and it took them four hours to get there. Clarke's back was tight when he got out from behind the wheel, but he didn't think anything of it. He had a job to do and any excuses wouldn't be worth a damn afterwards.

When the game finished, Down had completed what they had set out to do. Their three point win more or less secured their passage through to the Division Two final, even with one game remaining. It wasn't that easy though, and with eight minutes remaining, they trailed by seven points until they hit the gas and edged home. Clarke felt the rot set in after he messed up on a high ball just after half-time and he was back in the mental torture-chamber afterwards.

'I was talking to a few boys who were saying that maybe I was too hard on myself but Jesus Christ. I got away with dropping a ball in the first half but the first ball in the second half, I shouted for it cleanly and I was going to take ball, full-forward and everything else out. I totally missed the ball. It bounced to the full-forward, he threw her up and just flicked it in the net. That was them two points in the lead and then they scored another one right after that.

'I don't know what it is. I always try and do those simple things right but by Jesus, I'm not doing it right so far this year. It would have been my fault if we'd lost, plain and simple. That goal was a joke. If that was any other goalkeeper, they'd nearly have been taken off. It was an embarrassment. I don't know if I should start trying to train with O'Neills balls and get used to catching them or what. We're training with these Gaelic Gear balls and they're as dead as hell. Once it hits your hand, it's in your hand, whereas with these O'Neills balls, they could go anywhere.

'I think I'm just going to have to start doing basic drills, like. Maybe it's time now for a few different drills where I'm concentrating that wee bit more on dropping balls, bouncing balls, stuff like that. I have serious work to do here now because I have to sharpen up my eye. Croke Park is on the horizon and you can't be going down there with no confidence, no matter what Division League final you're playing in.'

At the moment, Clarke is trying to balance a savage equation. The 168-mile long drive before the game was enough to tighten his back and strain his brain to near breaking point. His life has never been as hectic and his hurling never as poor. He's trying to find the correct medium in the centre, hoping that time isn't going to catch him out somewhere along the line.

After Sunday's match, he jumped into the car and drove another 160 miles to Ballygalget. He'd driven 328 miles and played an important match but he still had a job on in Belfast the following morning. When

Clarke's alarm went off at 7am, Mary asked him to lie on for an extra hour and not to risk running his batteries down further. Clarke wouldn't hear of it. He's trying to mentally steel himself now.

'I just said to Mary that I didn't want to start feeling sorry for myself. Even though I'm wrecked, I'm just disgusted with myself. I'm not happy because I'm starting to doubt myself now. I've just turned thirty, I've a wee child there and I'm just after starting a new business and I'm wondering if I'm not concentrating enough on my hurling?

'Donal Óg Cusack wouldn't have done that drive before a game and Davy Fitz wouldn't have done it without a driver, but I have to think of my family as well. It's just hard. I don't know but you have to be honest with yourself. I could say to myself that the full-forward was pulling on that ball, but I should still be able to deal with that. I apologised to Crossey after the game for that performance because it was a joke.

'If we had lost and it cost us a game in Croke Park, that was me gone. That would have been it. I'd have fired my sticks into Strangford Lough on the way back and left them there for good. I just don't know what I'm going to have to do to get myself out of it. I'm just going to have to forget about all that shite now, get my head sorted out and get myself right. Jesus Christ, this is too important to go and screw it all up now.'

ON THE EDGE

Down might not be there just yet but at least they're within touching distance of Division One hurling next season. Wexford, Offaly and Antrim meanwhile are clinging onto Division One with their fingertips. The dirt is gathering under their fingernails from trying to claw their way to survival but one of them is going to go down to Division Two on Sunday. Wexford and Antrim have one point from two games in the second phase of the League while Offaly have no points. Antrim seem set for the drop but with the prospect of Wexford and Offaly free-falling ahead of them can't be discounted.

Dublin wiped out Offaly the previous weekend by eighteen points and they have to beat Laois now to have any hope of surviving. Although Antrim took a point from their game with Laois, they look doomed with an away fixture to Kilkenny that will torpedo their scoring difference. Wexford have a point and a decent scoring difference and while they look set to avoid the drop with a home game against Dublin, anything is possible with the way they're going at the moment.

Nine months on from drawing with Cork in one of the best championship games seen in the last fifteen years, that match seems like a lifetime ago now and they're staring into a potential doomsday scenario.

It has been building up to a crisis for a while now because the squad has been haemorrhaging players since the start of the year. Liam Dunne retired in January, Larry O'Gorman walked away in February and there has been a steady bleed ever since. Darren Stamp, Ken Furlong, Anthony O'Leary, Robbie Kirwan, Robbie Codd and Jim Morrissey have all left while Barry Goff pulled out just before Kilkenny hammered them last weekend. Even training in general over the last few weeks has become an issue. In one week attendance went from twenty one to fourteen and back up to nineteen and none of those numbers was satisfactory. Some players whose attendance at training had been poor were still being picked in League matches and, inevitably, tension has been building.

A new training regimen placed the first strain on relations. After nearly a decade of service Seán Collier stepped down as team trainer and Jim Kilty, a highly respected athletics coach who had just finished three years with Tipperary's hurlers, replaced him. Management decided on a tough programme in the close season and Kilty set it up. He told the players in January that the regime was designed with a specific target in mind; to win this year's All-Ireland would entail having to beat Kilkenny twice. With that in mind, between training and weekend matches the panel would gather four times a week, with two other gym sessions to be done by the players in their own time.

Some players were doing both gym sessions while others were doing none but the general mood amongst the players was that the training schedule was too much. Unable to trust everyone, management were forced to change their original plan and organise one supervised gym session a week. That only alleviated some of the unrest though, because more serious issues have been festering for weeks now.

Some players had been guilty of indiscipline and at times management were guilty of poor decision making. Senior players feel that management has accommodated certain squad members and now before their crunch game with Dublin, they've made another bad call. Their decision to drop Darragh Ryan was like firing a rock at a hornet's nest.

'Something could be about to happen in training tonight, because the boys were on to me there earlier on,' said Damien Fitzhenry on Thursday, three days before the Dublin match. 'They're going to call a meeting because it's crazy that they've dropped Darragh for Sunday. Management said he wasn't playing well but everybody could be dropped if that's the case. You don't drop the best man we've had for the last four years.'

An excellent player as well as a diligent trainer, Ryan has been crucial to this Wexford team since he was captain for the 2001 season. His form has been patchy during the League in an unsettled full-back line; for the first five League games Wexford changed their right corner-back five times; in the next game against Laois both corner-backs were taken off. Ryan didn't have one of his better days against Kilkenny and by dropping him management hoped they might re-ignite his old spark. Instead all they've done is throw more petrol on the flames of unrest within the camp.

'There's just mass disillusionment there at the moment and lads don't know where they're going or what they're doing or what is going on, like,' said Fitzhenry. 'There are lads getting chances that have got them every day and don't really deserve them and then there's lads not getting chances at all. It's crazy at the moment and that's the truth of it. With the way we're playing at the minute, anything could happen. Absolutely anything. If we get relegated, it will be an absolute disaster.

'No disrespect to the Division Two sides, but who wants to go and hurl down there? Things are absolutely at their lowest now since I got involved with Wexford eleven years ago. When you start off with a panel of forty fellas and then it's cut to thirty and then the next minute there's two gone, three gone, four gone, five gone, there has to be something up. Everybody can't be wrong. I guarantee you, if the boys *(management)* do go or are gone in the next week, you'll have lads who have left who will be back. There's no doubt about that.'

They could really do with Niamh Fitzpatrick now. She was the team psychologist to the team that won the 1996 All-Ireland title and has been used sparingly by respective managements since Liam Griffin departed the scene that year. Fitzpatrick was considered by the players to be an invaluable conduit to the management and was enormously respected but manager John Conran wrote to her in the off-season claiming that she wasn't right for his set-up. That was before he had been critical of her preparation for last year's Leinster final, claiming she hadn't the players' heads right. The Olympic Council of Ireland obviously feel differently. They've appointed her as their team's psychologist for the Olympic Games in Athens in August.

They could probably do with Larry O'Gorman now as well. He was more or less told to go in February before he was pushed and while he hasn't been helping matters lately by airing his views in the media, he possibly should have been retained for the purpose of team morale. Just for his one-liners, to help ease the tension and to open the valve and release some pressure.

When the squad were on their team holiday in Las Vegas in January, a group of players happened upon an International Porn Convention one afternoon and decided to do some investigative work. They waltzed into the hotel and perched themselves at the top of the stairs to give themselves the best vantage point. When one of the best endowed women at the convention walked down the stairs, she eventually felt the glare of twelve pairs of eyes on the back of her neck. When she reached the bottom, she turned around and Larry O Gorman gave her the thumbs up. 'Nice shoes!' he roared. Just ten days later, the squad had their first outdoor session of the season in minus 4 degrees and that story helped to warm up the mood. They could do with some of that heat now to help melt part of the lead that has been deposited in the squad's collective will.

'Everything has just turned pear-shaped now,' said Fitzhenry. 'Lads can't believe what's going on. There were fellas ringing into one of the local radio stations last Monday saying it was the worst Wexford performance in forty years, saying they'd never pay to watch Wexford again. Stupid stuff like that, but that rarely happens. We have to hold our hands up as well but we're not going out three nights a week for some gobshite from the middle of nowhere telling you you're cat, like.'

The only reason Wexford have a point in the second phase of the League was down to Fitzhenry two weeks ago against Laois. He stopped three bullets in the second half to earn them a draw that they didn't deserve. Last week against Kilkenny, he'd have needed an altar on the goal-line and a priest beside him saying novenas to have any chance with the shots that beat him.

'The three goals against Kilkenny were from the edge of the square and if any of them had hit me, they'd have killed me stone dead. The first one especially, be the Lord Jaysus, it could have finished me.'

LAST MAN STANDING

On Thursday evening, training went as well as could be expected but the squad met afterwards and arranged a meeting for the following evening in the Ferrycarrig Hotel. Everybody was expected to be in attendance and one of the senior players booked the Táin room in the hotel to give them the privacy they needed to air all their grievances and to thrash out a way forward.

Democracy was going to rule but a clear decision was forming in the minds of a couple of the players with the loudest voices in the chorus; they felt that the point of no return had been passed and that the management had to go. But when those players sought more experienced counsel on Friday, they altered their views. They were advised that getting rid of the management six weeks before the championship could destroy their season and rip Wexford apart in the process. By the time the players met in the small conference room in the Ferrycarrig Hotel Friday evening, that option wasn't on the agenda.

There was a full attendance at the meeting and the main topics of discussion were the needs to split their differences with management and to come up with a new gameplan. Management hadn't come up with one so they decided to take it out of their hands and implement the gameplan themselves. Fitzhenry said he was after playing a game of tennis with the Kilkenny half-back line for the previous two years and bombing high balls on top of the Kilkenny defence in the Leinster semi-final was not going to work again. They needed an alternative.

'We're going to have to look ahead to the Kilkenny half-back line because if we don't break them down, we haven't a hope of beating them,' said Fitzhenry at the meeting. 'The last thing we probably need now is to change our gameplan but we won't beat anybody with the way we're hurling at the moment.'

They discussed short puckouts and moving the ball quickly. They didn't know if it would work but time was running out. They said they'd try it Sunday.

While the Wexford players were meeting on Friday night, DD Quinn returned home to Loughgeil in Antrim, fired his gear-bag into the corner and just left it there. He had planned to pack his stuff for the next day's trip to Kilkenny but he didn't have the heart for it. At the moment, his morale is inside in his boots, his mood as tossed up as the gear in his bag. Better to keep them unzipped for now.

Quinn has played in six of Antrim's seven league games to date and now, for the one game he really wanted to play, against Kilkenny, he's been dropped. Manager Dinny Cahill told him during the training session that they were starting young Ryan McGarry from Ballycastle in goal and it hasn't gone down well with Quinn.

'I'm disappointed, surely. Kilkenny were the one team I hadn't played against in the last few years at senior level. I said to him *(Cahill)* "are you trying to tell me something?" He said that I was still number one but I'm annoyed because I don't get too many chances to test myself against the likes of Shefflin and these boys. I wanted to see if I was up to it. Playing against the best, the All-Ireland champions. I wouldn't have minded if he'd left me off against Dublin or Laois. But not this one.'

If results go to form, Quinn won't get another chance to play against Kilkenny in the League until at least two years' time because Antrim look set for the drop. There are no guarantees he'll ever get to play against them in the championship because Antrim haven't met Kilkenny since 1993. If he has to wait two years for the sides to meet in the League, it's not certain that he'll still be there. McGarry is a good prospect and if Gareth McGhee, the Dunloy keeper, took a notion to give inter-county a serious shot, he could nail down the spot. A lot of other players may take a League game against Kilkenny for granted; Quinn can't.

Getting dropped now has just rubbed more salt into an already raw wound. He's been getting pummelled all season and so has the team. There were a couple of sides limping around the division and Antrim still couldn't knock any of them. One point in the second phase doesn't look like being enough and the fact that they are the only side out of twelve who haven't won a game means they don't deserve to stay up. They're relying on Laois now to do them a massive favour against Offaly and the fact that their survival is out of their hands has left some players disillusioned.

'He *(Cahill)* is giving a lot of young boys a go, you know, and that's a bit tricky away to Kilkenny,' said Quinn. 'At the start he would have liked to have won a couple of matches to stay up but as the League went on, he was saying that he didn't really care because we came out of Division Two last year and hurled bravely down in Croke Park. Dinny said he's not too bothered but I don't want to go back down to Division Two. I want to be playing against the best players and I know that most of the other lads don't want to go down there either. I'd say Dinny does want to stay up too but he's just playing it all down.'

Quinn has noticed the confidence seeping out of the team in the last few matches, while his own confidence is on the floor at the moment. His form is gone to the dogs and he's become frustrated with Cahill's ambivalence towards bringing in a goalkeeping coach to help the keepers. He didn't feel sharp last year but he survived and he only felt the edge return to his game when he worked with Niall Patterson before Loughgeil's county final against Dunloy. That opened his mind to the importance of goalkeeping coaching, to fine-tune the specifics and technicalities of his game. To work on his own and be lone-minded. Athletes in solitary sports are familiar with such a frame of mind when their performance depends on nothing but themselves.

'I want Dinny to bring somebody in to work with the goalkeepers but he seems dead against it,' said Quinn. 'Niall *(Patterson)* made some difference to me before the county final last year and I want Dinny to bring somebody like that in. When he comes up from Tipperary on Tuesday night, he wants to work with the outfield players. I can see his point but I said why not bring somebody in, let him work the two keepers at the other end of the field and bring us up when he needs us? But he just seems dead against it, you know. I don't know why.

'He said that the drills we're doing are good for the keepers because we're attacking a ball and all that, but I think we need a bit more than that. I need to work on my reactions and I can only do so much with those drills. I keep saying it but I might as well be banging my head off a brick wall because he doesn't seem to be listening to me. I wasn't happy with the way I was playing last year and I said that I wasn't going to go through another year like that, but he won't listen.

'If Dinny is not going to do it, I'm just going to have to go and get someone for an hour or two during the week myself. Every year Dinny has been there, he's done nothing to help the goalkeepers. I've had to ask Graham *(Clarke)* about drills that he does with Down and he's been very helpful but I feel I need a bit more help than that. I don't feel that sharp now.'

Even though he's not sharp and confident at the minute and Sunday's game is going to be a turkey shoot for Kilkenny, Quinn was looking at it positively and was going to use the match as a gauge to see what level his shot-stopping was at. He had a picture in his mind of saving shots from DJ Carey and Henry Shefflin in Nowlan Park but he has readjusted his expectations.

'A lot of the players feel that we're just lambs to the slaughter. We're just hoping that Laois can do us a big favour and beat Offaly because realistically we have no chance of doing anything against Kilkenny. And that's not nice for the players.'

Quinn spent the whole game behind the goal on Sunday, primarily to observe the Kilkenny attacking machine and their scoring tendencies. Kilkenny put thirty-one points over the bar and their three-goal tally would have been a lot higher if their forwards hadn't acted like Samaritans and gone for more goals.

'They went easy on us,' said Quinn. 'But I'd still like to have been playing.'

Somebody behind the goal had a radio and Quinn stuck his head out over the fence with twenty minutes to go to ask how the Offaly/Laois match was going. When he heard Offaly were winning well, he just accepted it in his own mind that Antrim were gone down.

Offaly led by six points with seventeen minutes remaining but then a twenty-man brawl erupted and all hell broke loose. Damien Murray and Cyril Cuddy got involved in a tangle along the endline and this quickly developed into an opportunity to settle old scores between Birr and

Castletown and the Whelehans and Cuddys. They were the only players who really got hit in the fight and it became so nasty that Brian Whelehan had to change his blood-soaked jersey after the fire cooled down. When it did, Barry Whelehan and David Cuddy were sent off.

The stoppage completely halted Offaly's momentum and Laois came back into the game. Four points in succession cut the deficit to two with five minutes on the clock. Over in Kilkenny, it was announced over the loudspeaker that Offaly were still ahead with two minutes to go and a Dylan Hayden point in injury time looked to have secured the win. But Laois wouldn't let go. Damien Culleton finished a loose ball to the net five minutes into injury time and Liam Tynan then landed the winner. Offaly had gone down.

'It's just a sign of the times and Offaly aren't what they used to be anymore,' said Offaly goalkeeper Brian Mullins. 'It's sad to say that but that's the truth of it. Our confidence isn't great now. No matter how good you are, when you take a couple of pastings, you start to question yourself. I know we're missing a lot of players but we're still a bit unsure about how good of a team we have. To be honest, it's not good for the confidence.

'I had one good game against Tipperary but since that I've let in a couple of bad goals and I've had a poor enough League. I need to knuckle down now myself or forget about it. We all have to look at ourselves now and ask a few hard questions. Are we going to bother at all now? We might as well throw our hat at it if we're going to keep giving performances like that. Getting relegated is an embarrassment but we just have to hope now that it will be the kick up the arse that we need.'

Down have a great chance now of replacing Offaly in Division One after their passage to the Division Two League final was paved by Meath's failure to show for their game in Portaferry. The ferry across Strangford Lough was off because of fog but Down had agreed to put back the match so the Meath bus could take the longer road trip.

Instead the bus just turned around and headed for home.

Everything is going to plan for Clarke and for Down. They are playing well, have reached the League final against a Westmeath team they are confident of taking, and they have secured a match in Croke Park. The only worry Clarke has in the back of his mind is that things are almost going too well to be true.

His biggest fear of the lot was confirmed a day later. Waterford and Galway qualified for the Division One League final on Sunday and the match has been fixed for Limerick. Not Croke Park. The Division Two final has been pencilled in as the undercard to the main event. In Limerick. Not Croke Park.

'It's just crap, like,' said Clarke. 'It's just put a downer on everything. Our goal was to get to a League final in Croke Park but maybe it's our own fault for putting too much emphasis on Croke Park. It's just one of those things but I'm sort of used to it by now and you kind of become cynical towards the whole thing. You just accept that you're probably never going to play in Croke Park but it still knocks the heart out of you. No disrespect to Limerick but even if the game had been fixed for Thurles, it would have been a lot nicer. I've never played in Thurles either.

'There would be way more of a buzz about the place if the game was on in Croke Park but there's nothing you can do about it. It's a League final and we're just going to have to forget about this Croke Park thing and win it. At least if we get into Division One next year I might get a crack at Thurles.'

With Offaly losing on Sunday, Wexford didn't have to win against Dublin to cement their Division One status but they beat them anyway by seven points. They were happy with how their new gameplan worked but the players held a meeting amongst themselves in the dressing room afterwards and it was decided that a delegation from the players' committee would meet with management after training on Tuesday evening.

They wanted to iron out any further problems players had and they remained in the dressing room for nearly forty five minutes after management had left. Some local reporters were still waiting outside and the meeting was interpreted as a simmering revolt. The story grew wings and it was on local radio that evening that a putsch was about to take place. The following morning, it was reported in a couple of national newspapers that it was only a matter of time before the first shots were going to be fired.

Fitzhenry, John Conran and County Board Chairman Seán Quirke went on SouthEast Radio on Monday morning to clarify that there was no disharmony in the camp but Fitzhenry's comments were governed by diplomacy. He and the players wanted certain grievances addressed by management and they knew which path they wanted to pursue. After the 2003 Leinster final, Fitzhenry, Liam Dunne, Adrian Fenlon and Darragh Ryan held a heated meeting with management and it was the turning point in their season. The players said that all they wanted was a clearer and more progressive form of thinking for the good of Wexford hurling and the players could see no reason why a similar turning point couldn't be reached again.

After training on Tuesday evening, Fitzhenry, Rory McCarthy, Declan Ruth and Darragh Ryan approached the management for a meeting. Management were well aware of the degree of unrest and they said they would be receptive to what the players' committee had to say.

'We went to them and said we had come up with a gameplan,' said Fitzhenry. 'We were going to continue hurling like we had against Dublin on Sunday. We were sick of asking them for a gameplan and all they kept saying was: "Ye're big enough men now, just go out and hurl." We weren't going to accept that any longer and they were willing to take it on board. They had seen how we had worked it on Sunday and they were happy to go with it.

'We weren't happy with how everything was going but we told them that all thirty lads had made up their minds and decided to work hard for the next six weeks. If we left it any longer we were in trouble. The time to change it around was at the weekend and I think we're after turning the corner a small bit. As the slogan says "a lot done but by Jaysus, a lot more to do." That's the way we're looking at things.

'At the very end of the meeting I made the point to everybody that what we wanted and what they *(management)* wanted, were the very same things and it was just a matter of everyone rowing in together. And not having three lads pulling one way and thirty lads pulling the other.

'That's what was happening. They were pissing people off but everybody knows where they stand now. They know that they don't start pissing lads off who are training like lunatics the whole time, or if not, they'll walk. It's up to us now to make the most of the next six weeks and we just have to give it everything for June 13. We have to give it one hell of a shot.

'Even though we're going terrible, we have a chance if we can turn it around. Kilkenny are going to be thinking now: "Sure we beat the shite out of them with only half a team." I don't care what sort of a man you are, it's going to be quare hard to get that out of your head. I know they'll be mentally strong but if we train like dogs and get our heads right, you don't know what could happen.'

A lot done. A savage amount more to still do.

THE CAROUSEL

Sometimes life is just a bitch. Liam Donoghue has been waiting his whole career to play in a national senior final and now five days before Galway take on Waterford in the National League decider, his chance looks like short-circuiting up in a puff of smoke. A throbbing sensation started down the side of his face over a week ago and its intensity has been building up every day since. By Friday it was so bad he couldn't go to work and he was unable to train over the Bank Holiday weekend. Donoghue didn't sleep for three nights and the ordeal was prolonged even further because he couldn't go back to the dentist until this morning.

He'd been to the doctor a couple of times but the dentist confirmed that he had developed neuralgia - an undiagnosed, intense facial pain. A series of X-rays were taken and nothing showed up so he was booked in for an MRI scan in Galway City the next morning. In the afternoon though, Donoghue got a call back from the dentist to say that a second look at one of the X-rays had discovered the problem. A badly infected tooth was the source of the pain and it can be sorted with root canal treatment later on. He doesn't like injections but at least tomorrow morning, he won't feel like someone hit him on the side of the face with a baseball bat.

He's relieved because aside from missing the opportunity to play in a national final, Donoghue doesn't want to give someone else a chance to jump on the Galway goalkeeping carousel that has been turning constantly ever since Richie Burke left in 1995. Morgan Darcy, Pat Costello, Burke again, Damien Howe, Michael Crimmins and Donoghue have all played championship for Galway in the last eight seasons. In the same timespan, five more keepers have got a spin in the League and another four have got runs in challenge and tournament games. And yet, the best keeper in the county for the last decade - Kenneth Walsh from

Carnmore - hasn't played at all. He's just not interested.

Donoghue was consistently on and off the Galway panel for about four years until the door opened up for him two seasons ago when Michael Crimmins was dropped from the squad after the 2001 All-Ireland final defeat. Donoghue was in pole position after helping steer Clarinbridge to the All-Ireland club final but he slipped back down the grid again after the decider against Birr. After conceding four goals against Tipperary in the League quarter-final a month later, he could feel the Galway Goalkeeping Grim Reaper calling. In the dressing room afterwards he could see the black cloak and the staff coming around the door.

'We were annihilated and John Carroll was just walking clean through us. I got the message when I heard the management saying in the dressing room afterwards "we'll have to be looking at Liamy now." There was nothing said about what was going on out the field. Blame the keeper, like. We were being beaten all over the park and yet I was the one who was shafted.'

Crimmins was recalled a couple of weeks later and after Galway swatted Down with the back of their hand in the first round of the championship qualifiers, Donoghue walked. His departure scarcely registered as a tremor.

'They brought Mickey back in and after a few weeks he was back in goals,' said Donoghue. 'I didn't feel I deserved to be dropped but when I wasn't going to be in goals that was it, good luck. I was gone straight out the fucking door.'

Crimmins had enough after the 2003 championship and Donoghue was recalled along with Damien Howe by the new management. Howe had been the championship keeper for the 1999 drawn All-Ireland quarter-final against Clare before getting dropped at 11pm the night before the replay a week later. He spent the following three seasons in the wilderness but after conceding two bad goals in the first half of a League game against Clare in March 2003, he was substituted and walked afterwards.

Donoghue finally went on to play championship in the summer of

2003 and he performed reasonably well in his debut season. A couple of good games has never been enough to insulate Galway keepers from the cold winds of change but at the beginning of the 2004 League campaign, manager Conor Hayes publicly said that Donoghue was their first-choice keeper and that he would get every chance to establish himself.

'That meant an awful lot to me,' said Donoghue. 'It's an unbelievable load off your shoulders when you know you can make a mistake and you're not looking over your shoulder afterwards or looking at the bench. There are better keepers than me in Galway but nobody showed any faith in them. I'm the first keeper in the county in about seven years to have gone through a full League campaign and that makes a huge difference.

'This management are the first set of men that showed any faith in me. Management over the years have just made a scapegoat out of too many keepers and it hasn't helped Galway hurling. No matter what you say, it's only been in the last four years that Brendan Cummins has become a household name. I'm 100% convinced that it takes you a couple of years to get comfortable in there and to have the same confidence that you'd have with your club. If Cummins is honest, I'm sure he'll tell you that himself.'

Cummins agrees totally. 'When I started off in 1994, there's no way I'd have brought off the saves I'm after bringing off in the last three years. Your positioning and your reading gives you a chance but you can't inject that into someone. That has to come from being left there and being allowed to make mistakes, like I was years ago. The only problem with being a goalkeeper is you might only get two games or just one season to prove yourself and you won't be left in there to make all the mistakes you need to make to become a good goalkeeper.'

Donoghue has worked a lot harder on his game this year but he had to. Management informed him of issues in his game that they wanted addressed: flexibility, concentration, movement across the line, his tendency to shout too much at the wrong time. And his puckout.

One strong theory in the county is that Donoghue could have been in goal for Galway sooner if he had a better puckout. It was too inconsistent and too high and he wasn't able to line-drive the ball with a low trajectory. It was known within the Galway camp two years ago that some of the forwards weren't happy with his puckout and that they influenced the management's decision on dropping Donoghue. He knew himself it had to be addressed so at the outset of this season, he changed his puckout hurley and began working harder on the technicalities and specifics of his striking.

He has had a fine League campaign to date but it has been a long road back to arrive at this point. Donoghue could reasonably have been Galway's first-choice keeper nearly a decade ago. He had a decent underage pedigree and after Richie Burke got injured, Galway didn't have too many options after 1995. But Donoghue spilled a ball that ended up in the net against Kilkenny in the 1995 drawn All-Ireland Under-21 semi-final and smeared his CV at just the wrong time. In Galway, it can take almost a decade to live down a goalkeeping error like that.

Donoghue turned to soccer afterwards. That season he steered Kiltulla FC to the last eight of the FAI Junior Cup, scoring in every round and notching up forty goals in the whole season. He joined Galway United that autumn and although he never played League of Ireland, he lined out consistently with United for two seasons in the Connacht senior league.

Due to turn thirty in September 2004, a lot of heartbreak and disillusionment have woven their way around his soul in the last nine years. The Galway goalkeeping position has become labelled as a poisoned chalice but it is the high managerial turnover that has really been the poisoned chalice in Galway. It's easy to see why a part of Donoghue thought Sunday would never come. Only the carousel kept turning, it probably never would have.

'It all boils down to getting games,' said Donoghue. 'When you're playing, the whole world is rosy. When you're sitting on the bench, it's torture and all you do is bitch and complain and the whole world is against you because you're never going to get a game. In one way I had given up hope of ever playing on a day like Sunday because the management has changed so often in Galway over the years that it's down to someone's opinion whether he's going to like you or not.

'Then in another way, it's down to your attitude and I never gave up all hope because when you're hurling, you always think you're as good as what's out there and you will have a chance. But I still know that you can never take anything for granted in Galway.'

He learned that a long time ago.

Aside from the fact that they haven't won an All-Ireland in the last sixteen years, one of the many sorrowful mysteries of Galway hurling in that timespan has focused on the goalkeeping position. The county has continually produced some of the most artistic and skilful players in the country but they haven't been able to mine a single bluechip keeper from all their seams of underage talent from the last ten years.

Lack of senior success has engendered an abject sense of apathy in the Galway hurling public towards their players but they have developed an inherent distrust in their goalkeepers, who they've treated as the focal point for a lot of their angst.

Even John Commins, who won two All-Ireland medals with Galway in 1987 and '88, is still remembered by some for all the wrong reasons. He was a decent keeper with an excellent puckout who kept clean-sheets in successive All-Ireland finals. His displays in both finals went a long way towards securing those All-Irelands for Galway. But in his last championship game, he conceded five goals in the 1990 All-Ireland final against Cork and that was the end of him.

It was a sad finish to his inter-county career because Galway conceded four crazy goals that day. He should have stopped Kevin Hennessy's goal in the first half, but two more goals were scored from outside the edge of the square, he was unsighted for Mark Foley's strike and John Fitzgibbon should have been pulled for taking too many steps for the fifth goal. There was no point pleading his case to the defence: the jury had their minds already made up.

'I still hear the joke the odd time,' said Commins. ''What time is it? Five past Commins." It hurts me and it really bugs me when fellas say it to me. I'd still even get it to this day. I don't want any recognition for hurling for Galway but the only regret I do have during all my time was the way I left. I'd rather have been gone in 1989. I didn't want to be remembered as the lad who let in five goals in an All-Ireland final and never played another championship match for Galway. But that's probably the way I will be remembered.'

Although Michael Conneely is probably the most fondly remembered Galway goalkeeper of all - because of his man-of-the-match display in the 1980 All-Ireland final - he was dropped more times than he was selected and endured plenty of difficult days during his career.

Although Commins was a fine keeper who played in four All-Ireland finals and won two All-Stars, he wasn't regarded as the natural successor to Conneely at the outset of the 1980s. Back then the county had the great white goalkeeping hope of Galway hurling: Tommy Coen.

When Conneely retired in 1982, Coen was expected to fill the number one spot for the rest of the decade. He was an absolutely diamond shot-stopper who made his senior championship debut in 1983 and went on to win an All-Ireland Under-21 medal that September. He had already played in an All-Ireland minor final in 1981, had spent three years with the Under-21s and was underage again the following season.

Yet the visceral distrust of their goalkeepers was also burned into the psyche of the Galway management back then. Galway got blitzed by Cork in the 1983 All-Ireland semi-final, Coen conceded five goals - only one of which he was responsible for - and it was deemed sufficient evidence to build a case against him. Even though Coen was the Under-21 goalkeeper a year later, the senior management decided to select the Under-21 subkeeper, Tommy Kenny, for the 1984 All-Ireland senior semi-final against Offaly.

Kenny had a bad day at the office and was never seen with Galway again. When Cyril Farrell took over the senior team that autumn, he reconstructed a new side around the All-Ireland Under-21 winning squad of 1983. Galway would contest five All-Ireland finals in the next six years and when Farrell drew up his initial blueprint, Coen was part of the master plan.

Nobody remembers Tommy Coen now and for anyone who does, there is one dominant image lodged in the memory bank. Coen just happened to be the Galway keeper in the 1983 All-Ireland semi-final against Cork when Jimmy Barry-Murphy doubled on John Fenton's shot to score one of the greatest goals of all time.

'I thought that Barry-Murphy was trying to catch the ball and it had glanced off his hurley as he was using it to protect his hand,' said Coen. 'I read the flight of the ball all right but it was lifted higher than I expected. When I was picking it out of the net, Conor Hayes came back in beside me and asked me if Barry Murphy had hit it. I said he did, but I didn't realise then what he had done. It was an unreal strike.'

Coen felt his career was set to take off but he always had that drive necessary for survival at inter-county level. When Coen was in college in Thomond in Limerick in the early 1980s, everybody looked up to him. The football wing of the college had already created their own bit of history in 1978 by winning an All-Ireland club title but the hurling club was a joke. In 1982, they had to field a couple of camogie players to make up the numbers but Coen became player/trainer and transformed hurling in Thomond. Within a year, they had won the colleges title for Third-Level institutions who didn't play in the Fitzgibbon Cup.

The following season, the squad was training one cold and wet evening in October 1984. They were pucking around before the session cranked into full gear and Coen was standing between the posts. He jumped up and caught a high ball but as soon as the ball was in his hand, another shot was fired in from out the field. Martin Killeen put up his hurley to stop it but the ball deflected off his stick and hit Coen with full force into his left eye. The impact turned him upside down and he collapsed in a heap on the goal-line.

By the time he got up off the ground, his eye was closed. Initially he thought nothing of it but when the pain started knifing through his head, his team-mates packed him off to the Regional Hospital in Dooradoyle. The surgeon couldn't tell the extent of the damage because of the swelling but he was detained that night. Coen was still confident of being able to play for the college that Saturday but the following morning, his whole life changed.

He had a massive haemorrhage at the back of his eye, which knocked him out cold. The surgeons operated immediately to clear the blood and diagnose the extent of the damage it had caused. The retina had become detached from the wall of his eye and Coen went on to have five operations in the space of sixteen months. He was permanently blind in one eye. He forced himself to believe that it was only a matter of time before the sight would return. It never did.

His dream of hurling for Galway died a silent death that cold October day. He had to take the year out of college and before long depression set in.

'I just lost my way because hurling was number one for me really,' said Coen. 'There's so much of a routine attached to it that your whole life almost revolves around hurling. I was at sea for a while afterwards. I didn't know where I was going or what I was doing.'

In college they could see the trauma it caused him. 'He wouldn't have been a drinker up to the accident but it did hit him hard for a while,' said Martin Killeen. 'He was the best keeper Galway had at that time and even with one eye, he would still have been better than some of them. Tommy knew the possibilities that were out there for him and it was fierce hard for that to be ripped away from him.'

Coen's friends in college organised a small fundraising venture, while his own club, Mullagh, held a fundraising drive at the 1985 county final. Frank Burke was the County Secretary at the time and since the incident occurred in Limerick, he arranged an injury-compensatory payment from the Munster Council. In total, Coen received just over £3,000 as a way of compensation.

'It didn't matter what I got,' said Coen. 'If I had got £20,000 it wouldn't have made any difference. I had lost the chance to play for Galway.'

He travelled over to Boston in the summer of 1985 and seriously thought about staying out there permanently. Watching Galway reach the All-Ireland final was bittersweet but he coped. One chapter of his life had ended and another was just beginning.

Rita Divilly was a PE student in Thomond at the same time as Coen and he often spotted her when the team was playing in the college grounds. He never really knew her but when he was laid up in hospital she began visiting him out of the blue. She was a Galway camogie player but when she finished college in May 1985, she travelled to Boston and Coen followed her out there. Even though he had still to finish his degree, they were married later that summer.

'I suppose in some way, if I hadn't got the belt, we may never have met,' said Coen.

When Coen returned home, he had a wife, a family on the way and his college degree to think of and he went back to Limerick with a fresh outlook. Even though he couldn't play, he resumed his role as the college's team trainer and guided them to another Third Level crown. When he had his degree in the bag and another set of exams passed to allow him teach woodwork with his sight impediment, he secured a teaching job. With his life back on track, Coen re-boarded the hurling train.

Even though a lot of people questioned his sanity, he went back hurling in 1987. He just trained with Mullagh that season but in 1988, he played his first competitive game since his injury, lining out midfield for the senior team. He rotated between midfield and the forward line and when the regular keeper wasn't producing the goods, he went back between the posts.

'You'd be jittery in goal and you wouldn't have the same judgement,' he said. 'The ball that was coming in direct was fine but the ball that was hopping, I couldn't judge it. I would have smothered balls, but I couldn't control them or catch them cleanly. It was uncomfortable really.'

Everyone on the club scene in Galway knew Coen's predicament but that never guaranteed him any special privilege in the most cut-throat club championship in the country at the time. He never looked for any charity and he didn't get it.

He got on fine for two years until Mullagh played Kiltormer in the 1990 championship and Coen was lining out at corner-forward. He came out the field to collect a ball on his right hand side and never saw Ciaran Lynch coming for him like a train on his left. Coen ended up on the ground with a badly dislocated shoulder and he quietly conceded defeat in hospital that evening. He played the following year more in body than in spirit and he eventually walked away from the game in 1992 without any regrets.

'I often met John Commins but I never felt "that could have been me",' said Coen. 'I never even thought about that. In fairness to him he did well when he was there. He wasn't a spectacular goalie but he made a few vital stops and he deserved the success he got. It could have worked out differently for me but my attitude was that what happened to me certainly wasn't my fault and it just wasn't meant to be that I would go further with Galway.

'I always counted myself lucky to be involved in an All-Ireland minor final and to win an Under-21 medal with a lot of the guys who won senior medals in 1987 and '88. I felt kind of part of it all. I don't have a senior medal but I would never regret not having it. The medal was never the be-all and end-all for me; it was always about being the best I could be. And I felt I was as good as I could have been.

'It was an awful chunk out of my life when it was taken away from me but I never once felt bitter about it all. I probably felt a bit lost, but never bitter. That's why I did go back playing, because I was lost. I used to be very jittery and nervous and I'd be delighted when the game was over. But I'm glad I did go back because if I hadn't I'd always have been asking myself why I didn't. I was too young to give it up.'

Before the League final on Sunday, the Waterford team bus arrived in Claughan just before 3.15pm, their pre-planned departure time to leave for the Gaelic Grounds on the far side of the city. The players were no sooner off the bus when they had to re-board again and the minor puckaround they had managed in the meantime was too rushed to be of any benefit. The physio Shay Fitzpatrick had just laid out his massage table when he had to fold it up again and by the time Fitzpatrick had fully packed up, the bus was pulling off.

They set off in a mad dash across the city with a garda escort clearing a path for them through the traffic. A mini-bus from Dunhill spotted the opening and jumped on their trail and before long two other cars were on the track. The convoy careered through traffic lights and was even brazen enough to charge up the wrong side of the road after the blaring sirens. At the back of the team-bus, the prime ticket holders were laughing at the trailing circus.

By the time the bus pulled into the Gaelic Grounds, Waterford had arrived with the urgency of a fire engine. The players made for the dressing room with the haste of a batch of fire fighters chasing a blaze. Galway had arrived in the Gaelic Grounds at 3pm and appeared a lot more relaxed in the puckaround. Waterford weren't fully tuned in and they could sense it.

'When we were walking around in the parade, it felt like we were walking up the street,' said Stevie Brenner.

They armed themselves for the white heat of battle but as soon as the game began, they were caught in a Galway backdraft and burned to a cinder. Galway might feel aggrieved the margin of victory was only five points but from an early stage there was only going to be one winner.

The week ended well for Liam Donoghue.

TOO HIGH A PRICE

At 3.10pm on Sunday 16 May, Clare emerged from the darkness of the Semple Stadium tunnel and into an orb of brightness and light. Seán McMahon led them out, with Davy Fitzgerald just behind him. The goalkeeper bounced up the field like a coiled spring, jumping and bounding until he got to the goal where he belted his hurley off the crossbar. He ran around the goal for nearly a minute until the subkeeper Ger O'Connell arrived for their warm-up.

'I'm bollixed,' Fitzgerald said to O'Connell.

Both men just smiled because they know the routine. Fitzgerald's legs were like jelly and as O'Connell began gently throwing sliotars at him to catch and control, the energy didn't return to Fitzgerald's body until he got his second wind at 3.20pm. The goalkeeper's opening ritual completely exhibited the changing shades of his personality because after the fire comes the ice. Then the fire rages again as the battle begins.

'It just happens,' said Fitzgerald. 'I just let myself go and that's always been the way with me. I love that adrenalin rush and that's just my way of dealing with it. I always run out second because I want to hear that roar and I want to let myself get into the middle of it. I just want to live it. I have to let everything I have inside me get out. That's basically why I do it. I don't do it for any other reason.'

Energised and pumped up, it's time for Fitzgerald to go again after his two-month suspension. In the meantime he has compensated for his layoff with supreme preparation, so much so that by last Sunday evening he was hardly able to walk. He was wiped out from the obsessive routine of overdrive training he puts himself through before big matches.

For the last month, he has gone on four-mile runs, five days a week. That's outside of his intense core work, personal hurling training, Clare training, swimming pool sessions and his personal conditioning work with his personal trainer Darren Ward.

'I just wanted to be physically and mentally stronger than ever,' said Fitzgerald. 'I just wanted to lift it another gear. A lot of that was to say to the fellas who gave me the two months "you can do what you want to me but I'm coming back stronger than ever." That was my attitude. I thought I was soft and Darren hardened me up big time. I've often trained unbelievably hard but I've worked harder than ever over the last couple of months on my own game. This suspension thing has just motivated me more and I've used it this way.'

Fitzgerald is ready for this game and so are Clare. They're delighted with their preparations and they have absolutely no fear of Waterford. Right up the spine of their side they have leaders whose greatest stimulation is championship and the spice in their training game last Sunday evening really underpinned their belief that they are ready for a massive championship onslaught.

Fitzgerald hasn't trained since because he never does anything the week of a game. He cleared the clutter of work-related business from his head on Monday night and he's been mentally preparing himself for this game ever since. Fitzgerald's systematic practice of imagery facilitates the concentration skill that is the real key to his success.

'Focussing my mind is the biggest part for me,' said Fitzgerald. 'You can do all the training you want but it's no good to you unless you get your head right. I mentally put myself through the wringer all week. Lived, ate, slept it, I visualised everything. Thinking of every situation under the sun and preparing myself for all of it. Preparing myself for the crowd and how I'm going to handle it.

'Paul Flynn or (John) Mullane taking shots, I thought about all those things and I thought about nothing else only that. I put so much thought into it, I never sleep great the week of a game. I only start to sleep better coming in towards the match because I've so much done, that I haven't anything left to think about. I'd be a lot more relaxed on the Friday and Saturday nights than I'd be during the week because my mind is working overtime on all that stuff.

'I'm ready for anything then and nothing will go through my head. If the crowd are abusing me, I'll just answer them with my hurling. Every ball I'll get I'll clear it twice as hard. My body language has to be everything and that's the only thing I think about. That's the only way I can answer them, I won't open my mouth to any of them. Whatever they throw at me, I'll be ready for it.'

Clare were out on the field five minutes before Waterford emerged but in the meantime, the Waterford players were getting ready to unleash their own unmerciful onslaught. On Tuesday night they played a training game amongst themselves where the dimensions of the field had been tightened to allow for hard-hitting and championship simulation. There and then they had grasped the full measure of the difference between a League final and the championship.

Last week, most of the players would have taken a League medal before a championship win over Clare but when the moment arrived and the pressure came on, they mentally backed off. Their pre-match preparations hadn't done them any favours either and they looked at it all in cold blood afterwards. When they forensically analysed the video of the League final, they noticed that 2-10 of Galway's total score of 2-15 had originated from basic Waterford hurling errors.

They knew they could correct those with proper application and a restructured team would strengthen their base. Dummy teams and unorthodox selections had governed Waterford's league but Justin McCarthy was keeping his powder dry. They sacrificed Ken McGrath at wing-back and played Michael Walsh at midfield against Galway when both were going to line out at centre-back and centre-forward now against Clare. Team trainer Gerry Fitzpatrick had set this game as their perfect peak date and Waterford's season was never about a League final: today was always Judgement day.

'You don't have to be mean,' Fitzpatrick said to the players before they hit the field. 'Just go over to the man you're on, shake hands with him and then stare him in the face and make sure he looks away first. If he does, then you're getting to him and you're three-quarters of the way there.'

Waterford never blinked for a second. They came out and simply exploded. From the throw-in, Eoin Kelly passed the ball back to Ken McGrath, who lofted his clearance into John Mullane to land the first point within fifteen seconds. Waterford were leaving scorch marks all over the field with the pace of their hurling and they burned a huge hole in Clare's defence in fourteen minutes. Tony Browne drove a long ball into the square and Dan Shanahan, who had drifted in from wing-forward, fielded the ball over Conor Plunkett and slapped it past Fitzgerald.

The goalkeeper was calling to the sideline but nobody responded to him. After Dave Bennett drove a 65 over the bar two minutes later to put Waterford ahead by 1-4 to 0-00, Fitzgerald began hobbling on one leg and waving his hands frantically once more. He shook his head when nobody responded a second time.

'I wanted them to bring up the doctor so I could stop the play, just to break up things,' he said. 'They never copped what I was on about. I wanted us to try and regroup ourselves. I knew at that stage we needed to stop. I knew we were in big trouble because they had a lot more aggression than we had. They were like dogs, savages. They had everything worked out and we weren't able to match them. They were so savage and even looking at their body language, we didn't look like we'd be able to match them that way.'

It got worse on twenty eight minutes when a long Bennett delivery broke between Shanahan, Plunkett, Seamus Prendergast and Brian Lohan. Prendergast flicked the ball into Shanahan's hand and the forward slipped it past the advancing Fitzgerald.

The Clare full-forward line had still to touch the ball at that stage but in Clare's next attack, Frank Lohan had a great goal chance. His shot was saved, controlled and cleared by Brenner. Clare were listing hopelessly on the swells and dips but they had a chance to bail some water out of their sinking ship on thirty three minutes when Tony Carmody was fouled by Tom Feeney for a 20-metre free. Fitzgerald came up to strike it and the second he arrived the heat was turned up on the Waterford terrace.

'Here comes the little bastard, let's sow it into him now!' roared one so-called Waterford supporter on the terrace. Then the taunts and chants about Fitzgerald's private life rang out with a sickening sense of triumphalism.

Every goalkeeper in the country gets some form of verbal abuse during a game but Fitzgerald has become the focus for the most sustained level of vitriolic, hateful, vindictive and spiteful abuse ever directed at a GAA player. It is a stain on society in general and a blemish on the GAA's conscience that it is tolerated and accepted in the terraces.

The GAA has always prided itself on the good nature of its supporters but there has been an increasing element of yobbish behaviour creeping into some supporters in the last number of years. Not all of it is fuelled by alcohol, and the sordid and crude verbal actions of some people aren't a million miles from the hooligan culture that still infests worldwide soccer. There is a raucous edge to the behaviour of some individuals at matches, which reflects negatively on contemporary Irish society.

'The abuse is something unreal,' said Fitzgerald. 'It's not just from ten or twenty people, it's from hundreds of people behind the goal roaring at me. About my personal life, which they know nothing about. They will comment on your marriage, they will comment on you as a father and they will comment on you as an individual. It's just terrible. I build myself up before a game that I'm going to deal with it and use it to my advantage but when I sit down and think about it afterwards, I'm pure disgusted. Absolutely disgusted. There's no need for it at all.'

Like so many in a remarkable generation of Clare hurlers, it is games against Tipperary which define Fitzgerald's career. Those games brought out the best in him but the attrition levels between him and some Tipperary supporters raised the stakes too high: he feels that the consistent level of personal abuse directed at him on certain match days was spawned on the Tipperary terraces.

During a difficult period in his personal life, he single-handedly saved

Clare from defeat to Tipperary in the 1999 drawn Munster semi-final. He made one of the best saves of the decade from a Paul Shelley shot with four minutes remaining before burying an injury time penalty to bring the game to a replay which Clare won. Then just two months later, he was trainer to the Clare Under-21 team which lost a sulphurous Munster final to Tipp in Ennis.

At the end of the game, a Tipperary substitute directed a personal insult at Fitzgerald, which was largely rooted in his separation from his wife a year earlier. Fitzgerald lost it with him and a huge fight broke out amongst players and substitutes from both sides. Fitzgerald was suspended and it subsequently cost him an All-Star award that he deserved.

'I got suspended for standing up for my family, which anyone would do. I went after that fella because of the abuse he was giving my family. The whole thing got out of hand as well because I had sickened Tipp twice that summer with the save from Shelley and the penalty. That's why I'm hated, without a shadow of a doubt. And Jesus, I've paid a tough price for that because the doing I've got off some Tipp supporters behind the goals, I wouldn't ask anyone to go through it. They're an absolute disgrace, and that's the truth.'

In a small hurling community, gossip often spreads like a disease and Fitzgerald has been plagued by it from some supporters in certain counties. It hasn't been confined to just Tipperary and Waterford because they talk about him in Clare too. He almost had enough three years ago but to retire would go against everything in his nature.

'I find it very hard to take it at home, especially when you get it in Ennis on a night out. I find that very hard. People paint a picture of me, which is wrong and no matter what you say, you can't convince them what is right. I'm only a human being the same as anyone else. I will make mistakes and I'll do certain things but that really kills me when I get it close to home. I think I'm dealing with it now a little bit better than I used to. But I found it very hard and I got very depressed over it.

'Being on the Clare hurling team isn't the easiest thing going. You're public property. It's an absolute disaster at times because you have no private life. People make up things about you and if there's something out there, they'll multiply it by ten. I want my own life, to go out and make the same mistakes as everyone else does. The only thing that keeps me going is that I have a savage passion to hurl for Clare. I fucking love it more than anything. People wonder why I put on a show. I can tell you that it's no show. I can honestly say that.'

There is sometimes a canyon-like chasm between reality and public perception but Fitzgerald makes it easy for the public to make up their mind with the way he lays bare every kink and quality of his character. Being a Clare hurler doesn't pose the same problems for other players because they don't court attention like Fitzgerald does on the pitch.

While a large part of his personality is refracted through the prism of bravado, like the mad dash from the tunnel before the game, many people are offended by that in-your-face style. More feel that he should conduct himself better and, combined with his abrasive nature on the field and his remorseless haranguing of officials, his exasperating temperament provokes strong reactions.

Even though he was wrong to say what he did to Pat Horan in March, he felt he was right because that is the way he thinks. Many people interpret his fanatical attitude and fierce competitiveness as repellent. More interpret his priorities as misjudged but he has still paid way too high a price for how he is perceived. The constant abuse to which he he has to listen about himself, his wife and his young son, Colm, hurts deeper than anyone can imagine.

'The bravado I have is, number one, I'll stand up for myself and I'll take no shit from anybody,' said Fitzgerald. 'And number two, I listen to so much shit behind the goal that I can't turn around and tell them to fuck off and leave me alone. So I'll jump and show my emotions for Clare, which will say to them "up yours" every single time. That's what drives supporters mad but it's no show or it's no act; it's how I feel. You have to let yourself go outside there and I've always told myself that. No holding back.

'People see me as an arrogant little bastard, but they don't know me. They don't talk to me. They don't see the other side to me that does a lot of stuff for people and who does a lot of charity work. But I'm not going to apologise to anyone for being straight out. That's me, that's the way I am and I can't change it.

'Nobody knows the ins and outs of me but I'm never going to try and change anybody's mind about the way I think. It's important to be yourself and let your emotions show. I don't care whether people like it or not but I always come back to my biggest belief in life: never, ever, ever judge anyone until you meet them, talk to them or get to know them.'

Fitzgerald drove the free hard across the goal, it was blocked on the line but Tony Griffin was on hand to fire the rebound to the net. A Niall Gilligan free just before the break left Clare just six points behind after being played off the park for thirty minutes. The game was still – implausibly – there for Clare.

'If we don't shake ourselves up, we can forget about it,' roared Seán McMahon in the dressing room at half-time. 'There isn't much point training like lunatics and then going out and producing that shite. There's a lot more in us and we better go out and get it out of ourselves.'

After Eoin Kelly missed an easy free after the break, Clare went up the field and reduced the deficit to five points and it looked like they'd turned the corner. Instead Paul Flynn landed a gem of a point and Waterford bounded clear. Clare had no response and as the match died, Waterford piled on the scores. Shanahan got his third goal in the last few minutes when a Michael Walsh shot came back off the post. Waterford never let up in the second half and neither did their supporters with the level of abuse targeted at Fitzgerald.

'I got it all through the half,' he said. 'I'm used to it now but I'm disappointed that they won't just leave it alone. I just don't think there's any need for it. We go out and have war with the opposition and we go head on into it. If I turned around and opened some fella, then I'd say "take me apart." I'd deserve whatever I'd get then. But I haven't done anything to deserve what I get.'

At the other end of the field, Brenner never had an easier time of it at a championship match. The Clare forwards didn't pose any problems in front of him and their supporters behind him had very little to shout about.

'You'll always hear a bit of banter with the Clare crowd but I never heard them as quiet,' said Brenner. 'I had a few lads calling me a fat bastard and a waster but it's never anything like what he *(Fitzgerald)* gets. It's going way too far when people start bringing your wife into it. He might bring some criticism on himself sometimes with the way he psyches himself up, but the abuse he gets is scandalous. It's hard when fellas that don't give a shit about hurling get to you. If they cared, they'd be concentrating on the match. But a lot of them don't know anything about hurling, they're only there for the session.'

The nineteen point victory was Waterford's biggest ever championship winning margin over the other top four Munster hurling counties. For Clare, it was their worst hurling day since Tipperary hammered them by eighteen points in the 1993 Munster final. Fitzgerald has lived through plenty of harrowing defeats before and since that mauling and enough time has passed since that landmark date in 1993 for him to survey the landscape in a calculated manner. In his mind, this earthquake measured the same force on the Richter Scale.

'Along with '93, it was definitely my lowest point with Clare. Both days were exactly the same. As low as you'd feel playing for Clare and I never thought I'd see another day like that.'

Clare had become an obstacle for this Waterford team but the Clare players placed too much trust in their belief that they had something over their opponents. Since they emerged in 1998, Waterford had beaten every other Munster county in the championship except Clare. When the sides met in the All-Ireland semi-final two years ago, Clare's experienced players said beforehand that there was no way they were going to lose and they eventually ground Waterford down. They were convinced that they'd do the same again.

'A lot of our lads thought it was just Waterford and we've always beaten them,' said Fitzgerald. 'We thought "this is Waterford and no matter what, we'll beat them." As much as we were told not to take them for granted, a lot of lads did. A lot of fellas didn't stand up and be counted when they had to be. That pissed me off completely. No matter what the story is, that has to be rectified.'

The statistics damned Clare. Waterford had fifty one more plays than their opponents throughout the seventy minutes while they won seventeen of Fitzgerald's puckouts uncontested. Tony Griffin's four high catches made him the only Clare forward to win clean possession in the air and out of Waterford's 3-21 total, 2-8 originated from basic Clare errors. Their collapse was so spectacular, it was almost unbelievable.

Clare have five weeks now to put an end to the requiems and obituaries and retirement talk. To show that the blood is still pumping and the will is still strong. Five weeks to prove that they're not dead men walking, waiting to be buried by some other hell-bent side on the back road to retribution.

'Bring them on,' said Fitzgerald. 'We're either good enough now or we're not. Guys are hurt and I reckon we will be there or thereabouts. I wouldn't mind whoever it is we meet. If it's Galway fine, if it's Limerick or Cork, fine. I don't think we should want to avoid anyone now or get a soft draw. Five matches to win the All-Ireland. Bring on the best of them.'

They'll be here soon enough.

WHAT COULD BE BETTER THAN THIS?

On Munster semi-final day, May 30th, the Cork players emerged from the tunnel in the Gaelic Grounds and sprinted up to the Ennis Road terrace. The Cork supporters were located at that end but the team's training drills had been mapped out at the other side of the field and after the team photograph, they made their way down to do their warm-up. As the players filed over to the sideline, Donal Óg Cusack jogged down to the goalmouth with Cork's two subkeepers, Paul Morrissey and Martin Coleman. When he got to the endline, Cusack took a sip from a water bottle, inhaled a few deep breaths and just smiled. 'OK lads,' he said, 'let's go.'

They began loosening out by jogging from side to side, changing on every fourth step like synchronised ballet dancers. They stretched loosely in the middle of the routine that Cusack was co-ordinating and were in the middle of a hamstring stretch near the endline when the noise from behind them built up to a crescendo. As Limerick took to the field, Cusack raised his voice: 'Let's go to the 14 and pick it up for ten!' he roared.

They broke into a triangle, belting balls from hand to hand. After a couple of minutes they switched to first touch, changing the direction every so often, before Morrissey and Coleman took up station on either side of the 65 yard line and Cusack went back between the posts. The subkeepers kept lobbing high balls in which Cusack would catch, pause, then work his feet by taking two sharp steps before drilling the ball back to one of the strikers.

It's a match simulation drill that Cusack uses to sharpen his mind. He was also judging the wind direction and while the sun was breaking out from behind the clouds, it was still high in the sky and not prohibitive like it normally is in Limerick for late evening games. While balls were flying in over Cusack's head, as the Cork players were going through their shooting drill, Coleman and Morrissey began lacing sliotars at him from the 20-metre line. He was stopping all of them but he tried to catch one rocket from Coleman and it went through his fingers. A cacophony of klaxon horns went off behind him. 'You're fucked now Cusack!' roared one Limerick supporter. 'You're going to drop them all day.'

After the teams broke from the parade, Cusack made his way back down to the goalmouth and Diarmuid O'Sullivan, Wayne Sherlock and Brian Murphy joined him on the goal-line. They wrapped their arms around each other and as the national anthem began, Cusack gripped O'Sullivan around the shoulder and they all stared at the tricolour flag above the scoreboard behind them.

'This is it lads,' said Cusack.

A long nine months had finally come around.

Three weeks before, Ger Cunningham had rung Cusack and told him that Donal O'Grady had asked him about coming on board as goalkeeping coach. Cunningham didn't want Cusack to feel that he'd been imposed on him and he wanted to know if he'd have any problem with it. Cusack told him straight out that he didn't as long as it didn't develop into an old friends' act. If he had to be criticised, he wanted the criticism to be delivered without a sugar lump to moderate the taste. 'If I need to be told I'm going poor, I need to be told,' Cusack told him.

Cunningham is a legend in Cork. He was Cork's greatest ever keeper and one of the best goalkeepers to ever play the game. He played in goal for Cork for eighteen years and twelve goalkeepers had come and gone as his understudy, none of whom had managed to break into the championship side. Some of those subkeepers had been excellent players and when Cork captain, John Fenton, introduced the players to his home crowd in Midleton the night after the 1984 All-Ireland final, he introduced his clubmate Ger 'the King' Power as 'the best goalkeeper in the country.' There was a huge rivalry between Midleton and the Cork city clubs at that time and the city players didn't take too kindly to it. They didn't go back to the Midleton clubhouse for the reception and Fenton subsequently apologised to Cunningham. Tom Kingston had got a sustained run in the 1993 League campaign but nobody had ever looked like taking over from Cunningham until Cusack . He spent two seasons in 1997 and 1998 as understudy and it was only a matter of time when he would take over.

In the finish, the end came sooner for Cunningham than he expected. Doubts had been raised after he conceded two late goals against Limerick in the 1998 Munster quarter-final and there was a minor clamour for Cusack to replace him. But in the semi-final against Clare, Cunningham kept a clean sheet and made one of the best saves of his career from a Niall Gilligan ground shot. Although Cork were beaten, he felt he had it in him to continue for another year. But he also felt management were avoiding him afterwards and three months later he was told in a pub one night by a member of the management that they had decided to go with Cusack as number one for the following season.

'Even after the Clare match, the seeds of doubt had been sown in people's minds,' said Cunningham. 'I knew a new team was coming and I probably felt a little bit unsure what the right or wrong thing was to do. But I had this thing in my head that I wanted to go before I was pushed. To be totally honest about it, after playing well against Clare, I had time to think about it and if there was any encouragement there, I would have played on and made myself available to play in 1999. A couple of things would have disappointed me with the way it happened. I felt I deserved better treatment after that length of time as to how the whole thing finished up. I felt I could have gone out with a bit more dignity. I suppose I felt let down.

'If I had played on in 1999, probably for the first time in my career, there would have been serious, serious competition. But I felt all along during my career that I was good enough to handle that competition and it would have been a huge challenge for me. If I had played on I knew there was a chance that I may not have made the team and if I didn't, I don't think there would have been any benefit of having a thirty-eight year old goalkeeper sitting on the bench. I wasn't going to put Donal Óg under that pressure either of having me there and him looking over his shoulder. I had a degree of loyalty to some people and I made my decision. But circumstances would probably have forced my hand into making that decision.'

Cunningham's return was his first involvement with the Cork seniors since he left but after his first two goalkeeping sessions, Cusack rang him and told him he had exceeded all his expectations. His drills were innovative and fresh and Cusack was absorbing every new tenet like a sponge. After his session with Cunningham last week, he wrote in his diary that it was one of the best goalkeeping sessions he'd ever done

Every Cork player was given a red and black diary book at the start of the year and they were all told to write down their goals before each session and each game. They were also told to tabulate the positives and negatives after every match they played. Not everyone does it with the manic, obsessive devotion Cusack does because he records everything like a monk in the penal times. He is still going to the gym every single morning at 7am and he writes out his goals for each session the night before.

After they beat Kerry in the Munster quarter-final two weeks ago, one of the negatives he scribbled into his diary was that he was talking to one of the umpires just before the Kerry goal. The second negative he wrote down was that he was way too relaxed when he saved Errol Tuohy's initial shot for Kerry's only goal. Cusack stopped the ball and tried to flick it back out to Ronan Curran in the one movement. When Tuohy fired it back in, the ball went under his hurley.

After the game, Cusack went straight home to Cloyne to coach the club senior team. Despite all the other demands on his time and everything he has on his plate, he agreed to become the club coach a few months back. When training finished, he began banging a sliotar off the wall underneath the scoreboard in an attempt to replay his position for the Kerry goal. He noticed that he has a tendency to sometimes stick his hurley out in an awkward position, where the angle of the stick is facing in towards his body in case the ball comes up. On Monday night he painstakingly went through his whole technique with Cunningham again because he knows he should have stopped that goal.

Some people questioned him again afterwards but he felt supremely confident heading into Sunday's game. He had an excellent League campaign and Cusack had dispelled any doubts that may have surrounded him.

'I would have heard the stories and a number of people would have said to me at the end of last year that Cork needed to look at the goalkeeper position,' said Cunningham. 'That was out there but his League form stopped the whispering campaign. But from my inside knowledge with the management, Cusack was never under pressure. It was never an issue.'

Outside the camp though, some of the criticism has yet to subside. Cusack heard the first rumblings of the clamour against him when Cloyne played Avondhu in last year's championship in Fermoy. He received such personal abuse from a supporter behind the goal in the second half that the Cloyne centre-back Maurice Cahill ran over to the wire afterwards. 'You're a brave boy standing up there!' Cahill roared out to him. 'Why don't you come in here?'

Although Cloyne won, Cusack was livid. After he'd togged in, he wandered up behind the goal to see if the guy was still there. He thought he might be staying on for the second game and when Cusack spotted him, he went over and stood right behind him.

'The abuse was so bad, it was like as if I'd rolled over the man's grandmother,' said Cusack. 'I wanted a look at his face to see if I actually had rolled over his grandmother. There were two guys with him and one of them looked around and saw me. I could hear him saying: "Jesus, you're not going to believe who's behind you." I stayed there for ten minutes and your man was too much of a coward to turn around.'

Cusack has received a lot of positive support around the county this season but there's always somebody waiting to have a go at him. When Cloyne beat Glen Rovers in the first round of the Cork championship last month, one supporter spent the whole second half behind the goal accusing Cusack of 'costing Cork an All-Ireland'. After the game Cusack turned around and gave the V for victory sign in the general direction of the abuse. Some Glen supporters thought he gave them two fingers and it stoked their fires further.

Even though he'd made three fine saves in that match, Cusack's father Donal came home one evening a couple of nights later and informed his son that he'd heard another story about him but that this one took the biscuit. A fella from the city came up to Donal Cusack on a building site and asked him where he was from. When he told him he was from Cloyne, your man rounded on his son.

'That Cusack is hiding in behind *(Diarmuid O')* Sullivan far too long,' he said. 'And Sullivan is minding him and looking after him.'

'What are they going to say next about you?' his father asked him.

His son just shook his head: 'That's the one thing I don't like about the hurling. I'm absolutely immune to the whole thing. I'm training as hard as I can and once I'm as honest as I can be to myself and to the boys around me, that's it. But I'd hate to think that the father would be in an awful state over stuff like that. My father always battles for me in the crowd and he would never lie down to anything but I know that he doesn't sleep before games.

'Mickey O'Connell told me last year that his grandfather got physically sick when people were on Mickey's case over the summer. It doesn't affect me in the least because I have no fear of facing any man. But I'd hate to think that my family would be affected. My sister would be at matches and she has to listen to that stuff.

'My mother doesn't go to matches. I know she feels most of the pressure but she puts up with it and she's always there for me. My brother Victor and my younger brother Conor, who has been an inspiration to me over the last few years, they have to listen to certain shit and I know it can't be easy for them either.

'It's tough even on my friends and the lads on the Cloyne team. Even the guys I work with like Mick Noonan and John Buckley, it's probably harder for them to endure the criticism in the crowd because I'm immune to it. It's bad enough to have to listen to it from supporters in other counties but it's a lot harder for people close to you when it's coming from your own crowd.'

It's easier to take from the opposition because it's expected. When Cork played Waterford in Páirc Uí Rinn in their second last league game, anytime Cusack went to take a puckout in the second half, all he could hear was the chant 'Tooooneeee Browwynne'.

Two years ago, Cusack allowed a long delivery from Tony Browne slip past him in the Munster semi-final against Waterford and Cork lost a tight match. The Waterford fans kept reminding him of it during the first half of last year's Munster final and it has almost become their signature chant when they play Cork and Cusack is in front of them.

It hasn't been confined to just the terraces either. When Cork travelled to Ardmore to take on Wexford in a challenge game a few weeks back, a group of young fellas hiding in the long grass in a field outside the ground were chanting 'Toooooooonneee Browwwne' at Cusack..

'After that they started saying some desperate shit to me. Like, why would those young fellas start saying that to me?'

He's immune to it but incidents like that are hard to forget. He has tried to remain positive. He wasn't to know that his place was secure and he had enough battles without having to fight another mental war.

Martin Coleman played in the League against Tipperary and really impressed with his handling and his puckouts. Paul Morrissey was excellent for Newtownshandrum during their successful All-Ireland club campaign and he decorated himself in garlands after a couple of class saves in Cork's final league game against Clare. Cusack always believed he was going to be Cork number one but he still had to work hard and discipline himself mentally and physically to get to this point.

'I would have trained a lot during the winter and I would have had a lot of bad thoughts in my head. I felt I needed to discipline myself more to be ready for a massive battle. You need that discipline to survive in the championship. Maybe that's a negative thing too in that you're saying to yourself "I'm going to hurt myself and remember this hurt so that when the time comes in the championship, I won't let my mind wander." But goals is tough because you can be at the top of your game and then one little thing can go wrong and just mess you up.

'I knew there were going to be fellas coming for my place but now I feel that I've a lot of hard work done and I feel that I'm better for it. I feel that I can be as good as there is in Ireland, all I have to do is go and prove it. I mean that. I'm an honest man, I'll tell you when I'm wrong and when I'm bad and I said it to Ger a few weeks back that I feel I can be one of the best in the country. All I need to do is keep working hard, learn more about the game and myself and then be able to produce it.'

They all have to produce it now. After last year's All-Ireland final, Donal O'Grady wrote each player a letter, which said that even though they lost the All-Ireland, Cork were never bettered. They believe they can go the whole way this year and when they held a team meeting last Monday night, the importance of focussing on the positives was heavily stressed. They're without Setanta Ó hAilpín, who left for a career in Aussie Rules Football last November, and everyone outside the Cork camp has deemed his loss incalculable. A spring spent in search of a big man to play full-forward didn't throw up any answers and it's too early to say if the return of Brian Corcoran will be the solution.

'People are going on about Setanta and the loss he is,' said Cusack. 'Setanta is one of us, he's a Cork boy and we all played with him. He went out to Australia by himself and took on a game he never played before and made some hand of it. He has serious balls. That's great for us. We are proud of him and we intend to use it as an inspiration rather than a negative which most people are making it out to be.'

When they were all sitting down on the grass in Páirc Uí Rinn at the team meeting on Monday, Cusack spoke forcefully as usual. As they got ready to re-launch their crusade and go back on the road again to try and heal the hurt that has been deposited in their souls all winter, Cusack asked them all one simple question. And then he provided the answer.

'What could be better than this? Nothing. Nothing can compare with this. If you look at the great rugby competitions they have in South Africa and New Zealand and the way they go on about them, we have an unbelievable competition of our own here. The Munster championship, a unique game played on this island that has everything to it. The warrior side to it and the artist side to it and here we are, as fit as anything, strong young fellas, loyal to each other. It's a great thing. Where else would you see it? It's all about this now. It's like as if everything is centred on Sunday. It's like as if your life ends at 3.30pm on Sunday.'

After Albert Shanahan injured his shoulder a couple of weeks back, Timmy Houlihan got a phone call from the Adare club secretary, Kevin O'Mahoney, to tell him that he'd been asked in to make up the numbers for a game in county training. Houlihan didn't get too excited about it because his clubmate, Jack Foley, had been asked in the week before and he hadn't made the squad.

He thought about not going in and then decided he would. He got out of his car in front of the Gaelic Grounds at exactly the same time as the substitute keeper John Cahill was making his way in. They chatted on the way to the dressing room but Houlihan knew it was probably just as awkward for Cahill as it was for him.

'When I went in I was thinking "Jesus, who do I sit beside?",' said Houlihan. 'In fairness to all the lads, they said it was good to see me back but I felt I shouldn't have been there. It crossed my mind that they *(management)* were giving me a taste of the action, but that was all I was going to get. I thought about not going in but I couldn't not go in. After being so disappointed not being there, it would have been total hypocrisy. And it wouldn't have done my chances any good for next year either because the same management will be there and I want to make it next year. It was no harm to see the lads either, but, Jesus you would be pissed off.'

Houlihan didn't hang around for food afterwards. He did in fact have to be somewhere else but he didn't want to feel uncomfortable either. That was hard going because aside from the few lads who are good friends of his, he hasn't seen any of the rest of the players over the last six months. He couldn't face going to see Limerick in the League and the only match he did go to – the Clare game – was because Tina wanted to see the Limerick footballers play Kerry in the League semi-final afterwards.

'I just said I might as well just face up to it and go,' said Houlihan. 'It was weird being there. Some fella behind me was asking if I was coming back on the panel but what are you supposed to say to that? It was great to see the lads win the match but it was still a strange feeling being there in the stand.'

At the moment, Houlihan is physically in great shape. He's lost nearly a stone in weight, has toned up and has never trained as hard with the club. The former Tipperary player and selector Liam Sheedy is training Adare and he lets Houlihan do his own specialised goalkeeping training whenever he wants. Houlihan is staying really positive and is feeling the benefits.

'I can't wait for the club championship to come around. Not to prove to anyone else, just to myself that I can still do it.'

He still calls Ger Cunningham for advice. They were supposed to meet last Tuesday but Adare had a challenge game and Houlihan is planning to take a day off work in the next couple of weeks to travel down to Cork and get a session in with Cunningham. He'd prefer to be squaring up against Cunningham and Cork on Sunday but he's accepted his fate now.

Houlihan used to live for weeks like these. The buzz of championship countdown and the sensation that nothing else in the world seems to matter except 3.30pm on Sunday. The feeling that Cusack has now. The feeling that Houlihan would give anything to experience again.

'I miss it desperately. Unreal, like. You'd be devastated even thinking about it but what can you do now? I can forget about it this year now and just aim for next year and just concentrate on the club in the meantime.

'I think about it all the time. Even watching *The Sunday Game* starting up would get you thinking about it. It would come into my mind a lot every day. You'd have lads coming into the office asking me about it and you can't help but think about it then. You'd see the lads going off training and you'd miss it. You know, going in meeting all the lads and having the craic but busting your balls at the same time. Now I'm just meeting the lads out and finding out how they're getting on in training and that. At times, you'd find it very tough.

'It's hitting me more now because this is always the best week. You're not doing much in training but you're hopping off the ground and you're mad for it to come around. I was just thinking about it at home this morning and again on the way home from work. If I was playing or involved I'd be thinking 'will Sunday ever come?'. If I was there I'd be dying for it to come around. But it will be come and gone now before I know it.'

When Sunday finally rolled around, Houlihan got up and went for a jog out around Corbally. He moved into a new flat on Friday night in the city centre, just off Henry Street, so when he returned he showered and changed and stepped out onto the balcony. The streets were a poppy field of red as most of the Cork fans were making their way from the train station out to the Gaelic Grounds.

Ollie Moran had been on to him all week about going and Houlihan hadn't fully made up his mind if he would. He had a ticket but he still wasn't sure that morning. In the end, he decided that he couldn't face it.

'I just said I'd leave it and watch it on TV.'

It was one of those afternoons of raw toughness and hard knocks. The prospect of a home win chiselled out against the odds drove Limerick on. The day was warm and humid and the match ebbed and flowed all through the first half. It was one of those days when scores are hard to come by.

Limerick led by a point at the break but six minutes after the interval, the underdogs were effectively broken on the wheel of fate. Ben O'Connor tried to pilfer a few feet on a free a little over 65 metres from goal. Had the referee not spotted him and made him move the sliotar back, the ball would have cleared the bar for a point. Instead it dropped precisely over Albert Shanahan's upstretched hand and into the net.

As soon as the ball landed in the net, the Cork corner-forward Jonathon O'Callaghan jumped in front of Shanahan, smiled at him and raised his two hands in a declaration of thanks for the Cork gift. Shanahan looked away with a blank stare. After spending the first half abusing Cusack, some of the Limerick supporters behind the goal turned on Shanahan.

'Wake up Albert, will ya? Wake up Albert ya bollox, wake up!' one fan continually kept shouting.

He was souped up on alcohol and eventually one guy near him pleaded the defence case for Shanahan.

'Give him a break, will you? The sun was in his eyes,' he said.

Shanahan had been wearing a cap when the goal went in but he threw it into the back of the net afterwards and left it there. Two minutes later, a steward made his way down to the front wall just behind the goal and started calling Shanahan. The goalkeeper never turned around so the steward jumped the wall and went into the goalmouth and offered Shanahan his cap. The keeper just declined the offer.

The game had clearly turned on the goal and Cork went into overdrive afterwards. A late Limerick goal put a gloss on the scoreboard and Cork won by two points. When the final whistle blew, Shanahan just swung his stick in disgust, before turning around and gathering his hurleys. A swarm of young lads descended on him like a plague looking for sliotars but he made his way for the tunnel, stopping to sign an autograph on the way.

The general view in the aftermath was that Shanahan's mistake had turned the game in Cork's favour. 'I still think,' wrote Ger Loughnane in his newspaper column the following morning, 'that Timmy Houlihan is the best option Limerick have.'

He isn't the only one who believes it.

LIKE FATHER, LIKE SONS

Immediately after watching Cork beat Limerick in the Gaelic Grounds, Ger Cunningham sat into his car and drove south. Just before he got to Charleville, he turned left and then left again out the Kilmallock road. Cunningham was heading for Effin, a tiny little townland about three miles out the road and a small distance away from the Cork border. He was going straight to the GAA field because the Cork Under-21s were taking on the Limerick Under-21s in the annual Tommy Quaid challenge game.

The timing was a little awkward with the senior match just having taken place but Cork are out against Clare in the Under-21 championship in ten days time and Limerick are facing Kerry on the same night. They tried to arrange it a couple of weeks ago but this evening was the only slot that fitted into the calendar. The grass was a little long and there was a breeze blowing down the field but otherwise it was a perfect evening for a game of hurling.

The game itself is an annual celebration of a legacy left by a great goalkeeper and although the match ended in a draw, Limerick were presented with the Tommy Quaid memorial trophy because they were the holders. Midway through the second half, Cunningham was walking behind the goal when he bumped into Breda Quaid and two of her sons, Nicky and Jack. Breda introduced the two of them and told Cunningham that Nicky had played in goal for the Limerick Under-14s last year. Cunningham shook his hand and just smiled.

'I know if Tommy was still alive, he would be thrilled with that, to see the name going,' said Cunningham. 'He probably still is thrilled.'

Tommy Quaid was the coolest dude of a keeper you ever saw. He used to always chew gum that projected an image of total abandon that wasn't normally associated with GAA players. He could throw himself around the goalmouth like a break-dancer. You knew he was deadly serious when he stood in goal but he could also have passed for some guy who was hanging around a street-corner, just chilling out. All he seemed to be missing when he stood between the posts was the black leather jacket with studs down the back. Tommy was definitely cool.

His hurling reflected his personality. When he was training or playing matches, it was like he inhabited a different orbit. Nothing focussed his mind like hurling. Before big games, he liked to go to bed as early as 9.30pm but the thoughts of a big day never spooked him. They excited him. His wife Breda wouldn't speak much about hurling to him before a big game because she felt he didn't want to. But outside of those pre-match moments, she could always see it in his face how happy he was when he was discussing hurling.

Tommy Quaid first met Breda Grace when she was doing six weeks' work experience in Castlemahon, as part of her college course in poultry nutrition. She was staying in digs with an aunt of Tommy's and they were introduced at a social in 1979. Aside from the initial attraction, hurling was an obvious magnet. Her father Nicholas was a first cousin of the legendary Paddy Grace and hurling had always been a constant presence in her life in Galmoy in Kilkenny.

Although Tommy had made his championship debut at just nineteen in 1976, they met at a high watermark for Limerick hurling. In 1980, Limerick won the Munster title and went all the way to the All-Ireland final, only to lose to Galway. In 1981 they retained the Munster title and between 1980-'85, Limerick contested four League finals, winning two. In between all of that Tommy and Breda were married in May 1984.

They were married on a Saturday and their honeymoon only lasted two days. Limerick were training on the following Tuesday and Breda was back to work the following morning. Two and a half weeks later, Limerick took on Cork in the Munster semi-final in the Gaelic Grounds and for the first time, Breda was a first-hand witness to the ever-present perils of goalkeeping at that level.

Limerick looked set for victory until disaster struck. First the full-back Leonard Enright was about to clear a ball near the Limerick goal-line when his footing went from under him. The ball slipped out of his hand, hit his leg and went in over the goal-line. It was a setback but the game was still there for the taking. That was until John Fenton floated in a sideline cut, Quaid stuck up his hand to grab but it passed through his fingers.

The following night, the bile began to channel its way in Quaid's direction. Feohenagh-Castlemahon were playing a club game in Mungret and Tommy was playing midfield. The game had barely started when the abuse began to flow in his direction and Breda had to stand just yards away and listen to it. She knew how much pain her husband was in from the previous day, and now this. 'The abuse that he got that night was very, very hard to take.'

His club and county team-mate and one of his closest friends, John Flanagan, hadn't the heart to tog out for the club that evening but he wasn't surprised that Tommy did.

'He played even though he had ten times as many reasons as me not to,' said Flanagan. 'I heard from a few neighbours that the abuse he got was crazy but they said that the more he got, the more it drove him on. I know that it was hard for him to take but it was hard to put him down as well. Another man would have thrown in the towel but that man just wouldn't. He'd always plough on and see a brighter day and a better day ahead of him. We'll never see his likes around this part of the country again.'

Tommy Quaid ran his own engineering business in Effin. He had made good contacts from the hurling and he worked long and hard to ensure that his business prospered. In October 1998 he was working on the Credit Union building in Charleville and on the morning of the 6th he left the house at 7am. There were steel girders being delivered to the site and he wanted to be there to take them in off the street.

After a few hours preparing the site, he left to attend to another job. When he returned around 11am, he looked up and saw his brother Pat above on a 14-foot wall. He shouted up at him to come down in case he fell. A couple of minutes later Tommy got up on the wall because they were cutting a steel girder in half and he wanted to fix it into position. When the girder was halved it was heavier than he anticipated and he lost his balance.

There was a ladder beside the wall and he reached out to try and grab it, but missed it by a couple of inches. He fell, landed on his bottom but coiled back and banged the back of his head. There was a small gash there but the initial prognosis didn't look too bad. Tommy was still semi-conscious and his brother and work-mates thought he might have escaped lightly. Internally, however, his brain got a knock and had begun to swell.

There was a slight delay with the ambulance but he was initially transferred to Mallow hospital. At that stage Breda had taken their second son Nicky to the dentist and on their way back to Effin, she stopped off at the church. She was there when the accident happened and she only found out what had transpired when she returned home.

She went immediately to Mallow and then followed the ambulance when he was moved to Cork. When she first saw her husband, the shock hit her like a hammerblow, but she was relieved after she spoke to the doctors. It looked like he would recover in a few days and she travelled back to Effin that night praying that her husband would make a good recovery. Sleep was fitful and by 5am Breda rang the hospital for an update. By that stage, Tommy's condition hadn't changed.

Tommy's parents travelled down to meet Breda on Wednesday morning and they set off for Cork at 9am. She had already dispatched clothes to her two eldest sons, Thomas and Nicky, who were staying with neighbours, before dropping her youngest boy Jack off to the babysitter. She was just trying to get on with life, hoping and praying that everything would be fine.

From there on the hours blurred into a haze. Tommy's eyes had started to dilate later that day and his condition had begun to deteriorate. Wednesday seemed to pass like an eternity and on Thursday the doctors told her the news that she was dreading. Her husband was clinically dead and would never leave a bed for the rest of his days. All she remembers after that is the feeling of complete numbness grabbing hold of her and shaking her to the core of her being.

Her heart was broken but at that stage, her main concern was for her children. She had to keep it together for them and she didn't want to break their routine. Their father was a selector with the Limerick Intermediate team that were playing in the All-Ireland final against Kilkenny on Saturday and on Thursday night, Breda rang one of the Limerick selectors and asked that her two sons be allowed into the dressing room before the game. They had always followed that ritual with their father and she wanted to ensure that things remained as normal as possible for them.

When Saturday came, Thomas and Nicky travelled to Thurles with relatives and took their place with the rest of the panel in the squad photograph beforehand. Breda meanwhile had gone to Cork that morning and when she got there, one of the doctors asked her permission to remove a tube from Tommy's chest to see if he could function without it. He warned her that he could die immediately if they did. She agreed but she wanted her two sons to be there in case that happened. She knew they couldn't be in Cork until later that evening and the doctors agreed to wait.

All week long the hospital had been mayhem. Droves of people had turned up to lend their support but with the match taking place in Thurles, Breda at last had some decent time alone beside her husband's bed. She had got into the habit of talking to him and she just kept on chatting.

'There were no other distractions around and I was just so entranced looking at him. Those twenty five minutes were very precious to me.'

Then she suddenly noticed that he'd started to sweat and his temperature had obviously begun to rise. One of the nurses came in and turned him over on his side and Breda caught his arm. She just knew.

'I said to the nurse "he's going to go, isn't he?" Then she left to get another nurse and I just knew he was going to go. I was just so glad to be there and it was very peaceful. He just faded out. It took a while, well that's what I thought but he obviously wasn't going to go cold that fast. I thought he might still be alive but it was very calm and peaceful and there was no deep breathing or anything like that. I remember thinking at the time how calm it was. And that was it. He was gone.'

Tommy Quaid passed away at 3.55pm on Saturday 10 October 1998. In Thurles his two sons were in the dugout roaring on a Limerick team that looked destined for defeat. Kilkenny were running away with the game but around the time Tommy passed away, something seemed to snap in the collective mindset of the Limerick side. People in the stand could sense that something had happened. Limerick stormed back and won the game.

'It looked afterwards like Tommy was lying in Cork and he said to himself "I better get out of here because they need me in Thurles",' said his first cousin Joe Quaid.

It was a moment of calm in a week of madness for Thomas and Nicky Quaid but when they arrived in Cork, their mother told them that their father had passed away.

'That was one of the hardest things I had to do and I can still see the way they reacted,' she said. 'We arrived home at 12.30 that night and I remember going into bed and at that stage I couldn't pray, I wasn't eating and I wasn't sleeping. I can still see myself lying down on the bed and throwing my eyes up to the ceiling and all I just said was "Almighty God, just please get me through these next few days." I firmly believe that he did. He kept me going, because I was able to stay going without food and sleep.'

Tommy Quaid's death, and the magnitude of the mourning which greeted it, gave an insight into the manner in which the GAA is a network of social capillaries linking people together. He was waked in their own house in Effin and roughly 20,000 people came to mourn him. Breda doesn't know how she had the energy or the heart, but anyone she didn't know, she asked them who they were and what their relationship was with Tommy. The funeral party sat down at 2.30pm and the coffin didn't arrive in Effin church until 11.30pm that night.

In her mind's eye she can still see most of the players that travelled to mourn him and honour his memory. She can still see the couple that her husband stayed with in America during an All-Stars tour arriving in the door. She remembers literally being in awe of the fact that so many people had travelled to the funeral. She found it hard to believe how some people thought so much of him to travel long distances. And how more people, who never even knew him, took the time out to pay their respect.

'At one stage this guy walked into the room and he didn't come near us,' she recalled. 'He came and stood at the heel of the coffin. He was a big tall fella who had come on a motorbike and he folded his arms and just looked at him. I found it hard to believe what he was doing so I actually got up off the chair and went over to him. I said "did you know him?" He just said "I was one of his admirers" and he left. I don't think he shook hands with me, he just walked out. I often think about him since.'

The size of the space Tommy Quaid left said a lot about the type of person he was and his understanding of the true perspective in which to view the game he played. He bequeathed a sense of the GAA itself. After giving his life and soul to Limerick hurling for nearly two decades, he began putting back what he once took out.

He was instrumental in the setting up of the five-year development plan in 1995, which sowed the seeds for the present Limerick football success and the county's three All-Ireland Under-21 winning haul between 2000 and 2002. He coached the Limerick minors and Intermediates and gave everything to his club. After he moved to Effin when he got married in 1984, he still travelled back the twenty three miles to Feohenagh three times a week to line out with the club. When his own sons started to play with Effin, he threw in his lot with them and steered them to three south Limerick junior championships. The week before he passed away he scored 1-5 in the county quarter-final victory over Fedamore. That night his two sons were on the line watching their father perform his magic. Then like a puff of smoke, he was gone.

'The memory of that time will always be there and I feel myself that he's an awful loss to the three children,' said Breda. 'That's what I always felt from day one because it was the three boys who needed him the most and they were going to really miss him. I just got on with rearing them. Just getting them up for school and proceeding on day after day. But as late as last week, I remember thinking how much of a loss to them he still is. I know people said to me that I had to look after myself as well but all I just wanted was to look after them. I remember the priest looking down at me during the funeral and he said "Breda, you have to be a mother and a father to them now." And that's literally what I've tried to do ever since.

'They're often referred to as Tom's sons and I can still see little pieces of Tom in them. Thomas is very like his father in looks. Earlier in the time when he had just died I would look at his side-face and think it was like Tom walking in the door. Thomas' hands are the very same as his father's. He has big hands and Tom had very big hands. He always claimed one was bigger than the other from catching the sliotar. Maybe I just pull those images out of the lads as well.

'Thomas was playing in goal against Feohenagh-Castlemahon last year and I was standing on the bank beside some Feohenagh people and they just said he was so like his father the way he takes the puckout. I thought I was the only one who saw that. They would be constantly looking at videos and they would take all those little things from Tom's game.'

Thomas and Nicky are goalkeepers now. Thomas went for Limerick minor trials this year while Nicky has played for the Limerick Primary Schools Team and was the Limerick Under-14 keeper last year. Jack is too young yet to play but he has only one position in mind when he does take up competitive hurling.

When their father was alive, Thomas and Nicky played a lot more of their hurling out the field but since his death, they have been drawn to goalkeeping. On the day their father was waked, the two lads spent most of the afternoon out the back playing hurling. After a lot of mourners had filed past the corpse, they stood outside the back door and observed them closely.

'That left an impression on them,' said their mother. 'I didn't know that at the time and they didn't know it either but it did. To me they would be two lovely corner-forwards. They can read a game very well and are well able to throw the ball around like their father was. But I think they realised that day how popular and good their father was and I suppose they wanted to carry on his memory. They were very young but they probably made up their minds that day that they were going to be goalkeepers.'

The abiding memory many people took from the day Tommy Quaid was buried was the sight of his two-year-old son Jack carrying his father's boots after the coffin. In his room Jack has the one and only photo the family have of him and his father. It's framed by a decorated little piece of cardboard and was taken when he was only a couple of months old. But in his mind, he has plenty more pictures of his father. He remembers going to the zoo with him once and of how his father pushed him around in his buggy. His father's image is burned deep into his memory.

'Jack is the child that keeps his father alive in this house,' said Breda. 'There is definitely not a week that goes by when he will talk about his Dad the same as if he was still here. He is the child that kept him alive. The other two got a little bit reserved about him and wouldn't bring up his name in an everyday conversation but we all had to answer Jack back and I suppose that is what has kept his memory alive. I wanted to keep Tom's memory alive and I felt that talking about him has kept the memory alive. I felt that we tried to keep him alive, in our own way.'

In her own way too, she just got on with life. Less than six months after her husband had passed away, she completed the Level 1 foundation coaching course and got involved with the Effin Under-12 team. She was with the same team at Under-14 level and was with them last year at Under-16. In a small parish, she does a bit of everything. She transports the players to the games, fills the water bottles beforehand, carries the hurleys and tries to pick the team as best she can. She is treasurer of the juvenile club as well. She knows it is what Tommy would have wanted.

It's the memories that keep her smiling. She remembers the time when her two eldest sons simulated playing in an All-Ireland final to the audience of herself and her husband. They filled their gearbags in the house before togging out in a caravan they had out the back garden. They ran out behind an imaginary band before marching around the garden. They placed one of their father's old trophies on top of their swing and when the match was over, Tommy and Breda were called out to present it to the victor. She and her husband got hours of enjoyment from watching their sons trying to carry on their father's legacy.

'My memories now are my sons. Nearly six years down the road, it has got a bit easier but for the first three years, I was convinced he was there. I was convinced that he was looking after us and that any good little thing that happened, it was Tom that did it. I still have great faith and I'm convinced that he's still watching them and he will pull them through their Junior Cert and Leaving Cert and he will get them there. I know he's up there looking after us.'

In the meantime, Breda Quaid will continue to watch her sons' love of hurling, and of goalkeeping in particular, grow stronger. She notices them becoming more aware of the Quaid name and of the respect that their father has left behind. She continues to see more and more of Tommy's traits in each of them every day. Of the pride they have in their father and their desire to honour his name. They are all goalkeepers because it is in their blood.

'I like goalkeeping and it's my ambition to play in goals for Limerick like my father,' said Thomas.

'It's my ambition too to play in goal for Limerick,' said Nicky.

'I still think that he's there with me and helping me,' said Thomas. 'If we were ever playing a game and we were losing, I'd say a prayer to him to help us.'

'I'd do the same,' said Nicky.

What they remember most about their father is travelling with him to training and matches and how much he always told them to continually practise the skills. Thomas recalls his father once showing him how to do a shimmy, while Nicky remembers him describing how to position himself correctly on the goal-line.

'I suppose I've tried to model my game on his and I'd take little parts from his game,' said Thomas. 'We don't have that many videos of him as a goalkeeper but we always watch the ones we have. He helped us a lot but it's the little things that we remember now. I suppose we'd like to keep his memory alive if we could.

'I miss the fact that he's not around to help us out. Even with schoolwork. We still miss him a lot but I like it when people just know me from my father's looks. I like it when they tell me that I'm the image of my father. I'm very proud of that.'

His younger brother looks more like his mother but people still recognise him as Tommy Quaid's son.

'I'm really proud of who he was and most people, that's all they really know me as,' said Nicky. 'People often come up to me and ask me am I Tommy Quaid's son and I don't have a clue who they are. I just know that a lot of people idolised him.'

If Thomas and Nicky ever do make it for Limerick, they may have another young goalkeeper snapping at their heels, trying to take over a position that their father occupied for eighteen long years.

'I want to be a goalkeeper too,' said Jack. 'I want to be like Dad.'

MUNSTER MADNESS

Before Tipperary and Waterford emerged onto the field for their Munster semi-final on June 6, Páirc Uí Chaoimh was rattling like a boiling tureen full of noise and giddy chaos. It was the warmest day so far of the summer and a simmering sense of tension and anticipation was bubbling all over the ground. Half an hour before the match was due to start, the venue was packed to near capacity and the atmosphere was electric.

The Tipperary players had just come up the tunnel from a stretching session in the Páirc Uí Chaoimh gym and Brendan Cummins went straight into the tiny shower-area at the back of the dressing room. The players were starting to twist the dial on the radio to tune into the required frequency and the volume was also being turned up, but all Cummins could hear was the hypnotic thud of the sliotar he was pounding off the shower wall. Shakedown time was almost upon him but every second felt like a minute, every minute like an hour.

'It's the longest ten or fifteen minutes of your life,' said Cummins. 'You're waiting and waiting and these little voices are telling you "do you really want to be doing this?"'

This is Cummins' thirty fifth championship game but it never gets any easier. He's more programmed now to deal with the game itself but the countdown, the waiting and the mind-games are all still hellish. Players learn how to adapt and accept them but the tension and empty feeling still tightens like a vice at the bottom of your stomach. Some players love it, others can't bear it but they all have to go through it.

'The nerves get worse as you get older,' said Cummins. 'Before the game the nerves are way worse now than they were five or six years ago. I'd be feeling sick and worried out of my mind but I think I'm only ready when I feel that way.'

Deep in the recesses of his mind, his primary balm to the pre-match mental anguish is the knowledge that he is as prepared as he possibly could be. Class is Cummins' mark and master but preparation is always the key to success. When he clears his head and thinks rationally, he knows now that he couldn't have done anymore to get himself right for this match.

Cummins remembers a sport psychologist saying one time that when the game starts getting easy that's when you're getting soft. When the League ended in April, he went through a dip in his form for a couple of weeks and he could feel the softness creeping in. For the following two weeks, he ran every night and visited the darkness along the way.

'I was only at 70% just over a month ago because I was trying to toughen my mind up again,' he said. 'You'll always be playing games in your head but there were a few gremlins telling me that I was getting a bit soft. I put myself through a bit of torture but you have to keep doing it. You get so many pats on the back that the next year is harder to go out again. Everyone expects the same thing to happen again but if you start expecting it to happen again, you're falling into a big trap.

'A lot of things have to fall into place before a big day happens and you can sometimes skip two or three little steps that help you to perform on the day and then you fall in a big heap. Then you look back and say: "Jesus, I never did that." The little ghosts were starting to pop up in my head a month ago so I decided to get rid of them by making sure that I was doing everything right.

'You have to be right because I'd often say to myself in the middle of a game "Jesus, what am I doing here?" Then you look around and think "Oh, shit!" And then you say "cop on, concentrate, concentrate." That goes on the whole time and you play little games in your head. The gremlins are there but they're not there to destroy me; they're there to keep me on edge and keep me focussed. I use them as constructively as possible.'

The key to cognitive control is self-talk. It becomes an asset when it enhances self-worth and performance and effective self-talk trains a player to focus on what they want to happen, not what they want to avoid. It reinforces the habit of making thoughts positive and Cummins continually tries to control his inner voice to his advantage.

He sets huge standards for himself and in his own mind, he wasn't right in 2003 until the All-Ireland quarter-final, when he made the second best save of the season from a Brian Carroll rocket that nearly took his head off. He knew after that game that he was back to where he wanted to be but his inner voice still gave him a dressing-down before the All-Ireland semi-final against Kilkenny.

'Before the Kilkenny game I had conceded a load of goals *(five)* in the League final against Kilkenny so I said to myself "these guys were the ones who fucked me up in the first place so I'm going to prove a point to them now." Every time you play you have to have something in your mind that drives you on.

'You have to have little things like that locked away in the back of your head so that when the gremlin comes in, it brings you back to why you're there and why you're bloody doing it. The standards that you set can be used as a stick to beat yourself with but I use them to put myself under pressure. I'd rather be under the pressure I am now than be the has-been goalie that could have made it.'

In an era of excellent goalkeepers, Cummins has become hurling's pre-eminent number one. He has won three of the previous four goalkeeping All-Star awards and has set a standard for everyone else to aim for. After winning consecutive All-Stars in 2000 and 2001, he wasn't even nominated in 2002 and it drove him on even more. He trained for over an hour the night of the awards ceremony and he went into a frenzy over that winter. He trained Christmas Day, St Stephen's Day and New Year's Day. There were hardly enough days in the week for him to train but he came back stronger than ever and won his third All-Star in 2003.

Not everyone rates his flamboyant, spectacular style but he is a brilliant shot-stopper, has an excellent puckout and is very safe under a dropping ball. In the All-Ireland semi-final against Kilkenny last year, he gave one of the best shot-stopping exhibitions ever seen in Croke Park. On the day he looked almost indestructible but his nature finds it difficult to sanction that level of inner calm.

'It was the best game I ever played but I was afraid of my life inside there,' said Cummins. 'I was thinking "Oh Jesus Christ, they're going to score ten goals here, what am I going to do?" I just kept saying to myself "keep blocking the next one and keep blocking them." That's the way it ended up. It looked on the day like I was totally in control and people were thinking "look at him below he's laughing at the Kilkenny forwards." I was dying.'

Now his focus has turned to the Waterford forwards who torched Clare to a cinder three weeks previously. Ever since that game, Cummins has been collecting, processing and analysing Waterford data in his head. Every seam of strength and every tic and switch of the opposition has been added to his database.

'In training I was picturing Waterford fellas in front of me hitting the ball at me. I had fellas taking 20-metre frees in case Paul Flynn will be hitting one. I've watched videos of lads, watching this and that just trying to get myself right so that I can find some little thing. If Flynn puts down the ball, I just try to see what he's doing, if he's going for a goal or what kind of twitch he has. Every fella has something that he does in his head.

'He doesn't consciously know that he's doing it but there's something there and I just have to find it. I think it helps me too to tune in to what's going on and on the day of a match, your awareness is just so heightened by what you looked at in the past that nothing is going to surprise you. That's the way I've been operating for the last couple of weeks. It hasn't been a case of looking at it every day of the week either. Jaysus, I'm not going into a dark room watching these things, trying to hover above the bed.'

Cummins doesn't do supernatural but he does do superstition. In a big way. He had it in his mind from early in the season that he was going to wear new boots this year and after they arrived from Adidas earlier in the season, it was only a matter of deciding when he was going to break them in.

'It's just the way I work but in the past I found myself getting caught up in loads of it. Thinking "you played well that day because you laced your left shoe first, so if you lace your left shoe first this day as well you'll be OK." You start this shit in your head and you're not concentrating on the game then at all. After the League I wasn't going well and I went through a dip of about three weeks where I was just useless. Something had to change because it couldn't be me that was wrong, you know that kind of thing. So the boots went and the new ones were in.

'Then I played a club match a few weeks back with the new boots and it felt weird. I don't know what the Jaysus it was because it wasn't a big game but I just felt uncomfortable. I was looking down at myself thinking "they don't look right." Pure stupid stuff. The boots don't make any difference in the world but that's just the way my mind works. I don't know how to explain it. You just get a feel for something being right and then it happens to be right. It's only all in your head, but Jesus, it works for me. I had it in my head from the start of the year that I was wearing the goldie-coloured boots. If I wore different boots, I wouldn't play well. Unfortunately, that's the sick reality of it. That's honest to God.'

Whatever works for him makes him happy. It's not voodoo potion or black magic but it just grants him peace of mind. When Cummins first started playing for Tipperary, he would wear a Manchester United T-shirt, a Ballybacon-Grange jersey and a Man United jersey under his own Tipperary garment. It was just what he wore and even if the game was on in the middle of the Sahara desert, Cummins wouldn't feel right if those layers weren't there to cushion his mindset.

The previous weekend, Tipperary played a training game amongst themselves and Cummins wore every stitch of new gear that he is wearing today. He ripped the jersey out of the plastic, slipped on the new togs and rolled on the socks. He trained in the gear beforehand and then played the match. Afterwards he handed the jersey back to John 'Hotpoint' Hayes and Hayes threw it back to him half an hour ago.

'When I put on that jersey I thought "Jesus, the last time you wore this you were flying." When I put it on I felt that bit bigger. I said to myself "the last time you wore this gear you were on fire, so what's the problem now?"'

It's all about finding a routine that he is content with and Cummins went through his normal pattern for the last couple of days. Although he moved into a new house in Cahir last summer, he still returned home before the All-Ireland semi-final against Kilkenny. He decided to do the same this time around, checking back into the Cummins household on Thursday. His family know what to expect because they know his moods and his mannerisms by now. And that the 'Do Not Disturb' sign was up.

'That edginess is always there and I was fierce contrary. I can't handle someone talking to me about something I don't want to talk about. If someone asked me to take out the bins just ten yards out the road, I wouldn't do it if I didn't want to. At home they just stayed away from me. I don't know what it is but I don't want to be hassled with anything else in the world only this game. Then you get frustrated and worry that you're going to hype yourself up too much and explode but eventually the right mix comes. It's not something you can force, it's just something you let your body go through.'

He felt cranky on his way up to training on Thursday night but once he togged off and went out onto the pitch, all the worries left him. It will be the same now once he gets out onto that field in Páirc Uí Chaoímh. A long year has been turning since last August and all the training and mental preparation ever since has been leading to this. This is his stage. This is what Brendan Cummins is meant to do.

'Once I go out there it's like something else takes over. I suppose that's what I'm here to do in life, to stand in the goals. It's like some fella who goes up heights. He stands below at the bottom and says "how do I do that?" Yet he goes up and does it. It's just what you do. It's just what I do.'

Waterford were first out onto the field and the city-end terrace crackled with electricity when the players made their way down to that end of the pitch. They were stretching and pucking around when Tommy Dunne jumped the barrier in front of the tunnel and Cummins leaped over it after him as Tipp tore out onto the field.

As the Waterford players jogged across the field in a military line, responding to the stretching routine that Gerry Fitzpatrick was calling, Stevie Brenner was facing shots on the goal-line from Ian O'Regan and Tom Feeney. He looked edgy and fidgety. At one stage he turned around and looked up at the baking sun high above the terrace behind him.

At the other end of the field, Justin Cottrell was lobbing high balls into Cummins and one of them hit the top of one of his fingers and it began to swell up immediately. He got an ice-pack on it straightaway but he told Cottrell that he was fine. He knew then that his mind was completely tuned in. When the teams completed the parade, they gathered in separate huddles and during the national anthem, Brenner grabbed the cross around his neck in his left hand.

Helena gave him the cross as a wedding present and he always holds it tightly just before a game to take his mind off the match. He thought of his wife and had a silent little chat with his late father Ger. When he lived at home with his mother, he used to visit his grave on the morning of a big game. But since he got married and moved to Tramore, Brenner changed his routine and now he asks his father to look after him on the field just before the throw-in. After the anthem, he made his way down to the city-end goal.

'I never get nervous before a match or during a match or anything,' said Brenner. 'Especially the big occasion. I could leave in five goals and it still wouldn't affect me. I'm so easygoing that it would make no difference. It never gets to me but it got to me just before the game. It was only when I was standing on the goal-line before the throw-in when I started getting this twinge. I was thinking "Jesus, what's going on here?"

'It was a funny feeling. Whether it was the pressure of getting to a third Munster final in-a-row or what, I don't know. That might have even got to the team as well because some of the lads looked really nervous. I was just trying to focus in on what I had to do. Maybe I was too relaxed. I don't know. I was kind of tired and I was wondering was the sun after getting to me. Usually I'd be grand and I'd be hopping about and watching things down the field but I was even finding it a small bit hard to concentrate. Maybe that was rubbing off a little bit on me as well.'

That edginess was visible. Waterford led by 0-3 to 0-2 in the seventeenth minute when Colin Morrissey drove a long ball into the square and it popped out of Brenner's hand. When he went to gather it under pressure from Eoin Kelly, the ball looped back in goalwards and Declan Prendergast just took it off the line to preserve Waterford's one point lead.

'I was just thinking "Jesus Christ, what's happening here?"' said Brenner. 'You think that it's not going to be your day.'

The fireworks really began in the second-quarter when the fuse was lit by Dan Shanahan on twenty minutes. He fielded a line ball from Dave Bennett and rammed it to the net from eight metres, nearly taking the head clean off Cummins in the process. Four minutes later, a high ball dropped in from Eoin Kelly with Shanahan and Eamonn Corcoran back-tracking under it. Cummins was roaring at Corcoran to flick Shanahan's hurley but the forward got a touch to it and steered it past the keeper.

'It all happened so fast and it carried that little bit extra,' said Cummins. 'If it had come another two feet, I might have been able to go out for it but experience told me to stay on my line. If he missed it I was there to catch it, but if I went out, I'd have looked like an eejit. I said that I'd play the law of averages, hoping he might miss it. But he didn't.'

Waterford led by seven points but it took just ninety seconds for the remarkable Eoin Kelly to wipe out that deficit. Benny Dunne flicked a ball into Kelly inside the 14-metre line, he was pushed wide but his shot squeezed in at the near post. Brenner was trying to take the hit on the body but the ball hit his hand and dropped into the net. Kelly nicked a point from the puckout before he latched onto a mistake from Declan Prendergast. He got clear with no one near him and directed his shot from fourteen metres across the goal with more accuracy than power. The ball hopped on its way into the corner of the net and Brenner should have stopped it.

'I was disappointed with it. It took a bounce in front of me and I was kind of looking at it in slow motion and I went down to push it around the post. I was waiting for it to hit the hurley and it never did.'

Brenner lay on the ground for a second before getting up like a shot and grabbing the ball in anger. He shook his head after the puckout, ambled outside the square and held out his hands, as if to plead for some leniency. He gathered himself and the nerves instantly left him.

'Initially the second goal made me worse,' he said. 'I was looking at Declan Prendergast fumble the ball and let Eoin Kelly in and I was saying "there's something going wrong here." Then after I pucked out the ball, the nerves went about a minute later. I don't know, a goal kinda brings you back down to earth.'

The quickened momentum continued and just before the break Michael Walsh put John Mullane through one-on-one with Cummins. You'd have fancied Cummins but Mullane drove it close to his body and it clipped his arm and grazed off his jersey.

'If that was against Kilkenny last year, it would have hit me,' said Cummins. 'You can't stop everything. There are only so many one-on-ones that you're going to be able to stop. You need a lot of luck in there. Sometimes they hit you, sometimes they don't.'

Waterford led by three points at the break but Cummins didn't realise what the score was and he called the backs into the shower-area with him. 'We've got to keep a clean sheet in the second half,' he told them. 'We've got to. Three fucking goals are gone in, there's no more going past me. We'll take every ten minutes as it comes. We'll deal with the first ten, then the next ten and the next ten and we'll keep going until the end.'

He felt perfect going out for the second half. Conceding three goals in thirty-five minutes would dent any keeper's confidence but Cummins felt so right that it didn't make any difference.

'If they scored ten goals I was going to block the eleventh one. Another day you could fall asunder. But I felt we were going to win the match.'

Tipp clawed their way back into the match with two quick points and then seven minutes into the half, Eoin Kelly arced a high ball from out near the sideline that appeared to go over the bar. The Tipperary crowd behind the goal was cheering the second it left his stick but the umpire waved it wide. Kelly ran it with his hands in the air to remonstrate with the umpire as Brenner got ready for the puckout.

'Ah Jesus, it was over,' said Brenner. 'It was, yeah. It was about two feet inside the post. I jumped in front of him *(the umpire)* and was just up in his face shouting "wide!". I couldn't believe it when he waved it wide. Some you get and some you don't.'

Waterford were still a point ahead when Cummins stopped an Eoin Kelly bullet on forty eight minutes but he surpassed his standards four minutes later. Paul O'Brien got past Martin Maher and let fly from fourteen metres. Cummins saw it late because it passed Diarmuid Fitzgerald but he got his stick to it and the ball flew up in the air about twelve metres from goal.

Paul Flynn was standing underneath it, he took a split-second glance at the goal and as the ball dropped, he arced his shoulders back and met it perfectly with his stick. It was going for the top-corner but Cummins reacted in a flash, dived and pushed the ball out for a '65. It was one of the greatest saves ever seen in Páirc Uí Chaoímh. Or anywhere else.

'Initially I was surprised that it went out as far as it did, but it was going a bit livelier than I thought,' said Cummins. 'Once it ricocheted out, I had time to settle myself and get my ground and get the hurley right in my hands. When Flynn leaned back, the way his body was shaping, there was only one place he could really put it. It all seemed to go in slow motion after that. When he struck it, I dived to where I thought it was going and next I saw the ball going around the post.

'I don't remember seeing it hit the hurley. I didn't follow the flight path of the ball onto the hurley, it was just something that happened. I can't explain it, I just reacted to it and it hit the hurley. If you asked me to do it again in the cold light of day, I probably wouldn't be able to do it. But you throw me in the middle of that and I might be able to do it again. It's just instinct, I suppose. When you start off, you wouldn't stop them. The longer you go on, the more you stop the ones that are the bonus shots.'

Flynn put his hands on top of his head in disbelief and Eoin Kelly went in and patted the keeper on the back. The Waterford fans behind him couldn't believe that the ball hadn't gone into the net but they still respectfully applauded Cummins' genius.

'If he was pulling off saves like that in the Premiership, he'd be a legend forever,' said John Mullane.

Before the '65 was taken, however, Cummins took a couple of seconds to settle himself. He was listening to his inner voice.

'I just said to myself "Don't get soft now." You have to think that way in goals. It's OK for a fella out the field after scoring a great goal or a point but you can almost picture the headlines. "Brendan Cummins saves wonder shot but drops the '65 into the net." What will they remember the most? That's what keeps the edge on me. I don't want to make the mistake that they'll remember me for. If I drop a ball, that save goes out the window.'

Dave Bennett drove the '65 over the bar to push them two in front but Waterford had still failed to take full advantage from a sequence of control and pressure and they were punished with little over ten minutes remaining. Colin Morrissey latched onto a massive Cummins puckout and he picked the ball on the 20-metre line before weaving inside three Waterford defenders to kick the ball to the net from close range. A super Tommy Dunne point a minute later saw Tipp lead by 3-12 to 3-9.

Waterford's world was caving in. Flynn had pulled back a point but he was substituted afterwards and then Ken McGrath was forced off injured. They still trailed by two points with a minute remaining when Brenner pucked out to Seamus Prendergast on the 45-metre line. He fielded the ball and drove it low through the heart of the Tipp defence. Philly Maher and Mullane slipped and Paul O'Brien darted in from the right corner.

'I thought it might run into me but your man came in like a rocket,' said Cummins.

The goalkeeper came out to narrow the angle but O'Brien pulled on it and the ball flew into the left corner, beyond the despairing dive of Cummins. Waterford had gone in front by a point and the terrace exploded.

'The first thing I thought was "right, a draw,"' said Cummins. 'I settled it down for a second. I didn't puck it out straightaway.'

Waterford won the puckout and the ball was fed to Dave Bennett, who floated a dangerous ball goalwards. It was dropping short and John Mullane was chasing it in but Cummins caught it brilliantly and landed it back down the field.

The game had slipped into injury time and Tipp were camped in the Waterford half, frantically looking for that one elusive score to save them. Mark O'Leary missed a great chance but the ball kept shooting around like on a pinball machine and Waterford defenders kept emerging from the Alamo with it. Three minutes into injury time, Eoin Kelly had one final desperate chance but he was blocked down by 'Brick' Walsh and the referee blew the final whistle when Walsh drove the ball up the field. All over the pitch, Tipperary players collapsed in despair as Waterford went through to their third consecutive Munster final.

Cummins picked up his sticks and walked out to Damien Young, Tipp's third choice keeper who was acting as a hurley carrier. He asked Young what he thought of the atmosphere, but the disappointment hadn't fully hit Cummins at that stage. Eoin Kelly came over and hugged him and they swapped jerseys. Then Brenner arrived, after making the trip up the field.

'Jesus, that was mad stuff altogether,' he said to Cummins while shaking his hand. 'One of those days. We could have let in a heap between us. I don't know whether it was the sun or what.'

'Yeah it must have been the heat,' replied Cummins. 'It was mad alright.'

Mad, for sure.

FORGOTTEN WARRIORS

At 6.10pm on Wednesday June 2, DD Quinn ambled out of his house in Scally Park in Loughgeil in north Antrim with his football boots and two hurleys. It was a beautiful evening as he strolled past the church at the top of the town before taking a right down Lough Road, passing Fr Barrett Park and then walking on for another 400 yards. The little rusty red gate at the back of Fr Healy Park was open so he didn't have to negotiate any hazards on his way into the GAA grounds. Perfect.

He walked across the gravel track behind the pitch, jumped over the little three-foot wall and made his way across the manicured field. He sat down on the concrete seating at the side of the pitch, laced up his boots and drove a couple of balls down to the bottom goalmouth. He was casually stretching in front of the clubhouse and pavilion at the bottom left-hand corner of the field a couple of minutes later when he spotted Niall Patterson's car pulling up along Lough Road.

Quinn jogged up the field and met Patterson at the top goalmouth. They exchanged a few words before Patterson dropped a clutch of sliotars on the 14-metre line and Quinn went in between the posts. Immediately, Patterson began to work the goalkeeper's feet, throwing balls constantly at him. Quinn was pouncing across the line, stretching from post to post before continually returning to the centre of the goal. After nearly two minutes, Patterson told Quinn there were ten balls to go and that he had to either catch or control ten-in-a-row.

'Keep it going, keep it going, when you get tired that's when you start making mistakes!' roared Patterson.

They continued to work on handling, first touch and taking balls into the chest. By the time the session ended, the Loughgeil minors were starting to arrive in the field for training and Quinn and Patterson were just chatting in the goalmouth. Quinn was happy that his touch felt good and that his eye was in. He felt lighter on his feet than he had in an age and lighter in his heart than he had for almost two seasons. In the last five weeks, Patterson has lifted a great deal of weight from him.

When the League ended, Quinn asked Dinny Cahill again about bringing in a goalkeeping coach. When Cahill refused, Quinn told him he wanted one night a week off training so that he could work with Patterson. Cahill still wouldn't budge and a couple of weeks later, Quinn was on the verge of walking. Doubts had beset him like a virus and he felt his game was heading for meltdown.

It came to a head one damp Friday evening in April. Antrim were training in Cushendun and Quinn's mood was as dark as the weather. One of the selectors, Tom McLean, picked up on it and he asked Quinn after training if something was bothering him.

'I'm just pissed off, Tom,' said Quinn. 'It's the same shit for me every night in training and I'm doing nothing to improve my game. I don't think I've done anything to improve my goalkeeping over the last few years.'

'Don't worry,' said McLean, 'it might be better the next night.'

'Well, I might not be back the next night,' responded Quinn.

The next night at training in Armoy, Cahill pulled Quinn aside and the goalkeeper told him that he'd had enough and he wanted specialist coaching. Cahill repeated that he wanted every player to do the same drills and that a goalkeeper's sharpening should be done on his own by hammering a ball against a wall. Quinn refused to accept that, so he decided to just go ahead and do one night a week with Patterson outside county training.

Patterson is a legend in Loughgeil. He captained the club to the 1983 All-Ireland club title - the only Ulster club to do so - while he played for Antrim for almost a decade, lining out in the 1989 All-Ireland final against Tipperary. He wasn't your stereotypical goalkeeper: he was a longhaired, eighteen and a half-stone rock star who played lead guitar in a band and ran a shop all at the same time.

After his father died in 1993, Patterson buried his hurley in the coffin with him and never lifted a stick again. He had drifted away from hurling until Quinn showed up at his door one night in 2003 looking for help before Loughgeil played Dunloy in the county final.

Patterson took him for a couple of sessions and he didn't hear from Quinn again until he called over a month previously. Quinn was desperate for more assistance and Patterson knew where he was coming from. Declan Ryan scored a goal past him from thirty five metres in the 1989 All-Ireland final and his confidence went to pieces afterwards. He didn't know if he had the nerve to perform on the big stage again.

'I could totally understand DD's situation,' said Patterson. 'He was keeping well but his confidence was still low and it's frightening when you feel like that in goal. I just got him back to basics to build up his confidence. I didn't want to burn him out either because the wee lad was training so hard but I was surprised when he wasn't allowed do his own training with the county. I wanted him to take a night off but we've just worked away ever since.'

Quinn meets Patterson now every Wednesday evening for an hour and although it means that he is out hurling six, sometimes only five, nights a week, that extra session has been the glue that has stuck Quinn's hurling and confidence back together.

'It's great to be able to talk to somebody who is a keeper and who knows what it's all about,' said Quinn. 'Niall has put the belief back into me that I can do it. He tells me I can do it. I said to him a few weeks back that my confidence was just gone. I didn't even want the ball coming in near me during games. The confidence just eventually goes and when you're not specialising on your own game in training, you feel as if maybe you're not the man for this at all. Whenever you go into a match not feeling confident, there's something wrong.

'I said to Dinny that I needed to be doing more than just normal training and eventually I just said enough was enough. I was beginning to seriously question myself and think "am I up to it and should I be playing at this level?" I sort of felt like one of the weak links on the team. In the last two All-Ireland quarter-finals I felt that I could have been the weakest link on this team. They were all doing things out the field and I was doing nothing myself.

'It was getting to me. If things aren't going well for me in hurling I would take it wild hard anyway. Ach, I just felt he wanted Gareth McGhee *(the Dunloy keeper)* in. I'm not saying anything bad about Dinny but me and him would never have chatted much, in any way. But we seem to be getting on a bit better now, maybe because I had a few words with him and told him I wasn't happy.'

At the same time that Quinn and Patterson were finishing their session, Down were beginning their own training an hour down the road in Casement Park. They've been really positive since winning the Division Two League title against Westmeath and they had travelled up to Belfast for a light workout. When the players were jogging around the pitch afterwards as part of their warm-down, Graham Clarke set the tone for Sunday's Ulster final.

'This is the place where it's going to happen!' he roared to the rest of the players. 'This is the place where we're going to show that we're better hurlers than Cahill thinks we are.'

When Dinny Cahill was manager of Ulster's Railway Cup team the previous year, Clarke was one of only three Down hurlers on a side dominated by Antrim players. Cahill was entitled to pack the side with representatives from the Ulster champions but Down still felt a grievance towards the selection. They felt they should have had more players in the side and it has festered with them ever since. Now is the opportunity to let the pus out of the sore.

'I thought it was pure arrogance on Dinny's part but on the other hand he was right to be arrogant because that's where Ulster hurling lets itself down,' said Clarke. 'We're not arrogant enough. We go down to Cork and these places and see Joe Deane and think he's a god. We pay too many of these boys too much respect and they pay us nothing. In Down we've even paid too much respect to teams in Ulster. The time for that crap is out the door now. We're going to tear into these boys on Sunday.

'Cahill doesn't really rate us and Antrim are looking further than us. They weren't even doing ballwork before they played us last year. Antrim have to do well this year. Dinny Cahill said he'd have an All-Ireland won with Antrim in three years and this is his third year. So they must be going to win the All-Ireland this year so Kilkenny better get a bit extra done!

'Dinny, not the players, would see us as just a good challenge match and a good test. Dinny has the mentality that he believes in what he has the Antrim team doing but John Crossey also believes in what he has us doing. He believes that our squad is as good as Antrim's and that's why there's a lot of belief in our side because Crossey has instilled it in us.'

The session went well and the mood seemed just right. After the players had completed part of their warm-down, they all went to the middle of the field and began their stretching routine. Everyone was concentrating on the stretches but Gary Savage was raving to a few players about how flexible and fit a young player from his own club in Ballycran was. The young lad had gone on a fitness craze over the winter and Savage reckoned that Brendan McGourty was the only player in the club fitter than him. Crossey overheard Savage and he strolled over to him.

'Gazza, I'll tell you something now,' said Crossey. 'You tell that wee lad that Sa'id Ouita was the fittest man in the planet in the '90s. But he wasn't much of a fucking hurler.'

The whole squad nearly cracked up. Crossey is a straight shooter. Sometimes too straight. When Clarke hit a puckout over the sideline in the League final, Crossey came haring down the line and asked him was the pitch not big enough for him. When Down beat New York in the Ulster semi-final two weeks ago, Crossey and Clarke nearly had to be removed to Madison Square Gardens to settle their differences.

Just before half-time New York won a penalty and Clarke hunched down low to speed up the reaction time in his feet. Michael 'Bonny' Kennedy rifled the ball to the net and Clarke didn't even see it but Crossey charged down behind the goals like a lunatic.

'I saw him coming and next thing I hear: "Stand up to the ball, man!",' said Clarke. 'I lost the head with him. I said: "John, get the fuck away from me." He said again: "Stand up to the fooking ball." I said: "Get the hell out of here and I'll have a word with you later." What kind of shite is that, like? You never see a keeper standing straight up facing a penalty. For God's sake, Davy Fitz is nearly on his knees anytime he's facing a penalty.

'Half-time came and Crossey came walking in and I could see him looking at me. I said to him: "John, I'm doing goals long enough now to know what to do and am I the only guy here who you start picking on? Pick on somebody else will you?" He's a pure character but I lose the head with him sometimes. It completely psyched me up for the second half and I made three good saves. Crossey comes up to me then after the game and says "maybe me and you will have to fall out a bit more." I said "John, I don't want that shite anymore during games."'

Crossey has his own methods of getting inside his own players' heads and the minds of the opposition. A couple of days later, he did a newspaper interview, the gist of which suggested to parents that they'd be better off not bringing their children to the match on Sunday. When Clarke read it, he just smiled.

'He's trying to build it up to be a bloodbath to bring more supporters to the game,' said Clarke. 'It was to build the profile up and psyche a few of their boys out of it as well. He wants them to think that we'll be going around like headless chickens, whaling and smashing all around us. Crossey would have a reputation of his team's being totally motivated up to the last. But he is an unbelievable hurling coach. He's brilliant. He said to us: 'I hope ye didn't read the paper because we're not going out like that, we're going out to play hurling."

In some ways Crossey has succeeded. Down are without their outstanding forward Paul Branniff – who scored 3-9 in the League final – after he tore a cruciate knee ligament against New York and Antrim don't expect it to be a high-scoring, free-flowing hurling match. They're confident that they can win the game.

'There's a danger that you would just see it as a formality but it's going to be like the Derry game *(Ulster semi-final)* and it's going to be another hard battle and struggle,' said Quinn. 'You don't really get any flashy hurling in Ulster. When Antrim play an All-Ireland quarter-final, they're allowed to hurl, if you know what I mean. Down and Derry don't really let you hurl. They're battlers and the game doesn't flow very well. Dinny has massive respect for Down but he still thinks that we should wipe the floor with them.'

On Sunday Down came out blowing up a storm but Antrim weathered it and when Michael Herron blasted to the net from close range on thirteen minutes, Antrim led by 1-4 to 0-2. That looked to be the signal for Antrim's ship to just sail through calm waters but Down whipped up the tide again. Three pointed frees from Gareth 'Magic' Johnson kept them in touch and after Martin Coulter Junior blasted a penalty to the net on the half-hour mark, Antrim knew the waters were going to remain choppy. They only led by a point at the break.

The Down dressing room was totally calm at half-time. Crossey told them that they had proved now that they were good enough, all they had to do was keep hurling the way they were and they would be Ulster champions. 'Magic' Johnson and Brendan McGourty were dominating up front and Crossey insisted on those players being put on the ball more often. Before they went back out on the field again, Clarke roared out two words.

'Belief, boys!'

Forty five seconds after the restart, Brendan McGourty levelled matters. Antrim hit the gas again and tried to pull away with a couple of points but Down wouldn't let them out of sight. They reeled them in and went ahead by two points in the fifty third minute. Antrim equalised two minutes later and the sides continued to trade scores. Two minutes from time Simon Wilson had a chance to push Down ahead but his 80-metre free came back off the post and was cleared. The sides had been level on six occasions and seemed set for deadlock. But then with less than a minute remaining, Darren Quinn looked to have turned the key in Antrim's favour.

He won a ball near the sideline, turned and drove it high towards the Andersonstown goal. The ball soared up in the air and before it had reached the posts, the Antrim crowd in the terrace was cheering. It looked about six inches inside the post.

'Wide ball, wide ball!' roared Clarke.

He noticed that the umpires were slow to raise the flag and he tried to profit further from their doubt. 'I just roared at one of them: "It's wide this time umpire, definitely!" Whenever it's that close you put your hands up and shout "wide ball!" Every goalkeeper in Ireland does the same. But the ball was over the bar. Definitely.'

Clarke wasn't sure if he'd managed to convince the umpires but after the referee came in to consult with them, the ball was waved wide and all hell broke loose. Some of the Antrim supporters in the terrace went wild and started spewing venom at Clarke. 'You dishonest wee bastard!' they shouted at him.

The Antrim mentors were going nuts on the sideline while out on the pitch Gabriel Clarke and Darren Quinn had squared up to one another over the incident and a melée had broken out. While that was being broken up, Paddy Richmond ran in to the Down goalkeeper in a vain attempt to try and get him to mend his ways and come clean.

'You know that ball was over the bar, Graham,' said Richmond. Clarke just smiled at him and shrugged his shoulders.

Antrim were furious when the match ended in a draw. They felt they'd been cheated out of the win but the draw had other implications for DD Quinn. In February, he had booked a holiday with his girlfriend Amanda and they were supposed to be flying out to Tenerife on Friday. Johnny Campbell, Karl McKeegan, Mickey McCambridge and Ciaran Herron also had foreign holiday plans that week while Liam Richmond was flying to Lanzarote with his wife the following morning.

They all met in the dressing room with selectors Ger Rogan and Tom McLean after the match and discussed it further at the meal in the

Glenowen. Liam Richmond couldn't change his plans but the rest of them decided not to go. Quinn went into the travel agent the following morning to see if he could rearrange the trip but the tickets had been issued and he had to cancel it. He hasn't seen much of Amanda in the last few months with his hectic training schedule and now this. The County Board has told him that he'll be reimbursed but that hasn't got him out of the doghouse.

'She's mad, boy. Ach, I don't blame her. I really had to put up with it on Sunday and Monday and I'm going to have to put up with it for a while yet. But that's life.'

The replay was fixed for the following Sunday in Casement Park at 7.00pm. Neither side was happy with the starting-time of the fixture but the Ulster football semi-final between Cavan and Armagh was scheduled for that afternoon at 2.15pm so the hurling replay looked like an afterthought that had to be accommodated.

The general consensus after the drawn match was that Down had lost their chance but the players didn't see it that way. Clarke certainly didn't. In his heart, he felt they were good enough. He believes they are but until they actually get over the line and win an Ulster title, he can't let emotion smother him.

'We know now we are good enough and an Ulster title would mean the world to us. The Ulster Council look like they don't give a damn about the whole thing but this is everything to us. To me anyway because it would give us a game in Croke Park. I don't even want to think about Croke Park because it would just make me nervous. Crossey said to us that if we beat these boys, there will be no more excuses and they'll have to let us into Croke Park then. If we win, we'll camp out in the place.'

From the throw-in, Antrim hit them hard. Nothing personal, just business. They had clearly upped the physical stakes and there was a more cut-throat edge to their game. On nine minutes, Simon Wilson went down near the endline to pick up a loose ball and Liam Watson pulled high and broke the hurley across his knee. Wilson was stretchered off and Watson only received a yellow card.

There was nothing between the sides in the opening twenty minutes but Antrim were driving through the tackles and were much more forceful and purposeful than they'd been a week earlier. On twenty two minutes, however, the plan started to unravel for Down when their excellent full-back Stephen Murray had to retire with a knee injury.

'I could sense the heads drop immediately,' said Clarke.

A minute later Paddy Richmond took full advantage of Murray's absence when he latched onto a pass from Colm McGuckian and hammered the ball past Clarke. Down were still hanging in but a minute before the break, Richmond fired home Antrim's second goal to leave them ahead at the break by 2-8 to 0-7. It left Down with a huge mountain to climb but Clarke was trying to fill the oxygen bottles at the break.

'Listen here boys, any Down team I've ever played on has never got hammered around Casement Park like the way we have been in the last thirty five minutes,' he said in the dressing room. 'We make up our minds here now that we're not going to be walked over in the second half. We're going to have to match them and drive through them, walk over the top of them if we have to. We're going to show these guys that they can't walk all over us.'

They dug in immediately after the break and dragged themselves back up the cliff edge. They chipped away with a series of points and Antrim had to rely on a smart save from Quinn from a Ger McGrattan shot on fifty two minutes to keep sufficient daylight between the sides. Four minutes later though, Brian McFall cut the rope that Down were dangling onto when he darted in from the left flank, danced past three defenders and whipped a half-volley past Clarke.

Clarke was hoping and praying in the last fifteen minutes that there was a way back but he had accepted in his heart that Down were gone, lying helpless at the bottom once more. A life in Down hurling had blessed him with that wisdom. And suddenly with a minute to go, it hit him like a train. His Croke Park dream had died. Again.

When the final whistle blew, he put his hand over his face and sat down on the goal-line against the post. After the previous week's match,

Clarke had exchanged heated words with Colm McGuckian over an injury to 'Magic' Johnson but McGuckian went in to shake his hand. Clarke was concussed by the moment and all he could do was nod. The words McGuckian spoke never registered. DD Quinn sought him out and the two spoke in the tunnel. Quinn knew he had no words of consolation for Clarke so he showed his respect through the power of his handshake.

The Down dressing room afterwards was a vision of desolation. Few words were said, but the silence was eloquent. Shattered bodies, splintered spirits and another batch of broken dreams. The forgotten warriors in hurling's world. A lot of the hurling fraternity doesn't even know they exist but this is only the Ulster hurling final after all. Nobody really gives a damn. The Ulster Council says they do, but you know they really don't.

'They said that there were 4,500 at the match, there were no more 4,500 than there are 4,500 hurling supporters on the fucking moon,' said Clarke. 'There was about 1,500 to 2,000 at it. The stand was half-empty but where else in the country would you see a provincial final on a Sunday evening? Where else in the country would you run out against a team you're trying to beat since 1998 and have to play them in their home pitch every year? As some of the boys said after the match, it's the only pitch in the whole of Ireland that you get booed running out onto the field. It's a joke.'

Down's season is dead in the water and that was confirmed as soon as the match was over. They drew Galway in the first round of the All-Ireland qualifiers so they're just waiting for the Grim Reaper to come now.

'They're ruthless bastards,' said Clarke. 'They'll grind us into the ground. We've a load of injuries and them boys have no mercy. They'll just try and blow us away.'

A couple of hours later, anger gave way to disillusionment when Clarke looked at it all in cold blood and dissected his own game.

'It's just heart-wrenching and it's even worse when I feel that I didn't play that well. I don't know. I make very few saves from ten yards and maybe I wasn't brave enough for a few of those shots. People say to me: "Graham, you're as good a keeper as there is in Ireland" and I just say: "No I'm not." I reckon I'm way down the list. I'm trying to push myself up the list but I'm not getting anywhere. *(Brendan)* Cummins would have got Paddy Richmond's first goal and that's the difference between Cummins and me. Cummins, Fitzhenry and Fitzgerald and these boys are making saves from ten yards that the other keepers aren't. It's devastating. I'm training every night of the week and I can't make those saves.

'Paddy Monan said to me afterwards that I was still the best keeper in Ulster. I said: "Paddy, where's it getting me?" There's no point being the best keeper in Ulster and going out against Galway and letting in ten goals. I have to be honest with myself. There's no point making great saves in New York and in Casement Park and no one in Ireland seeing them. You have to be making the real special saves and I don't seem to be making the saves in a match that I'm making in training.

'Maybe I'm not up for it enough either. I don't know. If I thought for a second that we're not going to win an Ulster title or get to Croke Park, my sticks would be fired out to the garage. Because there's no way it justifies hammering a ball about five nights a week when you've a wee 'un and a wife who has moved up from Killarney. Mary took Lauren out the road and out of my way all day because she knew I was trying to concentrate on the game. She knows I'm trying to push myself to the limit but I have to think of my family as well. It's just madness. I don't know. I'm just gutted.'

The following morning, Clarke got up at 8.00am and headed to Belfast for work. He had played a provincial final less than twelve hours previously but he is the sole employee of his own electrician business and he had a job to complete. It was a beautiful clear morning and as Clarke was opening his van, he took a look out across the Irish Sea and noticed that the Isle of Man was visible. He normally wouldn't take any notice but he did. His head was all over the place.

He drove out the narrow stoney driveway, turned right down Drumarden road and then right again at the top of Ballygalget road. The

Ballygalget pitch is less than 300 yards from that junction and as he passed by, he looked in. His mind drifted back to the long dark winter nights when he purged his soul and spilled his guts on that field. All for one dream.

'Back in January, when I was running around that field, I was thinking: "This will stand by me when we get to Croke Park." It just seems further away now than it ever was. It's not a sad story but you want to be playing in Croke Park and you want a bit of recognition. Every time I turn up in Ballygalget pitch, I push myself to the limit, striving to be as good as I can be so I can be up there with Cummins and Cusack and these boys.

'People probably think I'm big-headed but there's no reason why I couldn't be up there, if I just got that break and the team got a wee run together. I don't know if it's as big a blow to the other boys as it is to me but that's what keeps me going, that's what keeps driving me. If I didn't think I'd be in Croke I wouldn't be hurling but it's just getting harder and harder to keep going. I hope to God that I get to see Croke Park as a player.'

Some day, hopefully.

'But ... I don't think I ever will.'

DAVID AND GOLIATH

Although there have been some predictable attempts all week to inject suspense into the Leinster semi-final between Wexford and Kilkenny, nobody is buying any of them. Jaded references to 1976 when Kilkenny were reigning All-Ireland champions, had just won the League and were going for six Leinster titles-in-a-row, look ultimately futile. The best price you can get about Kilkenny winning the Leinster title is 1-8 and they look a sure thing to secure seven-in-a-row next month.

The public in Wexford certainly can't see their team putting a stop to Kilkenny. Their forward line is heavy on ball players and light on ball winners and the only traces of that legion expected to appear on the field after the match will probably have to be scraped off the tracks of the Kilkenny defensive Panzer division.

The internal strife of six weeks before is another debilitating worry for Wexford supporters because they're not sure if the squad have been galvanised or torn apart by the condition. There is a huge responsibility on the senior players to shoulder this team and take the fight to Kilkenny, but there is no suggestion that those players are in the form of their lives. The only given for Wexford fans is the knowledge that their most experienced player is guaranteed to produce the goods.

Damien Fitzhenry is probably going to have to play the game of his life if Wexford are to have any chance of defeating Kilkenny. That's pressure but Fitzhenry has been performing at the top for twelve seasons now and his consistent excellence has always been a surety to Wexford hurling. Especially given the disaster zone he walked into back in 1993.

After John Nolan retired in 1986 and before Fitzhenry arrived seven years later, the Wexford goalkeeping position was a standard joke around the country. If a Wexford goalkeeper walked out in front of a double-decker bus, it would have gone through his legs.

In 1987 Ted Morrissey made his debut and should have got the line within minutes for pulling straight across Liam McCarthy from Kilkenny. A year later Paul Nolan was between the posts and when the second half of the Leinster semi-final against Kilkenny started, Wexford realised thirty seconds later that they had no goalkeeper. Nolan was inside in the dressing room changing his boots.

The Leinster final that year was a nightmare for Nolan. He topped a puckout in the first half and drove it only twenty five yards. Joe Dooley pulled it down and drove it straight to the net.

'The hurley twisted in my hand because I was going for too much power,' said Nolan. 'It was like topping a golf shot. Except it was a lot more costly.'

Later in the half, he spilled a long ball from Danny Owens and Dooley pounced on it like a hawk and drove it home. Nolan was a fine young keeper who had captained the Wexford minors to the 1985 All-Ireland final, but he was dropped afterwards and never asked back.

Nolan's departure reopened the door for Morrissey but he continued to struggle to get by with an easy life. Against Laois in the 1990 championship, he caught a high ball but was adjudged to have grabbed it behind the line. When the umpire raised the green flag, Morrissey snapped. He went for the umpire and almost assaulted him.

'The wind blew Ted back over the line,' said Larry O'Gorman. 'So the boys said that they'd have to tie a cement block around his legs the next time we were playing against the breeze.'

The floodgates opened again the following year and finally swallowed him up. Morrissey was captain as Wexford went all the way to the League final against Offaly. Late in the second half he tried to control a high ball but it broke away from him and Daithí Regan flicked the loose sliotar to the net. It cost Wexford the match.

A month later Wexford were leading Kilkenny in the dying minutes of the Leinster semi-final when DJ Carey broke through the heart of the Wexford defence. He took eight steps before kicking the ball from the 20-metre line. It skidded off the wet surface, Morrissey got his hurley to it but the ball squirmed in over the line. Even though the ball had travelled the full length of the pitch, after John Conran had failed to rise the sliotar twice, and Carey had taken too many steps, the whole of Wexford wanted to tie Morrissey to a stake and burn him alive.

'People wouldn't talk to me after that game,' said Morrissey. 'For ages afterwards I would be walking down the street and people would cross the road to avoid me. It was like as if I'd committed some terrible crime and they were afraid to be seen with me.'

Morrissey got the chop afterwards and never wore a Wexford jersey again. By the following spring, Wexford still hadn't settled on a goalkeeper and they were getting desperate. Finally they turned to a Kilkennyman, David 'Stoney' Burke.

The commentator Micheál Ó Muircheartaigh once referred to 'Stoney' Burke as 'the man with the height of a bantamweight boxer but the body of a sumo wrestler'. He didn't look like much of a goalkeeper but he was a superb shot-stopper. When he gave the best ever display by a keeper in an All-Ireland Under-21 final in Kilkenny's win over Tipperary in 1984, he moved on to stratospheric heights in the mindset of the Kilkenny hurling public. Anyone who was at the game left Walsh Park in Waterford convinced that they had witnessed the successor to the legendary Noel Skehan.

Skehan had nine All-Ireland medals and after he called it a day in March 1985, Burke was immediately installed as Kilkenny number one. For the first time in thirty years, Kilkenny had a goalkeeper that wasn't named Ollie Walsh or Noel Skehan. The pressure was colossal.

'It was awesome really taking over from Noel Skehan,' said Burke. 'Anytime that you put on a jersey for Kilkenny you were expected to win and expected to deliver. And if you don't, you're in trouble.'

Skehan was convinced that Burke was going to have a long career. 'He had a great chance at the time because he was a good keeper. He just didn't grab that chance.'

The 1985 Leinster final was a catastrophe for Burke. And for Kilkenny in the long run. Prior to that game, Offaly had only ever beaten their nemesis once in a Leinster decider and many people regarded that win in 1980 as just a bad day at the office for Kilkenny. Seven minutes into the second half of the 1985 final, the theory that Kilkenny always had something over Offaly looked spot-on when they led by nine points.

Then a high ball dropped into the Kilkenny goalmouth and Burke went out to catch it. He spilled it and Pádraig Horan slipped it in past him for a cheap goal. Offaly pegged Kilkenny back and in a high scoring game, scrambled a draw. It was a watershed game in the Kilkenny-Offaly hurling relationship and when Offaly went on to win the replay by six points, it expelled any doubts in Kilkenny minds that Offaly were just a transient force.

It proved how much belief Offaly had come to instil in themselves when facing their traditional superiors and the drawn 1985 Leinster final is deeply embedded in the Offaly hurling psyche. For Burke, that was the day the line in the sand was effectively drawn under his Kilkenny hurling career.

The management went to Skehan after the drawn game and asked him to consider returning for the replay. Skehan refused and anyhow, he was sure Burke would recover. But he didn't. Afterwards, Burke walked away from Kilkenny. He was still only twenty two and decided to go to the US for a couple of years.

At that stage, Kilkenny turned to thirty-one year old Kevin Fennelly. He wasn't a long-term option but he still remained in the number one position for five years between 1986-'90. Burke returned in 1988 from the US and was immediately drafted onto the panel. He won an All-Ireland junior title in 1988 but DJ Carey was the subkeeper for the 1989 championship. Burke returned to the panel for the 1990 campaign and when Fennelly retired after the championship, the door finally reopened.

There weren't a lot of other options in the county but Michael Walsh had been excellent in Kilkenny's run to another junior title in 1990 when his father, the legendary goalkeeper Ollie Walsh, was the team manager.

Michael Walsh had played as a goalkeeper on successive underage and junior teams during the 1980s but he was also an excellent soccer player. He attracted enough attention in the early 1980s to be asked to sign up to the League of Ireland with Waterford United and St Patrick's Athletic. He never did play League of Ireland but Walsh went on to make a serious imprint in Junior soccer and captained Ireland at International level.

He got a run as a wing-forward in the 1984 Oireachtas and had a chance in goal with the Kilkenny seniors in 1987 when he played the first three rounds of the 1987-'88 League. Against Clare in Round 3, however, Walsh came out to clear a ball and decided to pull on it first time. He slipped and missed the ball and it crawled into the net behind him. He got the door afterwards and was never expected to be seen again.

Ollie Walsh only got the Kilkenny manager's job by chance in the autumn of 1990. Dermot Healy was the manager but when the County Board refused to let him choose his own selectors, he resigned. Walsh got the job for just one year but he stayed for five seasons.

With DJ Carey having graduated to the forward division after spending one year on the bench as subkeeper, 'Stoney' Burke was seen as the obvious successor to Fennelly. He would surely have benefited from his previous experience and his club form had been really impressive the previous season. Michael Walsh meanwhile was almost thirty and had no championship experience but both he and Burke were drafted into the squad.

'It was a huge gamble for him *(his father)* and looking back on it now, I probably wouldn't have done it if I had more time to think about it,' said Walsh.

Burke got the first three League games and played really well. Walsh finally got the nod for Round 4 against Limerick and didn't exactly crown himself in garlands with his performance. He honestly didn't expect to make the cut but when the panel was redrafted after Christmas Walsh was still there while Burke got dropped. Adrian Ronan, who was the hottest forward property in the county before Carey arrived, was given the loose title of subkeeper.

'One of the selectors came to me and said that Ollie wanted to make sure that Mickey was in goal and they could pick the rest of the team after that,' said Burke. 'If that was a lie, well then I was told a lie. But I know for sure that it wasn't. At the time I was the best keeper in the county and I felt I had a lot more to offer Kilkenny. I would have absolutely no time for Ollie Walsh.'

Ollie Walsh is no longer alive to defend himself and Michael puts the family case forward.

'Stoney is totally entitled to feel the way he feels but it certainly wasn't anything to do with me. There were five selectors there and I don't know how much of a say my father did have. All I will say is that if you were a selector, he honoured your opinion. He maintained until the day he died that it wasn't him who was pushing me. He said that there were other selectors pushing me and I can only take the man at his word.

'Stoney is entitled to his opinion and maybe he has a right to feel aggrieved but I felt the same way in 1987 when I was dropped after one bad game. I felt I was shafted and Stoney was brought back in as subkeeper but I just took my medicine and said nothing about it. When I got my second chance, the selectors made their decision and I think history will prove that they made the right one."

As well as the inevitable comparisons with his father, the innuendo that was circling the county exacerbated the situation. Along with that, Offaly had taken a stranglehold in Leinster by winning three titles in-a-row and the pressure to deliver a provincial title was overbearing in the county. All some of the critics were waiting for was Ollie Walsh to cost Kilkenny more success through nepotism.

'It was a huge burden for me but it must have been ten times worse for my father,' said Walsh. 'When I started out, I knew it was being said that the only reason I was there was because I was the manager's son. I just had to turn a blind eye to it. It's probably still being said to this day but I don't really care now.'

It was always going to take something special for Walsh to win over the Kilkenny supporters. In the end, it took throwing his head in front of a hurley. In the 1991 Leinster semi-final against Wexford, a ball broke to Jimmy Holohan just fourteen metres out with the goal yawning in front of him. With the ball breaking, Walsh was out of position but he gobbled up the ground, threw himself on the ground and flicked the ball to safety. Just as he did, Holohan's stick caught him in the face with the follow through and almost destroyed him. His nose was broken so badly that it was shunted across his face and he had twenty six stitches inserted in a cut around his mouth.

'That was the first time that I was actually accepted by the Kilkenny hurling public,' he said. 'From that day on I could feel a difference. Maybe it was my own imagination but I definitely could sense an acceptance of me. We both knew that if anything had gone wrong for me that day, both of our heads were for the chop because I was a lovely scapegoat. Although it was painful at the time, maybe something like that needed to be done. That was a big turning point for me.'

Ollie Walsh's goalkeeping strategy though, could still have potentially damaged him that day. Although Adrian Ronan was technically regarded as the subkeeper, he never played there in training and the kitman Denis 'The Rackard' Cody used to stand in goal for training matches. Ronan only had a cast removed from his leg the Wednesday before the match after injuring an Achilles tendon and he just ambled into Kilkenny training that evening for a look. He nearly collapsed when Ollie Walsh told him that he would be travelling to Croke Park with the squad on Sunday.

'I said: "Sure, I can hardly walk",' said Ronan. 'And Ollie said: "Sure you know yourself, you won't be needed."'

Apart from hobbling around on one leg, his only goalkeeping experience had been a few games for his club years earlier. On Sunday Ronan was inside in the dugout with his boots off and his feet up on a bench when he heard somebody say that Walsh had gone down. His mind was a million miles away and out of the corner of his eye, he spotted the wing-back Liam Walsh on the ground. He thought he was saved.

Then a selector told him he was going in.

'I said to myself: "What the hell do they want me for?",' said Ronan. 'They had to say it to me two or three times before I copped it that Mickey was gone down. Then in the panic I couldn't find my boots. I was going around looking for them like a headless chicken. I only had one hurley and it was a complete joke. When I got in there I just said to myself: "Please don't let the ball come near me."'

Ronan survived and Walsh returned for the Leinster final. Although Ronan managed to secure an outfield spot, he felt the whole goalkeeping set-up compromised his position.

'Mickey was a great keeper but when I look back on it, they were shafting Stoney,' said Ronan. 'Stoney was just as good a keeper but Ollie couldn't carry him. He could always have the excuse that I was the sub-goalie but that came to my detriment as time went on.

'I know privately that the other selectors wanted a proper subkeeper because it was unheard of in inter-county hurling at the time that you wouldn't have a proper sub-goalie. Then when the shit hit the fan, the boys hung me out to dry. In 1991 and 1992 I played nearly every championship match in those two seasons and I got dropped for the two All-Ireland finals at the last minute. They probably felt they needed a subkeeper then but that was too late for me and Ollie couldn't fight his corner for me anymore.'

'I'm convinced that it doesn't help you along the way when you're a character and a gallery for everyone. They kind of think they can do what they like with you. And I kind of learned that myself. Stoney was a character and a joker and people probably thought he could be dropped and mistreated because he wouldn't mind. I think that's what happened Stoney and he was able to be messed around. But his goalkeeping ability never changed and he was never appreciated.'

After Burke failed to make the Kilkenny squad in 1991, he packed in hurling later that year. His father was very sick at the time and he was working and living in New Ross in Wexford with a young family.

Above: *Why?: The boy prodigy Timmy Houlihan wasn't on the Limerick panel in 2004 after being cut from the squad for the second time before he'd even reached the age of 22.*
Below: *Wide ball: All Graham Clarke wanted was one game in Croke Park, but he didn't get it.*

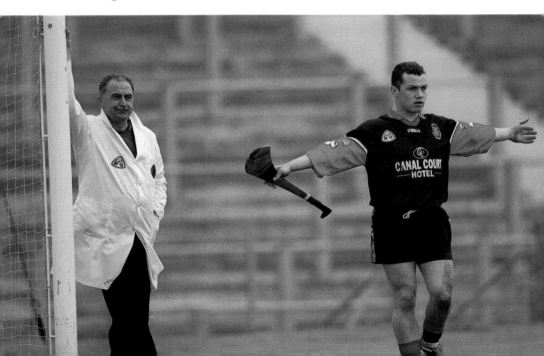

Above: *Like father like son: On a cold March morning in 1999, Nicky Quaid, son of the late Limerick goalkeeper Tommy Quaid, lines out between the posts in an U-12 Hurling-Shinty International match between Ireland and Scotland.*

Below: *Rage against the tide: After eight years as Dublin's first-choice keeper, Brendan McLoughlin retired six days before Dublin's 2004 championship season ended.*

Above: *Ice in his veins: After just two seasons with Offaly, Brian Mullins has already moved into the top strata of hurling goalkeepers.*
Below: *'If you only knew what was going on inside my head': some people thought Joe Quaid was the cockiest keeper they ever saw but he never felt that way.*

Above: *Peace before the war: Brendan Cummins emerges from the darkness of the Páirc Uí Chaoimh tunnel and into a kiln of heat and pressure as Tipperary prepare to take on Waterford in the Munster semi-final.*

Left: *Turn back the clock: Moments after Stevie Brenner conceded a soft goal in the Munster final, he tries to wipe out the memory and retain his focus. The mistake possibly cost him his place for the All-Ireland semi-final.*

Above: *Full force: Liam Donoghue pucks out on the day of a Galway meltdown against Kilkenny in the All-Ireland qualifiers.*
Below: *Keep on keeping on: Before the championship began, DD Quinn was beset by doubts but he rediscovered his confidence and was one of Antrim's best players in their All-Ireland quarter-final nightmare defeat to Cork.*

Above: *The loneliest place in the world: For eighteen years, Ger Cunningham was Cork's first-choice goalkeeper, fighting off a posse of pretenders to the throne during that time.*

Left: *Ball of fire: David Fitzgerald ignites and fires up his team-mates in their All-Ireland quarter-final replay against Kilkenny.*

Above: *The eyes have it: The best goalkeeper in the country during the 2004 championship, it was largely due to Damien Fitzhenry's heroics that Wexford were crowned Leinster champions.*
Below: *Nearly there: James McGarry celebrates Henry Shefflin's second goal in the All-Ireland semi-final against Waterford. Reaching the All-Ireland final was the zenith of Kilkenny's season but their dreams of three-in-a-row went up in smoke.*

Above: *The Save: Seconds after Donal Óg Cusack makes a fantastic save from Henry Shefflin in the All-Ireland final, he goes about launching an attack that resulted in a Cork point.*

Left: *Deliverance: At last Donal Cusack heals the hurt of the previous twelve months.*

Wexford had recruited Cyril Farrell from Galway as trainer and in the spring of '92 Farrell and Martin Quigley called to Burke's house and asked him to reconsider his retirement plans. He was still only twenty eight and they felt he had something to offer. They couldn't guarantee him his place but he decided to go for it.

Before long, Burke had nailed down the position and the management's decision to recruit him was completely vindicated when he played brilliantly in the Leinster quarter-final win over Laois. When Wexford got over Dublin and Kilkenny advanced past Offaly in their respective Leinster semi-finals, the plot thickened. For Burke, the Leinster final was going to have more angles than a compass.

'It was like David and Goliath with a twist,' said Burke.

Although his father, Michael Burke, was very sick, he was behind the goal with a Wexford scarf concealed inside his coat for the Leinster final. He was a die-hard Kilkenny man but he knew the pressure his son was under. In some parts of Kilkenny, Stoney Burke had become a hate-figure.

'I knew what was being said in the Kilkenny dressing room,' said Burke. 'I'm sure Ollie Walsh was saying "don't let that Stoney Burke win this." He'd never have lived it down if we had won.'

Burke's presence on the Wexford side was a definite motivational factor. 'With (Cyril) Farrell there and Stoney in goals, there was a lot going on but we were never as psyched up for a game,' said Michael Walsh.

Burke was in an impossible position but he had hurled with a lot of the Kilkenny squad and there was a small degree of understanding about his situation in the opposition camp.

'When I was walking around behind the band during the parade, we passed the Kilkenny dug-out and I looked over. I could see a few of the Kilkenny boys giving me the thumbs up on the quiet. They knew what had gone on.'

The game wasn't long on when Burke could hear the taunts behind him. He knew it was going to be a difficult day but he hadn't braced himself for the torrent of abuse that was flowing from the peaks of Hill 16 and the Canal End of the stadium.

'That was the most difficult day of my hurling career. The abuse that I got that day from Kilkenny people behind the goal, I wouldn't wish it on my worst enemy. What they didn't say about my kids and my mother, it was scandalous. They were shouting out that they hoped my father died.'

At one stage, a small section of Wexford fans on Hill 16 took issue with a group from Kilkenny over the tone of the poisoned comments they were aiming at Burke. A ruck started and a few of the Gardaí stepped in to break it up.

Down on the field, Burke was acting as normal as possible. He played solidly and kept his head but Kilkenny slammed three goals past him in a ten-point victory. It was one of the most complete performances ever from that Kilkenny team but Burke knew that, in real terms, the margin of victory was far greater.

'There was just a minefield of difference between Wexford and Kilkenny,' said Burke. 'When you're growing up in Kilkenny, you never expect to lose. So if you were either a fourteen-year-old or a twenty-four year-old going out against anybody, you were already three points ahead of them. You knew in your heart and soul going out against Wexford that they were going to die midway through the second half and you were going to pull ahead. The Wexford fellas knew that too deep down and you could sense it. I saw it myself that day first-hand.'

Kilkenny and Walsh went from strength to strength after that. They won their first All-Ireland for nine years later that summer and they retained the title a year later. By the time he was thirty in 1991, Michael Walsh had yet to even play championship for Kilkenny. Two years later he had two All-Ireland medals and two All-Star awards. A year after that, he was Kilkenny captain.

After Ollie Walsh passed away suddenly in March 1996, Michael's drive and ambition died with him. He had always travelled to the matches with his father and he didn't have the heart for it anymore. He was thirty five and after Wexford beat them in that year's Leinster quarter-final, he retired with a cornucopia of memories.

'It was a total fairytale story for me really when I look back on it,' said

Walsh. 'I thought my chance had passed me by and to even play for Kilkenny in one match would have done me at that stage. The fact that I was Ollie's son, I'm sure I was judged twice as hard but the fact that he trusted me was a huge thing for me. I couldn't do anything about what other people thought but I hope I repaid the faith he showed in me.

'He took a huge risk. There were four other people involved and he was a man of his word. But if it all went wrong at the end of the day he was the one who was going to get the rap, not the other four. The deepest impression that was left on me after the whole thing was how much pressure my father was under and never, ever did I once recognise it. I didn't think of it. It was an impossible situation for him and when I think back on it now I wonder how he did it.

'If I started thinking about him being manager, I definitely wouldn't have done anything. I tried to put all that stuff to the back of my mind but you don't really realise how deep your ambition is until you actually get there. I had only one ambition since I was growing up but I never really realised that until I got my chance. Maybe it took that situation for me to realise what was inside me. When I got the chance I said to myself that I had to make it work.'

After the 1992 Leinster final, David 'Stoney' Burke never hurled again. Wexford also lost the Leinster minor final that day to Kilkenny but at least they had seen some shard of light cast on the day. The minor keeper was brilliant. He was the future.

His name was Damien Fitzhenry.

BLACK AND AMBER AMBUSH

On June 13, the morning of the Leinster semi-final, the Kilkenny squad met as usual in the Newpark hotel in Kilkenny City. It was their first championship trip back to Croke Park since the previous year's All-Ireland final and James McGarry was one of the first players to arrive at the hotel. As the other players started to trickle in, they began milling around the car park before it was time to board the bus. McGarry surveyed the scene and immediately, warning flares started going off inside his head.

The efforts around the country all week to inject box-office appeal into this game have failed spectacularly. The pay-per-view option hasn't been taken up by the normal ratio of subscribers, as the majority of Kilkenny supporters aren't even travelling to Dublin.

Naturally, for the last couple of weeks, the management and squad have had to try and guard against that outside complacency, that insidious disease that can infiltrate a panel and silently tear it apart. Kilkenny are sure that they've taken all the precautionary and preventative vitamins and that they are in full health. They've trained hard, they feel fresh and are quietly confident. But before the bus departed, McGarry ambled over to manager Brian Cody in the car park.

'I didn't think the attitude was right,' said McGarry. 'I could sense it. I said to Cody: "Do lads realise that we're going up to play Wexford?" He said: "Yeah, it hardly feels like a championship day at all." When some lads were getting on the bus, other lads were arriving late. It might have only been a couple of minutes but they were still late. If you're tuned in you'll be there early.'

At roughly the same time, the Wexford team bus was collecting the players from the south of the county in Wexford town. The bus arrived at the SuperValu carpark in Enniscorthy at 10.30am, where Damien

Fitzhenry and the mid-Wexford crew jumped on board. After the bus had made its last pick-up at Gorey just before 11am, it was straight into south Dublin.

Fitzhenry normally moves around the bus on match days like a drifter. He'll always base himself at the back and then work his way forward but today he sat down beside Mossie Mahon for the first half of the journey and then went up beside Paul Carley until they got to Dublin. He knew both would be tense because Mahon was just beginning to establish himself on the team and Carley was making his debut. Fitzhenry wanted to help melt any tension they might be feeling and they chatted about everything. Except hurling.

The bus arrived at their base in the Stillorgan Park Hotel at midday. Everything was timed perfectly. They immediately sat down to their pre-match meal of soup, pasta and chicken salad before heading for the team meeting room. Normally Fitzhenry will wander around the lobby for a while to chat to local people up for the game but he didn't. Not today.

Before any of the players or management spoke, they were all addressed by Fr Odhran Furlong, a priest based in Templeudigan near Rathnure and one of the most progressive young priests in the country. He runs an alliance scheme in Wexford, which fosters leadership skills and mental awareness, primarily in secondary schools throughout the county.

He has studied psychology and was approached by John Conran a few weeks back about speaking to the squad. Initially it created a bit of unrest in the camp because some of the players didn't feel he was an adequate replacement for the sports psychologist Niamh Fitzpatrick. He first addressed the panel when they stayed in Dungarvan after playing Cork in Ardmore in May and he has kept reiterating the importance of teamwork ever since. He hammered this message home once more in the meeting.

When Fr Furlong had finished speaking, management went through their gameplan. The squad had worked relentlessly hard in the last five weeks on adapting and fine-tuning the system the players devised before they played Dublin in the League. The half-forward line was to play deep and leave plenty of room inside for the full-forward line. And all over the field, they were to keep the ball moving, whether it was in the air or on the ground.

Two weeks before they took on and beat Galway in an eighty-minute challenge game in Rathineska, outside Portlaoise. Fitzhenry didn't play because of injury but Matty White stitched his puckouts perfectly into the fabric of Wexford's gameplan and they won an extremely high- scoring match. Their forwards had ripped Galway's defence apart with their pace and movement and Wexford felt they were coming good at the right time.

'We know if we can do it against Galway that we can do it against Kilkenny,' said Fitzhenry. 'But to make this work, everyone has to be tuned in.'

Mentally they were ready. 'Everybody looked at each other in the circle,' said the goalkeeper. 'And the feeling was: "We can do this."'

They departed the hotel at 1.30pm and it took them the best part of an hour to get across town to Croke Park. When they got into the dressing room, everyone felt focussed and relaxed. Nobody more so than Fitzhenry.

'I wouldn't see pressure from one day to the next, let alone one year to the next. It's just the way I am. To be honest I try not to get worked up about anything because it's only a waste of time and energy. Outside of hurling, I get worried about very little. It's the only way, especially for my position.'

He put on his gear, lay up on the treatment table for a few minutes and then went into the warm-up area for a few pucks. When he came back into the dressing room, he repeated the mantra to reinforce the focus and guard against any degree of increasing anxiety. The gameplan was going to demand a savage workrate. Savage.

'If you're able to go for fifty minutes and you have to come off, then come off and give someone else a run,' he said. 'Everyone will go up to you afterwards and say "Fair fucks to you, you ran yourself into the ground for Wexford."'

Before they went out onto the field, everyone gathered in a circle in the warm-up area and wrapped their arms tightly around each other. Rory McCarthy stepped into the middle with passion blazing in his eyes.

'Listen,' he said, 'Kilkenny are heading for seven Leinsters in-a-row and it's about time some team did something about it. They're going to be beaten some day. Why not let it be us today?'

Wexford set about trying to liberate Leinster from a run of Kilkenny victories that looked like rolling on through all eternity from the moment Fitzhenry took the first puckout of the game. He sent it dipping to the left in front of the Kilkenny half-back line. Paul Carley sprinted across from the right wing, leaving Brian Hogan toiling in his vapour trail, and gathered the ball. The message rang out immediately. Wexford were going to try and stretch Kilkenny at the back.

Fitzhenry was crucial to the symphony Wexford were trying to play. With his puckouts, he was conducting a lot of the orchestra's music. And they were playing well. And sweetly.

Wexford were hitting crossfield balls and consistently moving the sliotar at pace on the ground. When they secured possession, they were looking up and trying to pick out a colleague with a measured pass. Of the puckouts and clearances that spilled loose, Wexford were quicker to the breakdown because they were sharper to react and much more tuned in.

Noel Hickey, Seán Dowling and JJ Delaney made ten overhead catches between them in the 2003 All-Ireland final so Fitzhenry certainly wasn't going to launch an air raid on top of the Kilkenny defence. He pucked out to players on the run and varied his strikes so intelligently in the first half that only two were caught by a member of the All-Ireland champions' half-back line. Of the fifteen puckouts he took, Wexford won nine and they secured four points, either from play or from frees. His team was managing fine; they only trailed by a point at the break.

It wasn't alien territory to Kilkenny because they had done most of their damage in the second half over the previous two seasons. There was no great panic in their dressing room but they knew they weren't hurling well and McGarry could sense what he feared earlier that morning.

'I felt we were off the pace,' he said. 'Our forwards weren't able to get away from their men and we weren't creating a whole lot. I thought we were in trouble.'

Down the corridor, some Wexford players were panned from the intense workrate and their tongues were hanging out.

'Lads were just fucked,' said Fitzhenry.

He called John Conran over and suggested moving out Mitch Jordan from the full-forward line for five minutes to give Barry Lambert, Paul Carley or Eoin Quigley a break from the half-forward line. They decided to keep rotating their forward line to share the workload and when they all gathered in the huddle again, Fitzhenry tried to set the scene.

'This time last year, we were in a similar position but they came out and got a goal and we dropped our heads. If the same thing happens this year, don't panic. We'll claw it back.'

Eddie Brennan nailed them with a goal just after half-time in the previous year's Leinster final and Wexford capitulated afterwards. Then just thirty five seconds after the restart, Kilkenny finally got some breathing space. The ball broke on the 20-metre line after a throw-in and Brennan snapped it. He made a brief charge at goal before kicking the ball past Fitzhenry.

'I thought we were on the pig's back then,' said McGarry.

Everyone waited for the Wexford collapse. Except the players.

'I wasn't that worried because I felt lads were ready for it,' said Fitzhenry. 'Heads didn't drop. You have to be ready for anything against Kilkenny and we were.'

Wexford continued to stick to the gameplan and they were rewarded in the forty-second minute when Eoin Quigley directed a long ball goalwards from just in front of the Hogan Stand. The ball was dropping between Michael Kavanagh and Rory Jacob.

'Go for it, hold him out and get the flick!' McGarry roared to Kavanagh.

Jacob though, managed to hold him off. He swung to get the deftest of touches on the ball and it bounced past McGarry. The goalkeeper and corner-back stared at each other momentarily. No words were spoken but they knew that Wexford were back in the match. Within a minute, Michael Jacob added a gem of a point to put the sides back on level terms.

A Fitzhenry puckout found Mossie Mahon, who flicked it into Mitch Jordan for the lead minutes later and Kilkenny really knew then that Wexford weren't going to die. Kilkenny put their foot on the gas again to try and burn them off and in the forty-seventh minute, Henry Shefflin got inside Darragh Ryan along the right flank of the Wexford defence. With the angle he was coming at, Shefflin hadn't too many options to pick his spot so he just let fly straight and hard from seven metres out. Fitzhenry stood up to it and somehow got his hurley to the ball just under the crossbar. The sliotar cannoned out over the endline in a flash for a '65. It was an unbelievable save but the goalkeeper wasn't looking for any credit. He charged out the field trying to convince the referee he hadn't touched it.

'I knew the second I turned around that the umpires weren't 100% sure what had happened,' said Fitzhenry. 'They were looking at one another and I shouted 'wide ball!' The game was so tight at the time, they were probably going to put the '65 over the bar and go another point up, so I tried to get away with it.'

Seán Dowling drove the '65 wide but Shefflin had another goal chance just three minutes later when he flicked a ground ball, swivelled and let fly on the deck from fourteen metres. Fitzhenry took off but he knew he was beaten. This time the ball did hit the post and it rebounded out to Darragh Ryan who drove it to safety.

Wexford bounced back from the ropes and they continued to hold Kilkenny by the lapels. The All-Ireland champions didn't score for twenty minutes but three points in six minutes pushed them back in front with five remaining. A Paul Carley free levelled the match and it was still deadlocked over a minute into injury time when Seán Dowling stood over a line ball. The sliotar dropped behind the Wexford full-back line and Henry Shefflin pulled on it. Fitzhenry got down low to keep it out and Malachy Travers got his body to the follow-up shot from Eddie

Brennan. The ball pinged loose and DJ Carey, who was only on the field thirteen minutes, flicked it up and blasted it over the bar.

'Who the hell would believe this?',' Fitzhenry said to himself. 'He *(Carey)* comes on the field and gets one stroke at it and puts it over the bar.' I could see the headlines: "Carey the saviour and Wexford pipped at the end once more."'

Fitzhenry pucked out the ball two minutes into injury time and waited for the whistle to sound. It didn't and the ball ended over the sideline. Adrian Fenlon cut it up the field, Peter Barry won it and released it to Pat Tennyson, who was hooked by Eoin Quigley. Sideline cut, nearly forty five metres from goal.

Fenlon had cut a similar one over the bar just after half-time but this was eight metres further out the field and the odds were stacked against him. The pressure was massive and he had one chance to save his county. He caressed the grass with his fingers and took a couple of seconds to place the ball. The ground was eerie with tension as he squared up to it.

McGarry, meanwhile, was organising his defence. He called Peter Barry back in beside him on the goal-line.

'You attack it and I'll stand my ground in case anyone gets a flick,' McGarry said to Barry beside him.

Fenlon got a perfect connection but the ball was floating and didn't have the distance to make it over the bar. It was dropping in the square.

'Take it!' McGarry roared to Barry.

Barry caught it perfectly. 'Keep going, keep going with it!' McGarry roared to him. Once the ball was cleared from the goal the match was going to be over but Barry took three steps and threw it up to off-load it down the field. Just as he was about to make the connection, Michael Jacob stepped in and blocked Barry down. The ball bounced on the ground, Jacob snapped it, turned and rifled it goalwards. The ball flew in over McGarry's shoulder and into the net. The roar went up and Brian Cody collapsed on his knees along the endline.

McGarry grabbed the ball out of the net and he heard Martin

Comerford roaring for a short puckout. No sooner had he struck the ball than the referee Barry Kelly blew the final whistle. One last pistol shot had just rung out to shake and stir Leinster hurling beyond all comprehension.

The All-Ireland champions had fallen. Finally.

Damien Fitzhenry had played a lot of great games for Wexford over the years but this was one of his best ever. The second the final whistle blew, he grabbed his hurleys and ran to Declan Ruth. The two rolled around on the ground for a couple of seconds before Adrian Fenlon joined them.

'It was an unbelievable feeling,' said Fitzhenry. 'Unbelievable. One of the best ever.'

Almost every Wexford supporter in the ground flooded the field and it took the players an age to make it to the dressing room. The possible Armageddon scenario of just six weeks ago had been wiped away by a glorious renaissance.

Down the corridor, the mood in the Kilkenny dressing room was as black as it had ever been. It was silent and the men were in shock. Peter Barry was crying over his mistake that cost them the game. It was a sombre backdrop to the scenes that Kilkenny have become accustomed to but one image kept coming into James McGarry's head.

'I could hear Cody beside me after the goal,' said McGarry. "No Peter, no!' And then him just going down on the ground. I can still see him and I'll see that image for a long time yet. I'll bring it with me to the grave.'

For now, Kilkenny's ambition of winning seven Leinster titles in-a-row is laid to rest.

BLUE SUNDAY

On Wednesday evening, June 16 at 7.30pm, the Dublin players and management convened for a meeting in Parnell Park ahead of Sunday's Leinster semi-final against Offaly. Three days before, Dublin had beaten Westmeath in their quarter-final but the performance was poor and they lost their best player, Conal Keaney, in the process after he received a straight red card. His loss has further shortened Dublin's odds and the only people in the country that believe they have a chance on Sunday are the group meeting in Parnell Park. And deep down, not all of them are fully convinced.

It's a known fact that a few of the senior players harbour visions of a doomsday scenario on Sunday. Positivity isn't exactly dripping from the squad and confidence isn't sky-high but most of the players still left the meeting in a positive frame of mind. They couldn't afford to be thinking any other way and anyhow, they hammered Offaly in the League and they're hopeful of pulling another rabbit out of the hat.

It has been difficult to get that into their heads and steel their collective mindset because a lot of the players feel that training hasn't gone as well as it should have. There has been very little pace and zip to their hurling and their immune system probably isn't programmed to deal with the pace Offaly are going to inject into Sunday's match. Their only vaccine is to mentally strengthen themselves and hope they can sweat it out on the day. Some of the new and younger players are confident that they can, while most of the more seasoned members of the panel are trying to remain positive. But Dublin's most experienced squad member is convinced that the team can't win. And that they won't.

'To be honest, it's probably the worst prepared Dublin team going into the championship that I've ever been involved with,' said Brendan McLoughlin after the meeting. 'Westmeath were poor and if they had two more decent forwards, we'd have been in trouble. I have no doubt that we have the players that would trouble Offaly but not with the way things are going. Unless Offaly have a stinker and we play out of our skins, we haven't a hope of beating them. That's being brutally honest.'

McLoughlin made his debut with Dublin in 1995, was dropped in 1996 but has been first-choice keeper with Dublin ever since this season. Now for the first time in eight years, he finds himself on the bench and unsure of where his future lies with the county side. 'I'm seriously thinking about walking. I'm going home to have a chat with my Dad because I'm near the end now.'

He has had lingering problems with his ankles and he damaged a couple of discs in his back two weeks before the Westmeath match, but McLoughlin was never going to be in goal for this championship. After he played against Waterford in Round 3 of the League he missed a raft of training sessions because he was waiting for the results of a series of scans on his ankles. By the time he returned to full training, Gary Maguire from Ballyboden St Enda's was ensconced as number one keeper after playing solidly in Dublin's remaining League matches.

Three weeks previously Dublin played a challenge game against a mixed side from the St Vincent's senior team and the Dublin Under-21s and McLoughlin had targeted that match as his opportunity to try and reclaim his place. When he didn't get a run, he rang the manager Humphrey Kelleher afterwards and a simmering tension between the two was brought to the boil. Kelleher told him he wasn't fully fit and McLoughlin rejected his viewpoint. When he wasn't selected for the championship, McLoughlin took it personally.

Matters came to a head the following evening, Thursday, when McLoughlin found out from another player that he wasn't on the panel for Sunday's match. When Humphrey Kelleher rang him on Friday evening to tell him that the decision was based on his lack of fitness, McLoughlin frankly told the manager that he deserved to hear that off him first, rather than from another player.

'I rang him to tell him that he wasn't on the panel for the game,' said

Kelleher. 'He was well aware of that prior to the game.'

Kelleher said that he wanted McLoughlin to follow a fitness programme that had been drawn up for him by the team physiotherapist and team doctor but that McLoughlin hadn't done so. Moreover, as a former goalkeeper himself, Kelleher has never agreed with McLoughlin's policy of playing outfield for his club and then wanting to play in goal for the county. Kelleher doesn't feel it's conducive for goalkeeping at the highest level and, deep down, McLoughlin knows that his inter-county career is over.

'It's really childish and I've basically been around too long now to be putting up with stuff like that,' he said. 'It's hard for lads who have seen better managers being treated a lot worse than Humphrey Kelleher has and he hasn't a clue. People might say that I'm only saying this because I'm not playing but I'm not the only one who feels this way. The only thing that's carrying Dublin at the moment is that the players are playing for their own pride.'

McLoughlin's pride has been hurt but he has his agenda too. For weeks he's been listening to some clubmates in O'Toole's telling him not to walk away and give Kelleher the satisfaction of ending his career. He has stuck to his guns but according to other players on the Dublin panel, McLoughlin has dug his heels in from the very start of the year with regard to Kelleher.

When McLoughlin's clubmate, Marty Morris, walked away from the Dublin managerial job last season, it created a serious amount of friction in the O'Toole's club about the nature of his departure and the political machinations behind it. No matter how good or how bad a manager Kelleher was, McLoughlin subconsciously carried over some of that residual bad feeling towards the new appointment.

Before Dublin's last League game with Wexford, O'Toole's pulled their players from the squad because they had a club championship match the following week. McLoughlin was one of those players but the roots of his present predicament are much deeper than a personality clash. Although he was injured, the manager and some of the players still felt he was able to train more than often than he did. It aggravated them too when McLoughlin declared himself unfit to train but was still able to line out for O'Toole's in both hurling and football. They felt that it created a negative vibe in the panel.

'Brendan has given great service and he is a fantastic clubman,' said Kelleher. 'I've watched him and he gives it all to his club but you can't be selective. To me the county team is the number one priority if you're on the Dublin squad.'

When McLoughlin first appeared on the inter-county scene, he was a fine goalkeeper. He made a mistake for one of Eamonn Morrissey's goals on his debut against Kilkenny in 1995 but he was only nineteen then and he went on to establish a solid reputation. He was excellent in O'Toole's march to the 1996 Leinster club final and he became an efficient keeper with a very good puckout.

Over the last number of years, however, mistakes had crept into his game and when he dropped a ball into the net and hit a fresh air swing against Clare in the 2002 All-Ireland qualifiers, people started looking to Maguire. Especially after he gave a flawless handling display in last year's Leinster Under-21 final against Kilkenny, on a nightmarish wet evening for goalkeepers.

Up to this year, McLoughlin had never really been pushed before because there was no outstanding candidate in the county snapping at his heels. He also luxuriated in being the most experienced member of the squad and what's more, he had almost become the face of Dublin hurling. With most of Dublin's players wearing face-guards, he was their most recognisable player and one of the very few Dublin hurlers that the general public could identify with.

There was also a flamboyant side to him that attracted attention. With his tanned Latin looks and his sleekly gelled hair, he gave off a confident aura that wasn't associated with Dublin hurling. In lots of ways that was good for the game in the capital. When Dublin played Laois in a Leinster quarter-final replay in Tullamore in 2000, the TV cameras picked up McLoughlin during a break in the play juggling the sliotar on the back of his neck in the same way that soccer stars perform the trick during an exhibition.

It was stuff like that which people remembered but it had to be backed up on the field and his demotion isn't a huge surprise on the ground in Dublin. Even if he is silently harbouring ambitions of continuing his inter-county career, it's not going to happen. He can hear the fat lady clearing her throat now.

'If a new manager comes in next year, he's not going to see me in goals. If I don't get in this year, it is curtains and I will walk. Well if Humphrey Kelleher is still there, I'll definitely walk. There's no hope that I'll hang around because I just wouldn't put myself through another year of that. There is the fear there now that I won't play for Dublin again and I will miss it. I love Dublin hurling and I love all the lads and the craic. They're all like brothers to me because I've hurled with a lot of them for so long.'

After the match on Sunday, McLoughlin walked. Dublin were hammered by fifteen points and when McLoughlin met a local journalist afterwards, he told him he was retiring and asked him to publish it the following day. It appeared merely as a footnote in one of Monday's papers and McLoughlin bowed out without the sound of blasting trumpets or any fanfare.

'Being honest, I'm very bitter about it,' he said. 'I put my whole life into Dublin hurling and then it's taken away from me like this.'

Aside from McLoughlin's ill-feeling though, yesterday was a disaster for Dublin hurling and it's not going to get any better anytime soon. Although they're playing Kilkenny in the All-Ireland qualifiers on Saturday, the team-captain Kevin Flynn is flying out to the US on Wednesday and one of their best forwards Liam Ryan is following him out on Saturday morning. Their imminent departure has loaded two more bullets into the chamber for McLoughlin to fire at the management and County Board.

'You have John Bailey *(County Board Chairman)* coming out saying that he wants the Dublin fans to be patient because no one said it was going to be an overnight success,' said McLoughlin. 'That sort of shite.

He's basically backing Humphrey Kelleher because he knows the County Board are wrong by putting him there. Make no mistake about it, John Bailey would get rid of Humphrey Kelleher as quick as he'd look at him.

'The County Board just have no interest in hurling whatsoever. It's lip service. They want it to be heard that they're doing things for Dublin hurling but what have they done? They haven't done anything. They say that it's equal rights between the hurlers and the footballers and it never was. It seems that they just don't want hurling and Bailey is two-faced.

'He wasn't seen throughout the League and after we beat Offaly by twenty points, in a game that meant nothing to them, he comes out and says we're going to win an All-Ireland. That's the type of rubbish that we have to listen to. I've been listening to that stuff for ten years but it's up to the clubs to speak up. They have to stand up and be counted but unfortunately there are too many people who just won't do it because they want to be in the clique. I've known that for a long time and I probably should have walked earlier. I was probably a bit stubborn myself but I just love Dublin hurling.'

Dublin hurling. The capital with the biggest population of any county should also have the biggest hurling population. Instead Dublin has the biggest stockpile of blueprints, visions, talking shops and good intentions. Too many of the powerbrokers are content to pay lip service to hurling and just live for the big football days. At the moment, the senior hurling team are so far behind the other counties in Leinster that they can hardly see them in the distance.

A lot of the Dublin players feel that training was very poor this year, that morale was low and that Kelleher just didn't command the players' respect in the dressing room. Most of the players didn't even know who he was when he was appointed the year before. But at least Kelleher tried to change the ground rules. When he first came in, he struggled to even secure hurleys for his players but he still went about introducing an increased level of attention to detail into the set-up.

He ensured that there were three chartered physiotherapists on call for the squad and he also had a sports psychologist on board. At the outset of the season, Kelleher recruited the highly respected fitness-coach Jim Kilty for a few sessions but he had committed to Wexford for the year. Shane Curran was subsequently brought in for a while to carry out Kilty's patented SAQ (Speed, Agility, Quickness) programme before Will Heffernan arrived in March as a strength and conditioning coach.

Dublin's back-up system was excellent but it was still essentially missing the one fundamentally crucial point that Dublin hurling as a whole can't seem to grasp: not enough emphasis on hurling coaching.

The problem is reflected right through the club culture in the county. There is the best will in the world amongst hurling people but there is a lack of knowledge of how the game should be properly coached and fostered. Great hurling people working hard, but working hard doing the wrong things. If certain clubs around the country had the enthusiasm, back-up, sponsorship, numbers at training and organisational skills off the field that some hurling clubs in Dublin have, they'd be winning All-Ireland club titles every second year.

There is fantastic work being done at underage level, and it should result in an underage provincial title in the next couple of years, but it's the lack of hurling know-how that is crippling them at adult level. It's almost as if many Dublin hurling people just don't understand the game and what it is about. The type of hurling some clubs play in Dublin is rooted in a game that was played over twenty years ago. All the back-up and enthusiasm in the world isn't worth a damn if the coaching quality and application isn't there to match it.

It appeared that Dublin hurling was going in the right direction in 2003 when the County Board appointed Diarmuid Healy as their Director of Hurling. Healy did his best to address that whole issue of coaching and application but he knew deep down that not enough time was being spent on hurling for it to improve in the manner he wanted it to. Most of the coaches on the ground were dual coaches and most of the focus was on football.

He tried to address that issue by broadening the hurling-coaching base and he restructured the underage situation to ensure that competitions were played over the summer. That was a step in the right direction but then the fixture issue over the summer was a complete nightmare given the dual commitments of so many players.

On the inter-county front, some of the best hurlers are still drifting to the football panel and although Healy tried everything in his power to secure those players' services for the hurling squad, he couldn't do so. That was just one of a number of other headaches and earlier this year, Healy left the job.

It has left a huge vacuum now. The County Board make some effort for hurling but it is primarily a football-orientated board with football ideas. That is unlikely to change in the near future so it is up to all Dublin hurling people now to grasp reality and face up to the future.

There are plenty of ways forward. There are hundreds of twenty and thirty-something guys who have retired, or walked away from, inter-county and top-level club hurling in recent years and who are living and working in Dublin. Some have trained and played under the best managers and coaches in the country and they know what top level coaching and hurling is all about. That is an untapped seam of talent that is just crying out to be mined by Dublin hurling. An intelligent recruitment drive could really help the game in the county because a sizeable proportion would only be too willing to help. Except they're rarely asked.

That would improve the club scene but the senior county team needs to get a progressive hurling coach. That can also be a two-way street. When Clare club hurling reached a peak in the 1990s, it was a direct spin-off from the inter-county scene. Clare's skills and hurling training were never really afforded the credit they deserved but it was revolutionary and every player brought something back from Clare training and introduced it into his club. When the attitude, application and dedication is there, anything is possible.

When Brendan McLoughlin says that he loves Dublin hurling, it is easy to believe him. He comes from a strong hurling family and he gave great service to the county. But what does to love Dublin hurling mean? To love something is to do whatever it takes to guard it, protect it, improve it and treat it with undying loyalty, always being prepared to subjugate individual needs for the good of the team and the crest.

The set-up with the county might not have been ideal this season. The gear might not have been as plentiful as what the footballers got. The County Board might not give a damn about them. They might never get a team holiday. The training may have been poor, but players have a choice. They know most things aren't going to change but if they're not happy with how they are being treated by the County Board, or how certain managers in the past were treated, it's up to the players to stand up to the board in order to try and create a culture of respect. But more importantly, if they're not content with the fundamental issues of training and internal discipline and feel that the pace isn't in their hurling, it's up to them to address those issues with management. Almost a decade ago, senior players weren't completely happy with aspects of Jimmy Grey's training and they approached him and the situation improved. Players can either choose to improve the situation by hard work and a positive attitude or they can just accept things the way they are. Some people just accommodate a certain situation that hurling people in other counties just won't tolerate. Dublin are going to get destroyed by Kilkenny on Saturday and they know it. Kevin Flynn has work commitments as a website designer in the US but the fact that their captain and vice-captain are absconding to the US has sent out a disastrous message. It has given a verdict on the manager and the whole set-up but Dublin hurling has taken another hit in the process.

Given the logistical problems with traffic and the lack of the kind of public support that players down the country just take for granted, it's not always that easy to be a Dublin hurler. But if you are a Dublin hurler, the county comes first and you do whatever it takes to improve.

And unless that mindset changes, Dublin are going nowhere.

ULTIMATE PAIN
AND ULTIMATE GLORY

When training finished on the Friday night before the Munster final, all the Cork players followed their normal ritual and walked to the bottom corner of the field in Páirc Uí Rinn. Ben O'Connor addressed the panel before asking Donal Óg Cusack to have the last word. The goalkeeper didn't have any pre-arranged speech made out in his head but he had an idea what he wanted to say. He told his team-mates what was in his heart.

'You know,' he said to the group. 'I have a dream for this winter. And in it, I'll call up to John Gardiner in Na Piarsaigh and we'll go for a few pucks in the ball alley in the northside. Or maybe I'll meet up with Seán Óg and go for a jog with him. Or I might meet up with TK *(Tom Kenny)* and Joey *(Deane)* and as usual when they are playing golf when everyone else is working, I might join in with them. Or maybe I'll call up to Timmy Mac *(McCarthy)* in Castlelyons and sit above in a hill with him and have a cigarette. When Jim McEvoy *(masseur)* is doing the marathon in Dublin we might drive him on and support him like he has supported us, even carry him around the course if we have to. Or maybe all of ye will come down to Cloyne and we'll go over to Christy Ring's statue, and then we'll call over to Mickey *(O'Connell)* with his new kid, please God, and we'll all go up to the Alley bar and get fucking locked. And this is the key to it all. We'll do all that without the pain we had all last winter when we didn't achieve what we set out to achieve. We all know what our goal is and anything which gets in the way of that must be overcome. Waterford must be overcome so we won't have that pain deep inside our heads. Whether you're in Cloyne or over in China or Australia or wherever, that pain won't be down inside your gut.'

Stevie Brenner felt good before the Munster final. Really positive and completely happy that he was right for this match. Earlier in the week, he didn't know if he'd be fit enough to line out because he was hardly able to move when he woke up the previous Monday morning.

He had strained a muscle in training over the weekend and it became inflamed on Sunday evening. It was still sore after training on Tuesday but a high dosage of anti-inflammatory tablets and an intense bout of physio had him sorted by Thursday. He felt strong and confident and so did everyone else.

'*(Justin)* McCarthy didn't have to say an awful lot to us before the game,' said Brenner. 'The last time I saw us as focussed was before we beat Tipp in the Munster final two years ago. We were unbelievably ready. I felt the best I ever felt. Just great.'

Cork felt equally as prepared to win and Cusack never felt stronger or fitter. Ever since losing the 2003 All-Ireland final, the pressure has been on Cork to deliver. The players have insulated themselves from the hype but it's impossible to escape the expectation that surrounds Cork when they reach a Munster final. Winning back the All-Ireland is the priority but Munster titles in Cork are regarded as a sacred treasure that you dare not lose.

'Look, a lot of fellas going up to Thurles don't have a clue,' said Cusack. 'They're looking out at the Munster final and they don't know what's going on. They don't understand the game. They're probably only there for the day. They don't realise that what keeps you going is the respect you have for your team-mates and the jersey. I couldn't give a damn about those guys but I'd die for the thousands of hardcore Cork fans. We carry the hopes of all those people on our shoulders and that is a responsibility I treat with total respect. I would do everything in order to do it justice.

'The Munster final is a big day but I always tell the younger lads to take inspiration from the crowd but not to be intimidated by it. Any fella that cares about Cork wouldn't be going in drunk to that game. They're the guys that will be abusing us if we lose but the way I look at it, these fellas are only individuals and you'd never be afraid of an individual. There's a bond between the players because they know what's going on. Even if you were a fool, if you'd played in goals for as long as I have, you'd understand the situation.

'If I get abuse, it won't even register. Even if I do, what can anyone do to me? What can any supporter do to me? What would you do, go out and fight him? If that was the case, you'd have a lot of people to fight. If a guy was abusing me from the terrace or stand, I know that if I walked down the street afterwards and that guy was by himself, he'd probably wet himself. I know everyone is, to some degree, a product of their environment and maybe what I've gone through over the last couple of years has pushed me down this road. But I know I'm not worried about it because if I was, I wouldn't be playing and I wouldn't be able to play as steady as I can play. The only thing I care about is being honest to myself, my jersey, the genuine supporters and above all, my team-mates.'

The game was on two minutes when Cusack suddenly realised that he had forgotten to mark out his goal. Two weeks ago, Cork played Clare in a challenge game behind closed doors in Ennis and Ger Cunningham told Cusack afterwards that they needed to re-examine his positioning. Cunningham felt he could have been better positioned for one of Niall Gilligan's goals and they looked at it on DVD the following Tuesday after training. Cusack was open to suggestions and he agreed to mark out his square to guide him on his angles.

When the ball was down the other end of the field, Cusack strolled out and raked his studs to make two marks at either side of the edge of the square. Even though he was annoyed with himself for a split second for forgetting to do it before the match, he felt good in himself. At the other end of the ground, Brenner felt just as positive. His back was fine and he had none of the nerves that had haunted him during the opening period of the Tipperary game.

Inside three minutes though, Brenner's world was in danger of caving in. Heavy rain had fallen before the match, which always makes the bounce on the hard surface difficult to judge. A ball slipped out of Tom Kenny's grasp about twenty six metres from goal and after Tony Browne went to control it, the ball flew up in the air. Garvan McCarthy let fly on it and knocked the ball harmlessly towards goal. Brenner was about two feet off his line as the ball rolled towards him with its ambling trajectory. He had the bas of the hurley a couple of inches off the ground, expecting the ball to hop up so he could control it. But the ball skidded and rolled and it went under his hurley and between his legs.

'It was bouncing and then it went flat and rolled,' said Brenner. 'I was nearly lifting my head to see where I was going to put it. I just couldn't believe it.'

Neither could anyone in the attendance of 54,000. Especially some of the Waterford crowd behind him in the Killinan End terrace.

'Wake up Brenner ya bollox!' roared one supporter. 'Is there a fucking hole in your hurley or what?'

Cusack had been in that position before against Waterford two years ago and he knew the feeling. He had suffered the wound and recognised the scar.

'For an instant, I felt for him,' said Cusack. 'I know that Stephen was on the opposite side and we were at war, but there is a bond between keepers and I didn't enjoy seeing it happening, Munster final or no Munster final.'

Even the umpire at his left post, Seanie Arthur from Clare, was a second slow in getting the flag up because he wasn't expecting it to go to the net. Brenner picked the ball up, took a deep breath, blew it out slowly and pucked the sliotar straight down the field.

'Nothing really went through my head at the time,' he said. 'The first thing that came into my mind was Donal Óg Cusack. He made a crucial mistake in the second half from Tony Browne two years ago and it cost Cork the game because it came so late. I was telling myself to relax because I just felt that we had plenty of time to get it back.'

Cork were tearing Waterford to shreds with their short game and their five point lead after eight minutes didn't flatter them. The Waterford half-back line was struggling and when Tom Kenny had a point on ten minutes that appeared to have gone outside the post and wide, Brenner lost it with the umpires. Waterford were in big trouble but at the end of the first quarter, Eoin Kelly picked a ball on the 45 and hared down the sideline. His was hooked by Jerry O'Connor but he picked the loose ball and cut inside the left flank of the Cork defence. He was close to the endline when he shot from a difficult angle and the ball flew just past Cusack's hurley and into the net.

'I moved to my right-hand side and tried to spread myself but the ball shot in over my shoulder,' said the Cork keeper.

The goal didn't affect Cork and they were still on top through the next quarter. With the Waterford midfield and halfbacks unable to establish control, the idea of a Waterford gameplan became irrelevant. Most of their attacks were coming from Brenner puckouts after Cork scores. They trailed by five points on twenty six minutes when Dan Shanahan ghosted in behind the Cork full-back line, beat Diarmuid O'Sullivan to an Eoin Kelly shot that dropped short and smashed the ball to the net from close range. It was a vital score and while Waterford hadn't been playing well, the three point deficit at the break wasn't irretrievable.

Inside in their dressing room at half-time, the mood was positive. They knew there was much more in them and every one of the players went up to Brenner and told him to keep his head up. He told each one of them in turn that he felt strong and that he had reacted positively to the mistake. Justin McCarthy told them that they were only three points down after not playing anything near their full potential. He felt that they were in a better position from twelve months previously when they led by six at the break. It was there for them and after McCarthy had the last word, the players gathered in a huddle in the tunnel before going back onto the pitch.

'Don't anyone come in here afterwards and say you left it behind you,' Ken McGrath said to his team-mates as they gathered tightly around him. 'We're going to leave everything we have out on that field and we're going to come back in here as Munster champions.'

Down the corridor, Cork were still in their dressing room. They were happy with how the first half had gone. They had been quicker, more focussed and more determined than Waterford. Cork had enjoyed 56% possession and they had played more intelligently as well. They were playing lovely low ball in from midfield and the Cork full-forward line had played the ball sixteen times compared to just six by the Waterford full-back line.

'Ye're going great and ye're making them look average at times,' Donal O'Grady told his players. 'But we have to go out and win the second half now.'

John Mullane pointed for Waterford within ten seconds of the restart but a couple of minutes later, he struck Brian Murphy off the ball and Seanie Arthur, the umpire, spotted it. As Seanie McMahon, the referee, ran in, Cusack ran out to him and slapped his hurley off the ground. After consulting with his umpire, McMahon sent off Mullane.

As Mullane was walking off, Cusack strolled out to Wayne Sherlock in the full-back line and pointed his finger to his temple.

'We box clever now Waynie, we box clever,' he said. 'We don't get complacent and give the ref the opportunity to even things up.'

At the other end of the field, the Cork supporters in the terrace had just got off Brenner's case.

'Mullane got me out of a hole because they were roaring at him when he was sent off and it seemed to take their attention away from me,' said Brenner. 'But after that, I couldn't believe how quiet the Cork crowd were. Unbelievable, now.'

They were quiet because Waterford's response was phenomenal. Every single player stepped up in Mullane's absence and there was a heightened focus throughout the team. Waterford were still chasing the match and every time they got close, Cork pegged them back. But the tide was slowly turning in Waterford's favour. Cork's decision to play Diarmuid O'Sullivan as the extra man looked like a bad call and the combination of having wind assistance and an extra man, plus the loss of territorial dominance in the middle third of the field, blew Cork's gameplan out the window.

Waterford had been least comfortable when being ran at in the first half and the change of tactics suited them perfectly.

The match turned at the end of the third quarter when Paul Flynn stood over a 30 metre-free on fifty two minutes. Cusack was standing in the middle of the goal and O'Sullivan was to his right when Flynn struck the ball with his characteristic topspin. It was going crossbar height and Dan Shanahan swung his hurley on the edge of the square as the ball dipped viciously. O'Sullivan tried to bat it as it dropped under him but the ball flew past him and into the net. Cusack just stood still for a moment, dropped his shoulders and picked the ball up for a puckout.

'The ball shot in over Shanahan and Sean Óg (*Ó Hailpín*) and that was it,' said Cusack. 'It was in the net. In situations like that, you just get on with it. It's a thing I have thought about and we have spoken about it as a defence. When something like that happens we just look for what we will do with the next puckout and concentrate on the next play.'

The score wasn't a coincidence. In Waterford's crucial last League game against Tipperary in Thurles, the side were six points down at roughly the same stage of the second half and were gasping for some momentum. They got a free from roughly the same spot in the field and Flynn stood over it. The ball ended up in the net, Waterford went on to draw the game and ended up in the League final.

'They're planning that,' said Brendan Cummins. 'They put Shanahan about six or seven yards out at the angle of the view of the goalie and the full-back. Flynn puts it over Shanahan's head and it goes no more than shoulder high but it's going like a rocket. In the League game, I knew he was going to do it but there was nothing I could do about it. It came over Declan Fanning's head, he got a touch on it and it landed about knee high. It came off the nose of my hurley and crept into the side netting. In the blink of an eye, it's in. You can't train to deal with shots like that.'

After the ball hit the net, Brenner turned around to the Cork crowd behind him and raised his fist. There was no reaction to the gesture and a firecracker went off in his head.

'A shiver went up my spine and I thought "Jesus we're going to win this game",' he said. 'I just thought, "the lads are really pulling me out of a hole here."'

But within a minute, Brenner was nearly back in the hole. Tom Kenny sent in a long delivery from midfield that was dropping in the square. Joe Deane was inside on top of the keeper and the ball popped out of Brenner's hand and just went out for a 65.

'Come on Stevie!' Ken McGrath roared into him.

Brenner just raised his arm and pointed to the sun. 'I couldn't see it,' the keeper shouted back.

The crowd never understand such things and just before Ben O'Connor pointed the 65, a gentleman sitting behind Brenner's wife, Helena, exploded.

'Will ye get that fucking Brenner off, he's fucking useless!' he roared out.

Helena turned around. 'He's not useless,' she said. 'He's doing his best.'

The scores were tied but Waterford were galvanised by the task of defending rather than chasing the lead. Cork meanwhile had changed their puckout tactic. In the first half Cusack had gone long with thirteen of his sixteen puckouts and Cork only won five of them. After Mullane was sent off, he began hitting short puckouts to their defence. While Cork secured two points from the six short puckouts out of twelve Cusack had taken up to that point, the defenders were lacing the ball down the field to diminishing effect.

On fifty nine minutes, Cusack nearly got nailed completely. He hit a short ball to O'Sullivan on the 20-metre line and Paul Flynn nearly dispossessed him. The forward fouled O'Sullivan just before he handpassed the ball back to the goalkeeper, who in turn passed it out to Seán Óg Ó hAilpín.

'I was after finding Seán Óg in space and we have practised that tactic hundreds of times in training,' said Cusack. 'I give it to Sully, I move out towards the 21 and he gives it back to me to set up an attack. We had planned to do it in last year's All-Ireland final. It's a high-risk game and it's putting me at serious risk but it's our team tactic and we feel short puckouts have to be done for the end result. If it takes that messing around with it, we're prepared to take that risk. A lot of the balls Sully hit ended up in front of Joe Deane.'

Cork came back to edge in front again but the lead only lasted a minute. Eoin Kelly responded with an excellent point from the right wing and as the game became tension-packed, both teams' wide tally began to soar. This match was going to the wire.

Flynn pushed Waterford ahead as the clock ran down but with a minute to go, Kieran Murphy latched onto a breaking ball and fed Jerry O'Connor at pace inside the 14-metre line. He was right through but Declan Prendergast intercepted the ball and cleared it down the field. The sliotar ended up with Prendergast's brother Seamus, charging forward at full-tilt and hitting a great point to restore the two point margin.

Cusack showed remarkable composure to pick out Tom Kenny on the sideline with the puckout and the midfielder cut the lead to a point. The game had slipped deep into injury time and Waterford were fighting for their lives to hold out. On seventy three minutes, Ronan Curran launched one final attack from defence but Ken McGrath rose above Diarmuid O'Sullivan and majestically fielded the ball. Timmy McCarthy fouled him and McGrath triumphantly raised the ball aloft. Flynn ambled down the field to strike it and as the ball dropped from the sky, Cusack caught it. Just as he handpassed it out, the referee blew the final whistle.

'Oh Jesus Christ no!' he said to himself as he slapped his hurley off the ground. 'Not this feeling again.'

Pandemonium was raging all around him as Waterford supporters charged onto the field. Cusack stood motionless, showing no emotion. He doesn't believe in grieving in public, but he felt like crying. Then Wayne Sherlock came into Cusack and shook his hand.

'What a game to lose,' he said to the keeper.

Brenner meanwhile had picked up his hurleys and was making his way to the centre of the pitch. He passed Diarmuid O'Sullivan, who had relocated to the attack in the last few minutes, and tapped him on the back.

'Hard luck big fella, ye got us last year and that's the way it goes,'

Brenner said as he kept moving.

Brenner had prayed to his father just before the game to help him out but somebody ripped his cross from around his neck in the throng afterwards and he never spotted it dropping on the field. After Ken McGrath raised the cup in front of a sea of blue and white, Brenner spotted his mother Charlotte crying her eyes out in the stand. She is the secretary of the De La Salle club and the pressure of allocating tickets all week had been overbearing. But it was nothing compared to the sickening worry she had to endure during the game after her son had conceded a soft goal after three minutes. Her mind was trying to suppress the horrific ramifications defeat would bring on her son and when the final whistle blew, she could no longer contain the pent-up emotion.

'She'd be wicked quiet,' said Stevie. 'I know it was getting to her for a while, what people were saying about me, even at club level. People were abusing me above in the field, especially earlier in the year when I wasn't on the team. I know well that she had to listen to that shit during the game as well but my mother would never react. But my father, God be good to him, would have turned around and let fly.'

Ger Brenner passed away on September 6, 1993. Stevie was playing full-forward for De La Salle in a Under-21 football game in Polberry in the city and his father was doing umpire. Just after the half-time whistle was blown, the players noticed a commotion down near the goalmouth. They all went down to see what was going on when they realised that Ger had collapsed and died.

'We all went down and that was it,' said Stevie. 'It's something you'd never think could happen but it did.'

At the time, Brenner's older brother, Johnny, was the hottest young property in Waterford hurling and Stevie was struggling to cut it as a forward for the De La Salle senior team. When Donal Treacy retired as goalkeeper, Brenner went into goal but he didn't have much of a choice.

'I kind of went a little bit crazy for a while after my father died. I just went a bit mad on the beer and I didn't have much interest in the hurling and football. I was going through that stage where I was just too lazy and drinking on a Saturday night and I wasn't able to play out the field anymore. Just going crazy. I was working in a pub and drinking lights-out.'

When Waterford played Limerick in the 1997 Munster championship, Brenner arrived into the match with twenty minutes gone. He was there with three friends and they were all destroyed from a morning's drinking. They lasted just five minutes into the second half before heading back to a pub in Thurles. At that stage, an inter-county hurling career was a distant fantasy.

He had just started to date Helena Quinn though, and he began to refocus his energies and thoughts. He had a good year with De La Salle in the local championship and he did enough to earn a call-up to the Waterford senior panel that winter. The next time he visited Thurles, he was standing in goal for Waterford against Tipperary in the opening round of the League.

It was a long road back for him but it has been worth it. He was twenty seven when he made his championship debut but now he has two Munster medals and has played in three consecutive Munster finals. Each Munster final has been like a glorious stage - a stage of nobility and grace and beauty that is as good as sport gets. Anywhere in the world.

Sometimes the hysteria of Munster final day gets the better of perspective and matches which are hailed as classics don't deserve the term. The occasion is steeped in history and mythology and is always bound up with the iconography of hurling's giants of the past. But this match would surely rate as one of the truly great Munster finals.

So many big sporting events are bloated and soulless but this match was remarkable for its moments of pure artistry and genius. Brenner is just glad that this day will be remembered for all the right reasons in Waterford. The ghoulish thought of defeat in his circumstances doesn't bear thinking about for a millisecond. If Waterford had lost, he'd have been blamed for the rest of his life.

'It's just fucking horrible, like,' he said. 'It would have been unbelievable if we had lost and that goal cost us. It would have been almost suicidal kind of stuff.'

Later that night, Brenner sat down alongside Ken McGrath. Brenner remembered what McGrath said at half-time when the captain asked his team-mates to leave everything they had on the field. They had that feeling that the American Football coach Vince Lombardi once famously spoke about. That in any man's finest hour, the greatest fulfilment of all he holds dear is that moment when he has worked his heart out in a good cause and lies exhausted on the field of battle – victorious.

'Did you ever think you'd see the day when you'd win two Munster medals?' Brenner asked his captain.

'Jesus, I didn't,' said McGrath.

'Did you ever think that you'd see the day when you'd captain Waterford to a Munster title?' asked the keeper.

'No way.'

Then McGrath grabbed Brenner by the hand.

'Jesus, bud, it's unreal, isn't it?'

At roughly the same time, Cusack was on his way home to Cloyne from Cork City. He sat into a taxi in the South Mall, tired and sore and not in the mood for talking hurling. The second he sat into the car though, the talk drifted to the day's game.

'I blame Cusack anyway boy for that goal,' the taxi-driver said to him in a perfect Cork accent. 'I wouldn't blame Sullivan at all boy.'

'Yeah, grand job yeah, you're probably right,' the passenger responded.

A few minutes later at 2.30am, one of Cusack's close friends, Killian Cronin, rang him. Cronin plays full-back on the Cloyne senior team and he runs the Alley Bar in the town and he told Cusack that a host of his friends were still waiting for him at the pub.

'Grand job,' said Cusack in a loud tone down the phone. 'But you know what you might do there, Billy Paw *(Cronin)*? I'm going to pull up in a taxi and you might get the boys out because when I get out of the car we're going to turn the fucking thing over.'

Cronin nearly collapsed.

'Jesus Christ, Donal Óg, what the hell is wrong with you?' he asked him.

'Just get the boys outside because we have to turn the car over,' Cusack responded in a very calm tone.

'Jesus lads, Donal Og has lost it, he's gone mad,' Cronin said to his friends.

The taxi-driver was craning his neck in the mirror to see what kind of a drug-crazed nutcase he'd picked up. For all he knew Billy Paw could have been a Mafia ganglord with an itchy trigger-finger. Fearing an LA style gang-riot was going to erupt, he nervously turned around and Cusack stared at him.

'How's it going?' the passenger said. 'I'm Donal Óg Cusack, pleased to meet you.'

The driver's tone changed immediately and the apocalyptic vision in his mind had faded by the time the car pulled up outside the Alley Bar. Cusack just paid him quickly and went inside to try and numb the pain.

'I'm not proud of it but I drank inside for a few hours.'

After a while, Cusack, Cronin and Owen 'Pom' O'Sullivan, corner-back on the Cloyne team, walked down the town. Cusack's brother Victor was just leaving for work and he stared at them with a look that suggested that they'd all lost the plot.

The three turned left at the gable end of Cusack's home house and made their way in along the pathway to Christy Ring Park, through the red gate at the corner of the field and over to the top goalmouth. They sat down in the goal and began chatting about the day. Seagulls from Cork harbour were flying overhead and the dawn was just breaking. The scene was idyllic and serene and Cusack felt safe. And at home. The only place in the world where he would have wished to be at that moment.

'There are parts of my character that I keep to myself or only for my closest friends,' said Cusack. 'And you'd just hate the thought of the morning and all the bullshit attached to it.'

Although it had been a long and difficult day, Cusack didn't want it to end. He wished that time would stand still and he could prolong that feeling of serenity. But a new day was beginning and it would bring with it a fresh raft of inquisitions and recriminations. And all the hurtful memories would come flooding back. Before he got up to head in his back door seventy five yards away, Cusack thought of the feeling he had in the dressing room immediately after the match.

'It's a desperate feeling. It's just terrible. You can't describe it because Cork means so much to me. It's just one of those feelings where you ask yourself "Why the hell do I do this?"'

That pain is still deep inside his gut.

THREE GOALS, ONE TARGET

On the morning of the Leinster final, Brian Mullins left his house in Sandymount in Birr just after 8am and travelled out to his home place in New Road. He shot the breeze there for almost an hour before picking up Dylan Hayden and Niall Claffey and driving on to Tullamore with his team-mates. The squad were meeting in the Tullamore Court Hotel at 9.30am and after breakfast, they lounged around the lobby for a while before boarding a train for Dublin just before 11am. They headed east, their mood bright with anticipation.

They arrived in Connolly Station just before 12 noon, where they immediately got a bus to Parnell Park. Rooms had been set aside in the venue to cater for injury-treatment and rubs and the players togged out in one of the adjoining dressing rooms for their warm-up. As Mullins was pulling on his socks, he looked up as the rain battered off the windows. It was a wet and gusty day and conditions were deteriorating. Mullins can handle rain but he hates wind. He'd have preferred if the day was better but it didn't bother him. This was his first time back on the Leinster final stage in nine years and he was determined to make the most of it.

Offaly's 1995 Leinster final win over Kilkenny was possibly the county's greatest ever display against their nemesis but Mullins has nothing but bad memories from the day. In the minor final between Offaly and Kilkenny that preceded that match, he endured a nightmare experience. Four goals went past him, three of which were caused by fundamental errors. The ball went through his legs and dropped out of his hand. One of those days that either makes or breaks you. It was the making of Brian Mullins.

'It was nerves,' he said. 'I used to get fierce nervous and they used to eat me up. Afterwards I went home and thought about it and just said "enough is enough." I just said that there was no point getting uptight about it and it kind of changed me. The worst had happened that day and the nerves haven't come back since. That game changed my whole attitude towards hurling. I'm more light-hearted and relaxed now and it's served me for the better.'

Mullins is certainly light-hearted. In a county that became stereotyped in the 1990s as the greatest bunch of hurling lounge lizards who never let a quiet pint turn into anything less than a savage drinking session, Mullins appears like the ideal modern prototype. He is the hip, laid-back, independent cool dude who hangs around with a non-GAA crowd. He is an excellent tennis player, who has won the last two Birr Opens. If you were to believe all the stories you hear about Brian Mullins, he'd be cast as a support act to Billy Connolly.

He is the quiet joker who enjoys his fun and while he doesn't command the same high profile that some of his illustrious predecessors did, he personifies the old caricature of an Offaly player who likes to hurl and who likes to party. But like the Offaly team of the 1990s, there is a germ of truth in how he is perceived and a wealth of hidden variables, which make him the player he is. Some may mistake his lack of hurling fanaticism as indifference, but he has still managed to develop into a brilliant goalkeeper and one of the most talented in the country.

About life and about hurling, Mullins might come across as non-committal. He's been known to arrive into a Birr dressing room five minutes before a championship game. But when you strip the mystique from the reality and put him on a pitch, he is as passionate as any hurling man and as proud as any other goalkeeper. He hates conceding goals and losing cuts him to the bone. But it's not in his nature to think that way outside of those seventy minutes when his reputation, honour and pride are on the line.

'Before a county final or a county championship match, I wouldn't cut loose or anything, but the week beforehand, I'd do what I normally do and I'd go out drinking no problem,' said Mullins. 'I love hurling but I always feel that I don't owe anybody anything. If I want to go for a few pints the week before a game, I'll do it. I'd be hearing about all the training the top goalies would be doing, but first of all I live my life, and second of all I don't think I'd be nearly as dedicated as some of those boys. I think the top boys are excellent. I possibly might have the ability to be up there all right but I don't think I'm near that level now.

'I never harboured any massive ambitions to make the county team, it just came around. I'm delighted it did but in terms of living a clean life and making everything revolve around hurling, I don't think I'd ever do that. That wouldn't be for me. But having said that, I know that if I want to continue playing for Offaly, maybe I should change my approach a bit. I realise that acting the bollocks and drinking, not even bothering totally about training on my own, I'm determined to change that. Whether I will or not is another story.'

Mullins certainly doesn't fit the modern goalkeeping stereotype. He looks and thinks differently. He is one of the few goalkeepers in the history of the game to wear a tracksuit bottom on championship days but that's what he has always worn and he never saw any need to conform to type when he began playing for Offaly. He takes it all in his stride and while he is growing tired of hearing how notoriously laid-back he is, the numerous myths and stories that circulate the county about him have all added to his local legend.

A good deal of how Mullins is perceived was unconsciously formed by his own innate shyness. When he first came on to the Birr senior team, he was surrounded by hurling Greats and he craved their acceptance and respect. He was quiet but he was witty and sharp and he used his dry humour as a means of announcing his arrival and stamping his personality on the squad.

Two years after Sarsfields from Galway had become the first club in the country to win consecutive All-Ireland club titles, they arrived in Birr one evening in 1996 for a challenge game. Mullins was on the bench and he was enthralled by the skill of the Galway side. 'Jaysus,' he said as he turned around to the rest of the subs, 'those lads aren't too bad at all, who are they?'

He knew who they were but the guys on the substitutes' bench almost collapsed in fits of laughter. Mullins was only a young lad at the time but he was carving a reputation as a jester who hardly knew what day of the week it was. Of course he did. He secured the points to go to college in Waterford IT a year later but when he was down there, he never even bothered playing hurling at a time when a galaxy of stars decorated the college side. He'd spend a lot of his days watching Ricki Lake and his nights out on the town. He didn't have the time for hurling.

All of those carefree and free-spirited moments added extra chapters to the most famous story ever told about Brian Mullins. The story went that Pad Joe Whelehan *(manager)* approached Mullins at half-time in the 1998 All-Ireland club final and told him to keep the puckouts away from the Galway legend, Joe Cooney, in the second half. To which Mullins responded 'Who's Joe Cooney?

'There's a lot of that shit going around the place about me that would sicken your rocks,' said Mullins. 'A lot of it has been blown out of proportion. Growing up, Joe Cooney would nearly have been a hero of mine and I knew well who he was. But I used to be in awe of some of those boys on our team. I'd be thinking a lot of the time, "Johnny *(Pilkington)* is really laid-back now and I'll just crack an auld joke here." So I just asked him who Joe Cooney was.

'I was having a bit of a laugh because I was beside Johnny. I could see that he was struggling to keep a straight face and he just looked away from me and said "your man in the green helmet." Then he went around afterwards and told everyone what I said. Most of the time I'd be making jokes and people would be taking them seriously. You might say you don't give a shit about hurling but at the end of the day, if you didn't care you wouldn't be playing. I suppose I'm laid-back enough, but I'm nowhere as laid-back as people think I am.'

How Mullins fitted into the broader picture was never his concern. All he wanted to do was to be true to himself and his sport and set his own standard to aim for. And no matter how he achieved it, that was good enough for him. He kept his head down with Birr and when he did arrive on the inter-county scene, there was nothing preordained about it.

He was asked to join the panel in 2001 but turned down the request and after spending a year on the bench in 2002, he wasn't going to bother going back in 2003. Stephen Byrne was a fine keeper and was in his sixth season as Offaly number one.

'If I didn't think I could make a team, any team, I'm not happy sitting on a sideline, especially being a subgoalkeeper,' said Mullins. 'I just wouldn't do it. I kind of got the impression from previous trainers that he *(Byrne)* was number one and unless he made a monumental fuck-up, I wasn't going to get a chance. At the start of the year I was kind of thinking that I wouldn't bother going in because I was just wasting my time.

'I was talking to one of the selectors, Paddy Kirwan, and he said to me "come on in, we'll give you a chance." I got the impression that the selectors *(Pat)* Delaney and Kirwan and these boys were pushing for me to be in goals, whereas Mike McNamara *(manager)* would have gone for *(Stephen)* Byrne every time but that he was outvoted. I was going well in training and in any matches I played in so they kind of had no choice but to give me a chance. But I could just as easily have walked away from the whole thing and never played inter-county. Absolutely.'

Byrne sat on the bench last year as Mullins was outstanding. Excellent against Wexford, he made the save of the year in the All-Ireland quarter-final against Tipperary from Conor Gleeson. Last year was a dream but Mullins is a realist. Most of the shots he stopped were set up for a keeper with his class.

'I was shit lucky last year. I got none of these big high-dropping balls that were dropping from the air for about five minutes or none of these yokes that were trickling along the ground. It was a dream the way the balls were coming for me last year and I know for a fact that it's not going to happen again. A day is going to come when a dirty awkward, hopping one is going to nail me. Or a big high ball is going to drop out of my hand. I'm well aware of that.'

Against Dublin a couple of balls dropped just beneath the crossbar and Mullins controlled them on his hurley. Standing at 5'8, the high crossbar in Croke Park can be a problem and controlling the sliotar on the stick can be a tricky business, especially with the wet conditions now. It's the only thing playing on his mind and in the puckaround in Parnell Park, he got the subkeeper Shane O'Connor to rain high balls down on him.

'I find that it takes an awful effort for me to jump and reach that crossbar in Croke Park. It's kind of a football goals. In my own field in Birr I can put my hand a couple of inches above the crossbar. But in Croke Park, you don't know whether you're going to take it in your hand or tip it over with your hurley. If it drops just underneath the crossbar you're going to have to time your jump perfectly and it's a little bit worrying. That's annoying me a small bit now.'

After the puckaround, the players had some food and they discussed tactics before boarding the bus for the short spin to Croke Park. The day had turned really messy, which was going to make the conditions treacherous for a goalkeeper. Low balls were going to kick off the hard turf and high balls were going to be difficult to judge with that gusty breeze and thick drizzle.

Mullins will deal with it because he has his strategy now: no fear and no nerves. He is on edge all right but that is a mental preparatory mechanism. Although he doesn't get nervous, that fact doesn't make him immune from introspection and the realisation that he could be guarding the gates to either heaven or hell in a couple of hours' time.

'I don't get butterflies in my stomach and that doesn't really affect me. I know the feeling because I've had it, but not anymore. That doesn't mean I wouldn't be worried or not conscious of making a mistake. I know it's possible that I could make a mistake and that helps keep me on edge. It keeps me sharp.'

After the Wexford team meeting in the Stillorgan Park Hotel, Damien Fitzhenry opened his wallet and took out the blue piece of paper where he had written down his three goals for the day. He penned them in blue biro after Father Odhran Furlong had handed the goal-setting papers out when speaking to the group on Thursday night after training. Fitzhenry quickly glanced at what he'd written: (1) to be a team player and to achieve what I know I'm capable of; (2) to give 100% in my position and to help out where I can; (3) to be the holder of a third Leinster medal by 6pm.

The mood was calm and relaxed around the hotel and Fitzhenry was slightly concerned that it might have been too relaxed. His only worry heading into the match was that the slightest element of complacency could completely derail them. For the last three weeks, Fitzhenry, Adrian Fenlon, Rory McCarthy, Declan Ruth and Darragh Ryan had been drilling into the players that their victory against Kilkenny would count for zero if they didn't win the Leinster final. All five players had been burned by Offaly before and they knew all about the napalm they were capable of unleashing. They were just making sure that every other player knew it as well.

Conditions worsened as the game drew near but a huge crowd had travelled up from Wexford. All around the ground, the seats filled with disciples of the purple and gold. They outnumbered Offaly by at least 4:1 and it appeared that the whole of Wexford had come for a coronation. In the Offaly dressing room though, their players were intent on crashing it.

'We never had any fear of Wexford,' said Mullins. 'Since Offaly became a force, we've always been able to take on Wexford and it's there for the taking if we want it badly enough. We're going to have to play well but we can win it.'

Just before they were about to hit the field, the goalkeeper called Brendan Murphy and Brian Carroll over to him.

'Keep the ball low,' he told them. 'The grass is greasy and if the ball hits the deck, it could go anywhere.'

Offaly were met with a cacophony of klaxon horns and cheers when they emerged out onto the pitch but it was nothing like the wall of sound that greeted Wexford moments later.

'The noise from the Wexford supporters was crazy,' said Mullins. 'The roar that greeted them was unbelievable and I never experienced anything like that before. It was enjoyable but for Christ's sake, there was a fierce disappointing crowd there from Offaly. There was a Leinster final there to be won and we couldn't even round up a decent crowd to go up and watch the game. It's a sad indictment. We must have been outnumbered six to one.'

From the start, Wexford were clearly struggling to recapture the zip that undid Kilkenny and Offaly were setting the pace of the match. They were well equipped to stand up to the fast and controlled game that Wexford delivered to such unexpected effect in the semi-final and three quick Offaly points emphasised that they weren't going to wait for the fireworks to start.

On six minutes, Offaly threatened to offload a huge cracker when Damien Murray came through the middle of the Wexford defence and got off a well-struck shot to the bottom left corner. It was a foot off the ground and Fitzhenry got to it and pushed it around the post.

'I was trying to read him but he was coming across his body with the shot and those balls generally go to your left,' said the keeper. 'I just took a chance on it that it was going to the left and I got across to it.'

It was a brilliant save but he had to make another intervention at the end of the first quarter when Brian Whelehan placed a pinpoint ball into Joe Brady, who flicked it into the path of Brendan Murphy. The forward kicked the ball but Fitzhenry spread himself and kept it out.

Wexford were on the backfoot but they got a huge break two minutes later. Mossie Mahon immediately moved the ball from a Fitzhenry puckout into the path of Rory Jacob. He shot across goal at an angle, Mullins got his stick to it and the ball deflected out to David Franks. The corner-back had the ball in his hand but he spilled possession and Mick Jacob clipped the loose sliotar into the net.

'I was happy enough to get a hurl on the initial shot,' said Mullins. 'I thought there was nothing more I could have done because I got as much on it as I could.'

Undaunted, Offaly kept coming but Fitzhenry's goal was impenetrable. Michael Cordial should have gone for a point on twenty two minutes but he elected to shoot and Fitzhenry knocked the chest-high shot down. In the ensuing scramble he managed to rise the ball, weave his way out past a couple of Offaly attackers and ship the ball to safety.

Offaly had another chance to put some daylight between the sides in the thirty-first minute when Brendan Murphy was deemed to have been fouled by Rory McCarthy and they were awarded a penalty. Damien Murray struck the ball hard but straight and Fitzhenry got his hurley to it. At the other end of the field, Mullins shook his head and turned around to one of the umpires.

'We're going to pay for those missed chances yet,' he said to him.

Offaly could have been ten points ahead at the break but they only led by one and that sense of missed opportunity was evident in their body language. In the previous two decades, the second half of Leinster finals had been Offaly's constituency and they always believed they would finish the stronger team. Between 1980 and 2000, Offaly teams were not always uniformly good but they were always proud and supremely confident. But in the last four years, that fireproof belief had seeped out of the county as though through a sieve and it wasn't easy to just lift the lid off the geyser anymore and wait for the confidence to come bubbling back.

'Management told us to keep going and the scores would come but I got the impression from looking around at the players, and even in my own head, that we were after missing too much,' said Mullins. 'We all knew it. I thought the heads were down and to be totally honest about it, I felt that if Wexford came out with any bit of fight at all, they had a good chance of taking us.'

In the other dressing room, Wexford's chief warrior was doing a war dance in front of his tribe.

'It's grand that nothing has gone in but on another day we'd be in savage trouble,' said Fitzhenry to his team-mates. 'Lads came up here and thought they'd nothing to do except tog off and win a Leinster final. Nobody is going to hand anything to you and we need to get a grip on things. Some lads are fucking waltzing around the field. Jesus, against Kilkenny we were hooking and blocking and hassling like hell for seventy minutes. We've done none of that for the last thirty five.'

He paused for a second and then lifted his voice even more. 'We went out and expected it to happen!' he roared. 'Unless you make it happen, it won't happen. Well we better go out and make it happen now or else we're fucked.'

Wexford came out on the warpath. They got the first two points of the half to reclaim the lead and then matters got worse for Offaly when Brian Whelehan had to leave the field with a hamstring injury ten minutes into the half. The game was tough and tight and hard but Wexford bounded ahead in the fifty second minute when Mossie Mahon won a ball in the middle of the field and drove it crossfield. Paul Carley was coming across at pace and he knocked it down and picked it on the run. With two defenders chasing him, he kept going at an angle and when he got inside the 20-metre line he drove it low and hard and across Mullins' body. The keeper reacted but the ball went past him and into the corner of the net.

'I was sure I had it but he slotted it,' said Mullins. 'Even when he was running in, I was confident I was going to save it. Sometimes when you're playing in games, you want lads to come in and take shots at you. It was kind of like that for me. I was disappointed with it.

'I know it would have been a good save but I kind of wasn't there for it. Up to that point they only had two shots on goal and they scored two goals. He finished it well in fairness to him but your job is to stop the ball going into the net. Ninety percent of the time when a lad comes in from that side, he's going to go for the right-hand corner and I thought I maybe should have moved a little bit quicker to the right-hand side.'

Adrian Fenlon soon extended that lead to five points before Offaly were thrown a lifeline when Gary Hanniffy punished some sloppy defending and pulled on a ground ball that flew into the bottom right corner of the net. Fitzhenry dived but he saw it too late.

The game was still there for Offaly but they couldn't manufacture the scores or the space that they had found in the first half. Paul Codd shot a couple of points and Offaly couldn't break the two-point barrier. Wexford went three clear as time ran out and two minutes into injury time, a Carley free put Wexford four in front.

Just as Mullins was about to take the puckout, the referee blew the whistle and the keeper laced the ball into the middle of the Cusack

Stand. He put his hands over his head, turned around and wiped his face on his towel. He lingered for a minute and then walked out to the 20 metre line where Barry Teehan and Ger Oakley were kneeling down. Wexford supporters were streaming onto the field beside them and a couple of them patted Mullins on the back. He just stood there. Motionless.

At the other end of the pitch, Fitzhenry was making his way up the field when his brother Paddy ran up and grabbed him. His arm was in a cast and he caught his younger brother around the neck and nearly choked him. The goalkeeper handed him his hurleys before getting swallowed up in the crowd.

When Fitzhenry got to the podium, he looked out at the massive crowd in front of him. The youngest member of a family of fifteen, he was trying to spot some of his siblings and his friends. Anytime he did, he gave them the thumbs up.

Fitzhenry deservedly won the man-of-the-match award and but for his display, Offaly would have been a disappearing dot on the horizon by the interval. He accepted the handshakes and the plaudits back at the Stillorgan Park Hotel afterwards but he allowed himself a wry smile too. He is a goalkeeper and his attitude is always framed by reality.

'I'd have been kicking myself if any of those shots had beaten me,' he said. 'Outside the first shot, if any of the other ones had gone in, I'd have been kicking myself. The penalty was head high, Cordial's shot was mid-stomach. Be the Lord Jaysus, me mother would have stopped that one. And that's not being smart.

'You could stop four in the first half and let in a shitty one with a minute to go and get beaten. Unless you think of goalkeeping in that way, I don't think you could be able to hurl in the position. It was just one of those days that you think you're going to stop bullets. People were coming up to me afterwards saying this and that and that I was the greatest Wexford man since Nicky Rackard. Bullshitting. And I was saying to them, "listen, if I let in a howler the next day, I'll be the worst man that ever hurled for Wexford."'

Once he knows that, there is no fear of Fitzhenry. His attitude had helped him meet his goals and achieve his target. He had been a team player, achieved what he was capable off and had given 100%. And he had his third Leinster medal.

Sweet.

WELCOME TO THE JUNGLE

Ever since the Munster final, Donal Óg Cusack and most of the Cork players have been picking pieces of lead out of their hides. They've heard it all since the defeat; losing the game to fourteen men, squandering a four point lead with the breeze in the second half and abandoning the gameplan. Cusack had known bad days before. Good days and bad days but this was one of the worst ever. The only way he could really look at it afterwards was by reminding himself that they had been in the abyss before and had still scrambled back up the cliff face.

Cork were drawn against Tipperary in the qualifiers on the night of the Munster final and Cusack begun clawing his way back up the cliff face the following night when he rang Ger Cunningham to discuss his performance. They spoke casually for a couple of minutes and then Cusack told Cunningham that he wanted it straight, with no holds barred. The former keeper had one major issue with Cusack's display so he spoke frankly.

'I know *(Paul)* Flynn was taking half a chance with his goal, but having seen him hit these top-spin shots, I would certainly have questioned Donal Óg's positioning,' said Cunningham. 'To me Flynn was going for the crossbar but I still felt Donal Óg was out of position. It was a bit casual as far as I was concerned because he is responsible for the set-up of the men in the goal area. Ogie wanted it straight out and I gave it to him and that's the real beauty of Cusack - he'll take it on board.'

When the squad returned to training two nights later, there were only fourteen players present due to injuries and the involvement of players in the local club football championship. The atmosphere was dead but Donal O'Grady addressed the players in the middle of Páirc Uí Rinn before the session begun. He began his speech by telling them that what kept the legendary basketball player, Michael Jordan, going all through his career was the chances he had missed. O'Grady spoke of atonement now and his words were like balm to their wounded spirit.

'We made mistakes and we took the wrong options at the wrong times but that's what the game is about, learning from them,' O'Grady said to his players. 'One competition is over and we're in another one now. And winning the All-Ireland starts here.'

Their training cones were set out as normal and when O'Grady blew the whistle after the speech, every player sprinted over to the first drill. Cusack was beside Seán Óg Ó hAilpín and he tapped him with the hurley. Ó hAilpín tapped him back and the fire that was glinting in his eyes told Cusack that the blaze was still burning inside.

'I remember thinking that we were at our lowest ebb but that Seán Óg was still going to drive on and that I was going to go with him. The whole of Cork were at us but we drove on and it was a great session.'

𝒪 𝒪 𝒪

After Cork trained on Thursday night before the Tipperary game, all the players gathered as usual in the corner of the Páirc Uí Rinn pitch. Ben O'Connor said his few words and then he looked across to Cusack.

'Ogie, do you want to say something?' O'Connor asked him.

'Victory,' said Cusack. 'That's all I'm going to say.'

Cusack is convinced Cork are going to win but he's had other things on his mind over the last few days. Only Diarmuid O'Sullivan, Ger Cunningham and Dr Con Murphy know that he had to have a pain-killing injection in order to be able to train tonight. Over a week ago, one of his ribs came away from his sternum after a collision and the pain has been ridiculous ever since. As usual, Donal O'Grady asked Cusack with ten minutes to go if he wanted any shots taken on him. O'Grady looked surprised when Cusack said no.

The pain was so intense during the session that Cusack wondered if Dr Con had just put water into the needle and the pain still hadn't subsided twenty four hours later. Cloyne were training and Cusack took the session but anytime he blew the whistle, he was nearly bent over with soreness. The more he blew, the more pain he was in but the session was still fused with a serious tempo.

It was a worry when he woke up on the morning of the game but he was prepared to go through the pain barrier for his team-mates. One of his best friends, Diarmuid Falvey, advised Cusack not to play because no amount of excuses afterwards would prevent him from being pilloried if things went wrong. Cusack would trust Falvey with his life but he isn't worried about the after-effects.

'I don't care about abuse, I want to play for the team and to start winning again,' he said. 'That's why I want to play. No other reason.'

Management still wasn't aware of his condition because Cusack had begged Dr Con not to tell Donal O'Grady. The manager wasn't happy when Cusack took an injection for his back at half-time in the League game against Galway and the keeper feared that he might be dropped if they knew he was injured now. Even though Cusack and Dr Con fell out for a period during the players' strike two years ago, Cusack has massive respect for Murphy and he trusted him. Totally.

Before the game, Cusack got a rub in the team room in the hotel in Killarney. There was very little talk and the mood amongst the players was very serious. The squad's music compilation was playing on the CD player and suddenly the *Guns'n'Roses* track 'Welcome to the Jungle' came on. Brian Corcoran got up from his seat and everyone thought he was going to turn the music down or else off. Instead, Corcoran turned it up full blast. Cusack just nodded to him.

'It summed up where we were headed,' said the keeper. 'Welcome to the jungle.'

When the squad arrived in the dressing room in Fitzgerald Stadium, Cusack and Dr Con went into a cubicle in the toilet area.

'Con,' said Cusack as the two squeezed into the tight space 'you better make this one hit the spot. Shove the needle in as far as you want and give me what you have to kill this pain because things are too important now.'

When Cusack went out on the field, Paul Morrissey and Martin

Coleman started hammering shots at him immediately but Cusack couldn't get his shoulder functioning properly. He didn't know if it was because he hadn't hurled properly for a week or if his form had just deserted him. Balls were flying in past him and the Tipp fans behind the goal were lapping it up.

'My head is still strong, I'm focussed,' he said to himself.

Before long the Cork supporters were baying at him. Cork were playing against a difficult diagonal breeze and their half-forward line weren't able to win any clean ball on Cusack's puckouts. He was picked off by Benny Dunne on three minutes. On eleven minutes he picked Tom Kenny out with a beautiful ball but the midfielder was bottled up and Tipp were awarded a free which they pointed.

'I'm amazed that Cork are at it again with the puckouts,' said Michael Duignan in the TV commentary. 'Tipp are ready for it, every team in the country are ready for it. This problem was there last year and it's still there and I'm surprised it hasn't been resolved.'

Yet anytime Cusack went long, he might as well have been hitting the ball off a glass wall. Of the six times he went long, Tipp won each ball and secured two points from the bounty. When Cusack hit another short puckout to Wayne Sherlock on twenty six minutes, it stirred the Cork crowd into a craze and when he was weighing up his options for another short one a minute later, the crowd lost it with him.

'I knew they were going off their game over it,' said Cusack. 'I could have started to play politics but I didn't care what the crowd were thinking. We were doing what we thought was best for the team.'

The match hadn't developed into much of a spectacle. Both teams were hell-bent on closing down the opposition and both full-forward lines were tending to drift out the field in search of possession, compressing the space even more. With the forwards closing in on each other, there was bound to be some turbulence and it resulted in a series of clashes just before the break.

It started when John Carroll bulldozed his way through the centre and Cusack came out and brought him down for a penalty. The collision shunted one of the goalkeeper's contact lenses over the far side of his right eye and while he was receiving attention, an outbreak of sparring took place on the 20-metre line. Dr Con Murphy always carries Cusack's spare contact lenses in his pocket and when he arrived on the field, Cusack looked up at him.

'Con, you have my contact lenses in your pocket anyway,' he said.

'Ogie, you're not going to believe this, but I don't,' replied Murphy.

'What? You're not fucking serious?!'

When Murphy managed to get the lens back out of his eye, he had to clean dirt and grit from it. Tensions were still simmering after three minutes of a delay and the referee Barry Kelly was urging Cusack to get back up.

'Jesus Barry, I've to try and save a penalty, I'm not moving until this lens goes back in,' said the goalkeeper.

When Cusack got to his feet, the referee booked him. Eoin Kelly drove the penalty hard and straight but Cusack got his stick to it. The ball was still alive but Cork couldn't clear the rebound and Kelly's brother Paul scuffed the ball home in a scramble. Then, three minutes into injury time, Benny Dunne pulled across Jerry O'Connor in front of the Tipp dugout and all hell broke loose. A mass brawl erupted and tensions were at boiling point as Tipp went in four points ahead at the break.

When Cusack arrived back in, Dr Con gave him another injection in the corner of the dressing room. There was no need for secrecy this time and the last thing on Cusack's mind was the worry of his team-mates thinking he was wounded. Cork were in the middle of a savage battle and every man had to go back over the top to face the gunfire in the second half.

'The dressing room was just fierce,' said Cusack. 'And I mean fierce. We were in a real battle and everybody sensed it. We knew that we were fighting for our lives and that the team would never play together again if we were beaten. Donal *(O'Grady)* was also gone if we lost and everything we had stood for would have been called into question. Donal gave a great speech and then he spoke about how important the willingness to fight for the inches was. And how he knew that this team was prepared to do so.'

In the other dressing room, Tipp were equally as fired up but Brendan Cummins felt slightly detached from it all. It was like he'd existed in a vacuum for thirty five minutes and he was struggling to process the thoughts running through his head.

'It felt unreal,' said Cummins. 'It felt like the game was happening and I was above looking down at it. I hadn't touched the ball and when that happens, it starts to get a little bit eerie in there. I came off at half-time and I was looking around like a boxer that was punch drunk. I don't know whether it was nerves or what. I knew going out that Cork weren't going to take a shot at goal unless it was unstoppable but it just felt weird.'

Cummins didn't have to wait long to get tested. Cork struck early and decisively two minutes after the break when Timmy McCarthy picked up a breaking ball at pace and hammered it into Cummins' net from inside the 20-metre line. The goal put Cork in the driving seat and reversed the impetus of a match that was drifting away from them.

Eoin Kelly had a clear-cut goal chance for Tipp midway through the half when there were only two points between the teams and he flashed it over the bar. With seven minutes to go there was still only a point between them when Niall McCarthy found himself inside the Tipp full-back line with nobody close. His attempt at a pick-up failed so without hesitation he let fly on his left and whipped it into the corner of Cummins' net.

'He didn't hit it on his natural run, he broke his stride to hit it on the inside,' said Cummins. 'My reaction was to hold the hand up. It looked like I'm trying to wave it wide but I wasn't. I was beaten and I left it off to God.'

Game over.

Cork had toughed it out but they had racked up an impressive tally of 2-19 in the process. Cummins was disappointed that the only two shots Cork fired at him ended up in the net but he had braced himself for that possibility.

'Cork won't go for goals unless they're sure,' said Cummins. 'I knew that I might only get two or three balls all day and my training beforehand wasn't as intense as before other games because I knew I wasn't going to be as busy. It was a matter of getting the head right, rather than the touch right. Cork were never going to give me the opportunity to get confidence. It's not just because it's me, they do that anyway. They'll tap the ball over the bar and think that they'll win by a point eventually and that's the way they hurl.'

Cork were never going to make a hero out of Cummins. In each of his previous four championship matches, he has made stops that would make up a huge proportion of the best fifteen saves of the last two seasons. Cummins was always a good keeper but in the last four seasons, he has taken shot-stopping to a new level and has developed into one of the greatest shot-stoppers the game has ever seen.

He turned a huge corner in his career four years before when Tipperary travelled over to Sunderland Football Club in England for a training weekend. Niall Quinn arranged it through his friendship with Nicky English and it was manna from heaven for Cummins. He consulted intensively with the goalkeeping coaching staff there. By the end of the weekend, his head was spinning with new ideas.

The most important data he collated wasn't rocket science but Cummins had never been informed before of the benefits a goalkeeper could accrue from strengthening his core area and improving his flexibility. Ever since, he works hard in the gym over the winter on both areas but he incorporates those training methods into his overall programme as the year develops. That was easier this year; last winter he set up his own gym in the house.

His flexibility has improved 80% from when he first started hurling for Tipperary, as has his body strength and leg power, which provides him with an elastic spring in his feet. Not every hurling critic would agree with his flamboyant style but he gets the job done.

'The only reason I've made more spectacular saves than I would have before is because of my core and my flexibility,' said Cummins. 'That's what causes the diving but if I can stop a ball without diving, I'll do it. It's not a case of being a showman. If I do a triple somersault and a backflip before I catch the ball and save it, teams would rather have that type of a keeper than one who throws a hurley and doesn't get near it.

'For every person that says "Ah, Cummins is the best in the country", you'll have somebody else saying "Ah, he's just pure show." But if anyone can say to me that I could have made that save below in Cork from Paul Flynn standing up, they can come to me and we'll have an argument about it. I wasn't consciously thinking "I have to dive after this" but I'm delighted I dived when I did. Look what it's doing for young fellas as well. A lot of them want to be keepers now because the days of a fella standing in there with a big pot belly are gone.'

Cummins is a big, strong man, with huge shoulders and powerful legs. He is almost the perfect mould for a soccer keeper and while he has refined his game by borrowing some soccer tenets, he has carved his technique from an amalgam of bravery, geometry and skill.

'I find it easier to play inter-county hurling than to play club hurling,' he said. 'It's way easier because when a fella comes through at inter-county level, you know he's going to really hit it. One thing I've tried to do over the years is narrow the angle. I reckon if I can get there, within three feet of his hurley, the ball is not going to have time to go at an angle and go past me. When it leaves a fella's hurley it takes about four or five feet for it to take an angle. So when a fella throws it up to hit it, I want to get within three feet of him, so it will hit me.

'All I see is the ball, I don't see a hurley. I just see a ball being thrown up and I look at the shape of his body. If you look at the hurley, you'll get psyched out of it. You just get days when it's not in your reach and you just let it off then because there's nothing you can do about it.'

He has been consistently producing excellent saves since 2000 and Limerick could have beaten Tipp in the first round of the qualifiers two weeks before only for two classy stops. It appeared that Tipp had turned a corner against Limerick but now they're back to square one again. In early July. In the dressing room afterwards, Cummins was devastated. Completely shattered. The worst he'd ever been after a match.

'It was unreal. The worst ever and an absolute nightmare. I was sitting there just thinking "Oh Jesus Christ, this is an absolute disaster." I'll be thirty in my next championship match and that was another hang-up I was having. Next year will be my eleventh year hurling with Tipperary and I've one All-Ireland medal to show for it all. It's not arrogance but you'd expect to be in at least in three or four All-Ireland finals during that time.

'The most disappointing thing was the way we just collapsed, as we've done for the last two years late in the game. Whether that can be put down to training or individuals, it's hard to know. But as a unit of Tipperary fellas, we just collapsed with ten minutes to go. We had a chance of winning the game but we never looked like winning it. We never got Cork edgy. We were the ones on edge and they just ran through us like a dose of salts.'

It took Cummins a while to tog in and gather himself afterwards. He just sat there, still concussed by the trauma of the loss. Maybe it was just him but he didn't feel the sense of desolation around him through the coma of defeat.

'I didn't get the end of the world feeling around me. Absolutely not and that's the way it is. In the past if you were beaten, you'd be devastated. There was hurt there but it wasn't as much as there probably should be. That's just my opinion.'

The cutting edge that Tipp had shown against Limerick and in the first half against Cork abandoned them in the second half when the match was going away from them. The zest that always marked Tipp apart in the championship was absent again when the game was there to be decided.

Tipperary teams have always had something in their demeanour and their bearing. Even though they've only won three All-Irelands in the last thirty three years, they have always had an inclination to think that they were always better than the opposition. Tipp players took sustenance from the success of generations, as if the special belief system they possessed was passed on by osmosis. Their intrinsic confidence was undiminished over many valley periods in the last three decades, but over this summer their assurance didn't look totally fireproof.

'We're not good enough in our total game,' said Cummins. 'No one will ever question the ability of the players but maybe the mental strength is something that could be questioned. If there was any difference that I've seen this year between a Tipperary team, and any team we've faced, it's probably that mental strength. That has been the difference. It's something that doesn't happen overnight and it creeps in over time. Over the last two years, we've conceded late goals in a lot of matches and a lot of that is down to belief.

'People would have always said that Tipperary were arrogant and cocky and maybe that bit of a swagger is gone from us. In dressing rooms in the past, it would never have openly been said that we're going to win today. But by looking at everyone, you just felt that we're going to win and that's it. Look at Kilkenny. Shefflin has an auld go about him. He has that swagger and you need that if you're going to be successful. When I looked around the dressing room before the Cork match, the same confidence and swagger wasn't there. You can't stand up and say "believe." That has to come from within. That comes over time and with this particular bunch of players, it's dwindled away from the fellas that had it and it's probably affected the fellas coming in.'

It was a bad day for Tipperary all round. Their supporters were heavily outnumbered by Cork's but they could still have had more to shout about if they'd taken the four handy points available in the first half and if their forwards had given Eoin Kelly more of a hand after the break. But once again, they came up short in key positions and they struggled to win clean possession in the air.

'You can't always be banging balls one hundred yards, sometimes you have to try something different but it's hard to hit the perfect ball every time from a puckout,' said Cummins. 'You need ball winners in the modern game. If you're first to the ball, you put your hand up and catch it. Kilkenny will win 80% of their puckouts, Ken McGrath has no hang-ups about sticking up his hand and neither does the Waterford half-forward line. That's where you win and lose matches and we're not winning enough balls around the middle of the field. That's really the key to why Tipperary aren't winning.'

For now, Cummins knows what's facing him for a few weeks. He won't know what to do with himself. He'll struggle to sleep at night and he'll be cranky. He won't want to look at a hurley for a while and next year will seem like a million miles away. But he'll just have to deal with it.

Privately.

When the final whistle blew, one of the umpires asked Cusack for his jersey and he gave it to him. Just as he was making his way off the field, a gentleman approached him and introduced himself. Although the keeper didn't catch his name, he said hello to the man and he walked on. Then the man put his hand on his shoulder and asked Cusack to come with him for a drug test. The thought of three pain-killing injections within the space of forty eight hours suddenly formed a different vision in his mind.

'That's all you'd need.'

He went to Dr Con straightaway and was told there was nothing to worry about. Cusack was tested along with Sean Óg Ó hAilpín, Eoin Kelly and Ken Dunne and although he started lorrying water into him, it took Cusack two hours to pass urine. Declan O'Sullivan (physio), Jerry Wallis (trainer) and Jim McEvoy (masseur) stayed with the Cork players until they had completed the test and Donal O'Grady had organised a garda escort to take them back to the hotel afterwards.

It had been a great day for Cusack. Cork were back on track, he had played well and had coped admirably with his injury. The only downside to the day came later that night when he discovered that his young sister, Treasa had been in tears during the match. She was wearing one of her brother's goalkeeper's jerseys and she was near one Cork supporter who copped who she was. He terrorised her with the abuse he was giving her brother.

'I wouldn't mind meeting your man, big brave boy probably after ten pints intimidating a young girl,' said Cusack. 'Cowardly fucker. But I just said to Treasa, "that's just it, that's what happens at big sports grounds.'"

From now on, Cusack is going to make sure that his sister is in the stands beside people she knows. And not beside mindless so-called Cork supporters in the terrace.

DARK FORCES

Before Donal Óg Cusack took the Cloyne training session on the Friday evening before the Tipperary match on July 10th, he got a phone call from Liam Donoghue. The two goalkeepers had never spoken to one another before but Donoghue wanted to pick Cusack's brain on shelling puckouts into Kilkenny's defensive territory and about the threat from their attacking front. He quizzed Cusack about Kilkenny's, and Henry Shefflin's in particular, goalscoring tendencies. Donoghue has played against Shefflin a few times but on two occasions, the Kilkenny forward beat him with a flicked goal. No amount of strategic pre-planning can totally prepare Donoghue for the onslaught Kilkenny are threatening to unleash but Cusack offered him whatever advice he could.

Forty-eight hours before the battle, Donoghue was confident, relaxed and positive, even if most people in the county outside the team camp aren't. The vibe on the ground is that they have no centre-back, no midfield and no bottle and one in every two Galway people will tell you that there are better players in the county who aren't even on the panel.

Even though Galway won a League title two months ago, playing some lovely hurling along the way, negativity remains chained to a huge proportion of Galway's hurling public. It stems primarily from the manner in which the game is run in Galway by the county board and the players have had to pay some of that price. Although the county lost six of the last seven All-Ireland Under-21 finals, those players had to go it alone because their hurling public wouldn't support them. The senior team isn't expecting huge support either on Sunday but some of that is rooted in the manner in which certain players aren't rated. Although Donoghue had a very solid and impressive league campaign, conceding only six goals from play in nine matches, he knows he is one of them.

'It's very hard to please people in Galway,' he said. 'Some of the papers you pick up here don't have an ounce of faith in me. Some of the analysts on Galway Bay FM wouldn't have much faith in me. It does piss you off at times and you wonder what you have to do. If I had a game like Fitzhenry had in the Leinster final, it still wouldn't be enough. A lot of people in Galway do rate me but a lot more will just build you up when you get in there, and then all they want to do is knock you and get you out of there.'

Donoghue is a fantastic shot-stopper but he will always have two charges levelled against him in the county. First, that his puckout isn't good enough for this level and second, that he's a cocky boyo who you'll always hear before you see him on the pitch. Some people don't like that on-field brash persona and they use it as a stick to beat him with when he doesn't back it up by producing the goods.

'I wouldn't say that I wasn't cocky,' said Donoghue. 'I would be like that anyway and I never just put it on for a front. If I thought I'd something to say I'd come out and say it, I'd never shy away from it. When I'm playing in goals, I'm very vocal but I find that if I'm vocal I'm playing well and it just helps to keep my concentration levels high. Some people might not like that but if you hear me quiet in goal, there's something wrong with me. After the match the players will often come up to me and say "shut up to fuck now, we're sick of listening to you." But when you're going on the pitch they'll always say "keep talking to us, keep talking." It helps the defence but when I'm talking, I'm concentrating.'

His puckout wasn't the primary reason he wasn't in goal for Galway at an earlier stage in his career but it didn't do him any favours and he appreciates that he can't get away from the perception people have of his puckout. He has worked hard on it, really hard, since the beginning of the year and he knows what he can and cannot do. He's not a pinpoint striker but he has added distance and Galway haven't had any great deal of reason to doubt their tactics on their puckout so far this season.

Galway's present forward line doesn't have the physique or self-sufficiency to win a high ratio of dirty ball but Wexford have proved that pace can take down Kilkenny. Galway have more class and pace than Wexford's forward line and of the 20-135 total they hit in nine league games, 18-93 came from play. Galway have the arsenal and the hardware up front but Damien Fitzhenry's puckouts were critical to Wexford's gameplan in beating Kilkenny and Donoghue doesn't have that striking ability.

'I know once I look up and see a gap, I'll be able to find a man,' said Donoghue. 'No doubt about it. I wouldn't be able to pick out Fergal Healy in the middle of the park and put it straight into his hand, not a notion. I might get one out of five of those but I wouldn't even try it to be honest. The boys would tell me that they'd come in and break a hurl across me if I try a short puckout. They'd absolutely kill me.'

Sunday's game is huge for Galway in every sense. They believe they have arrived now but they have to prove it. They have class but over the years that manic, obsessive, collective drive hasn't been as pronounced in Galway as it has in other teams. They haven't reached the level other teams have. To take that extra hit. To go that extra yard. Some individuals have been complacent but when the squad held a meeting the previous October, they made a pact to be true to one another. Sunday will be the real test of that agreement.

Last month they went to Loch Lomond in Scotland for a four-day training spin and they felt the bond had tightened even further. They know it's sixteen years since Galway won an All-Ireland and they appreciate that if they lose on Sunday, like last year, their season is over before it begins. The dice has been rolled but they feel they've more chips stacked up now in their favour.

'We can't wait to get out on that pitch,' said Donoghue. 'We know it's a huge game but we've trained since last October for it. We have no fear of Kilkenny. Wexford proved that they can be beaten and Cork should have beaten them in last year's All-Ireland. They're not anything above the norm. No team out there at the moment is a cut above the rest. OK, Kilkenny two years ago were but they're not anymore. They haven't the same appetite or hunger. If we're going to meet them, we're better off getting them now.'

Although the match was fixed for 6pm, the team bus departed Oranmore in Galway just after 10am on Sunday. The bus made the last pick-up at Portumna just before 11am where the final group of players and County Board officials boarded for the trip south. Six members of the Galway Hurling Board were on the bus but three of the delegates had brought their wives and one delegate had brought his young daughter along for the spin.

At 1.15pm they arrived at their base in Dundrum House, outside Cashel. Cork usually base themselves there before championship games in Thurles and while Galway were trying to replicate Cork's pre-match routine, an evening throw-in placed a different emphasis on time management. The players had two hours to wait before their pre-match meal and they ended up in the bar watching TV to kill some of the time.

When management consulted with the kitchen staff to reconfirm the time of their pre-match meal of chicken pasta at 3.15pm, they were told that the menu had been changed to beef. The menu was changed back again and when management asked a leading county board official why he had tampered with their plans, they were told that if beef was good enough for him, it was good enough for the players.

After the meal, some of the players pucked around in the lawn for half an hour before the bus departed for their puckaround in Holycross. The local side had just finished playing a challenge game against O'Loughlin Gaels from Kilkenny but when the Galway players began their drills, management discovered that they only had thirty sliotars, and not the sixty they were promised by the County Board. When they finished their stretching routine they headed to Thurles and were in the ground by 5.10pm.

The Kilkenny squad had met earlier in the Spring Hill Hotel on the Waterford road before departing for Thurles. James McGarry was sitting up near the front beside Martin Comerford and just as the bus was taking off, Noel Skehan hunched back from the seat in front and looked back at them.

'For Jaysus' sake, what are ye two looking so worried about?' Skehan said. 'We went up to play teams like this before that were built up to the last and we beat them before our breakfast.'

McGarry smiled at Comerford. 'He turned around then and sat down like a bould child,' he said of Skehan.

Kilkenny were never as ready or primed for a match. In a team meeting a couple of days beforehand, McGarry brought it up about Eugene Cloonan scoring 2-9 against Kilkenny in the 2001 All-Ireland semi-final and that he was going to score anything near that tally again over their dead bodies. They could feel it all week as they were driven on by the lash of Brian Cody's tongue. Cody was setting the tone of their mood. Completely.

'I never saw Kilkenny as tuned for a match,' said McGarry. 'In all my time, the 2000 All-Ireland final was the only other time we were as tuned in for a match. But it was the most psyched up I'd ever seen Cody. He was psyched up big time but he'd been like that all week. People were writing us off and it was make or break for us. The whole thing was over if we were beaten. He felt that the team weren't going well and he probably thought that he needed to do something special to get us right.'

On the bus journey into Thurles, there was hardly a word spoken amongst the players. Inside in the dressing room before they hit the field, they were hell-bent on proving that their overwhelming drive and power had been fully rehabilitated. The 2001 semi-final, when they were bullied around the place, was brought up again and Kilkenny went out ready to hit Galway with all the force they had suffered three years before.

'Everyone was tuned in and geared to go,' said McGarry. 'Nobody was going to beat us.'

Kilkenny came out of the traps like wild animals intent on devouring all before them and it was obvious too that Cody was wound up on the sideline. He was zig-zagging in and out of the field of play and he confronted the linesman on a couple of occasions and then turned on referee Diarmuid Kirwan midway through the half. His in-your-face style was being replicated all over the field by Kilkenny.

Galway gnashed their teeth and scrapped it out but just at the stage in the first half when the match needed a Galway goal, it was Kilkenny who scored it. A long free broke inside the Galway defence and Jimmy

Coogan grabbed it and handpassed it forward. Henry Shefflin had lost his man and he flicked it past the advancing Donoghue. Shefflin had just beaten Donoghue with another flicked goal and the Kilkenny forward wheeled away in manic celebration in front of a Kilkenny crowd that outnumbered Galway supporters by at least 4:1.

'Shefflin was jumping around the place and he was pumped,' said Donoghue. 'I remember saying to myself: "Jesus, we're not at this pace at all." They were way more tuned in. You could hear all their forwards roaring, you could hear DJ *(Carey)* roaring and shouting at everyone. It was just clicking for them.'

Galway were playing with the breeze but their sails were slack and they were craving some form of momentum. The match was beginning to slip away from them – indeed McGarry felt the writing was already on the wall.

'I knew it was over after ten minutes. We just brushed them aside and their whole body language was telling me everything. I saw Cloonan looking up the field at one stage and he kind of shook his head after we got a couple of points. I always look at the opposition's strong men and feel that if we can scrub them out of it, we have a great chance.'

The champions led by five points at the break and had the breeze to come but McGarry had added some make-up to the scoreboard's complexion just before the break when he reacted smartly and got his legs to an acute shot from David Tierney.

When the half-time whistle blew, Cody approached the referee as he left the field and clearly remonstrated with him over what he had felt were a couple of harsh decisions against his team. The linesman on the far side, Seamus Roche, told Cody to back off but the Kilkenny manager made his point and ran back into the dressing room.

'The only other time I saw him *(Cody)* so fired up on the line was against Limerick a few years ago,' said McGarry, referring to the 2002 National League semi-final in Limerick. 'I remember the Limerick lads, supporters and all, were baying for our blood and Cody got totally fired up. It was brilliant and all the players really responded to him.'

Galway knew they were in trouble at the break and the vibe in the dressing room wasn't helped by a County Board official abusively telling the management to take off David Tierney, within earshot of about six players. The team gathered around in a huddle before they went back onto the field but there were a lot of blank stares in the group and they weren't exactly exuding confidence.

'Hand on heart, I knew we were in big trouble,' said Donoghue. 'We were going out playing against a strong breeze, playing absolute crap. We couldn't win the ball in the first half so what were we going to do in the second half?'

Nine minutes into the second half, Galway looked to be back in the match. Kevin Broderick made the opening for Damien Hayes to fire past McGarry and reduce the deficit to three points. Eddie Brennan replied within seconds for a Kilkenny point but two minutes later, Adrian Cullinane found himself in front of goal after the ball flashed across from the right flank. He connected on it but McGarry reacted superbly to block the snap-shot from ten metres.

Within sixty seconds, Kilkenny had won a 20 metre free and Shefflin went for broke. He laced the ball towards the right hand post and it went through the wall of Galway defenders on the line. That was that. The game assumed engagement on terms Galway couldn't manage and they were pounded. Kilkenny outscored their opponents 2-8 to 0-2 down the home stretch.

Donoghue couldn't have done anything for Eddie Brennan and John Hoyne late goals and after the match, McGarry walked down the middle of the field and went straight over to the disconsolate Galway keeper.

'Nothing I can say to you is going to make any difference,' McGarry said to him. 'But keep your head up.'

Donoghue didn't know what to think. Before the game, he was convinced Galway were going to win but the optimism that had built up during the League was crumbling and giving way to despair. It was hard to know where they stood now but the scene in the dressing room afterwards offered a neat little encapsulation of where Galway hurling really was. And is.

'Guys were down on their knees, absolutely devastated and not knowing what the hell had happened,' said Donoghue. 'You're thinking, what's it all for? You're asking yourself what the hell is wrong with Galway hurling. The players have to hold their hands up but then you see the County Board boys sitting in the corner eating Jaffa Cakes and wondering are their steaks done in Portumna yet. Not giving a fuck.'

Galway were mown down but they had been annihilated on their own puckout and they couldn't win any clean possession up front to utilise their pace. They had tried to beat Kilkenny with an orthodox formation but the All-Ireland champions had packed the middle third of the field and contracted the space. Galway were hit and tossed around like rag-dolls. They couldn't get any space to breathe and Donoghue's puckouts hadn't provided any oxygen.

'I was told not to hit short puckouts but it is a failing of mine and I wouldn't have the confidence to go short,' said Donoghue. 'It cost us the match really. We just played right into their hands. In fairness, Wexford showed how it should be done, but personally, I didn't have the balls to go short. If I was good enough, I'm sure the management would have said to go with it but I have to hold my hand up. I have to be brutally honest. I didn't have the confidence but there weren't a whole lot of players looking for balls in space. Other players have to hold their hands up as well.'

Plan B was never discussed. 'From the start of the year, it was go along with everything. But to be honest it was successful during the League and we'd no reason to change it. We won a League final against Ken McGrath and Tony Browne in the Waterford half-back line. We'd no reason to doubt ourselves.

'The fact that my puckout wasn't long enough wasn't doing me any favours but now they want short puckouts. Donal Óg is doing it for the last two years and he's been slated for it. As far as I'm concerned, you could give one or two short puckouts in a match but the bottom line is if you haven't got ball winners around the middle of the field, you're in trouble. That's the bottom line.

'Our inability to win puckouts cost us but so did our inability to scrap and win possession. We need to try and rectify that and if I'm going to be in goals for Galway next year, I can guarantee you this much, I'm just going tunnel vision with my puckout. You just have to have it in your game now. I know it is a weakness with me. I just have to work on it. If it doesn't improve, I won't be there. I'm going to eat and sleep in the pitch pucking out balls. I have to.'

Donoghue's puckout was a key kink in Galway's system but it wasn't the main fault that caused the meltdown. Some of their old weaknesses, which they thought had been eradicated, returned to haunt them and when the heat came on, too many of their players wilted. Similar to the last few years, Galway weren't prepared to go into the depths of hell on key match-days to secure the victory.

Although the Galway club championship is one of the most cut-throat in the country, that cussedness has never translated into the county team over the last decade. It hasn't been part of Galway's make-up. It manifested itself in the 2001 All-Ireland semi-final against Kilkenny but it hasn't been collectively seen since.

That relentless style of hardness is stitched into the fabric of the club culture but there is an almost tribal nature in a lot of Galway's clubs that hasn't helped the county team. Some of Galway's players haven't been prepared to lay their bodies and reputations on the line for their team-mates. More key players who would do anything to win for their clubs come onto the county team with a diluted sense of that manic devotion to the Galway cause. That may only apply to a select few but that is enough to bring the system down.

Galway may have all the rich talent in the world but county hurling is a form of communism, where every ego on the panel has to be subordinated to the greater good. Not enough leaders have stood up either to lead the revolution. The leaders who briefly stood up in 2001 and 2002 have disappeared and Galway haven't won a game at the business end of the championship since. They have some beautiful hurlers but sharpshooters don't always survive when they stand in front of the cavalry.

'After winning the League and with Wexford beating Kilkenny, we might have been a bit too cocky,' said Donoghue. 'We were in a war and mentally we weren't ready for it. We gave up with twenty minutes to go. We thought we'd beat them without having to go to war. But it is a war and we weren't ready for it.'

Mentally, Donoghue thought he was prepared for the battle but he's not sure if he fully was. Outside of his puckouts, he couldn't be faulted for the shots that beat him and he dealt capably with any loose ball he had to mop up. But before the game, he made a decision that he was going to keep his counsel during the match by not roaring and shouting and he doesn't think he was totally true to himself.

It was only after Shefflin's first goal that he loosened up and took a stroll out towards the 20 metre line and began roaring at the half-back line to tighten up. He was annoyed with himself afterwards for altering how he has always operated as a keeper. He couldn't put his finger on why he had but no amount of perceived fireproof confidence and brash attitude can prepare you for reality on the goal-line. Vince Lombardi once summed it up perfectly when he called it the place of truth.

'If you know me I'm not shy but if I didn't know you and you walked in, I'd find it hard to go over talking to you,' said Donoghue. 'I wouldn't be that confident. My biggest problem in goals is that I'm not half confident enough. There was a ball near the end of the match that I should have come out and ate up. I kind of went around the Kilkenny lad and got a flick to it but that was a ball that I should have came and ate. Ate. That's another of my weaknesses.

'You have to be an arrogant bastard to be a keeper and if that's not in your nature, you have to develop it. I might seem arrogant, but by nature, I wouldn't be. No way. But then if you went into training and asked the lads they'd say: "That lad has an answer for everything, he's cheeky and he'd say anything to anyone." But it's different when you're between the posts. Maybe I'm all talk, maybe I'm full of shite, I don't know. You'd just wonder at times because it's incredible how mentally tuned and sharp you have to be to play there. Maybe you have to be a different person when you're in there because it's an amazing position. It just fucks you up so much.'

A few days after the detonation of Galway's season, the black smoke from the fall-out was still hanging in the air. They haven't been blown off the map but the mood on the street suggests that Galway hurling is a step closer to oblivion. That isn't true but it feels like it.

The public is bitching about the players, management and the County Board and nothing ever seems to change in Galway. Nothing ever will unless the players stand up and take on more responsibility, the management get their house in order and sternly refuse to accept interference from certain sections of the County Board, and the County Board realise that hurling is more than just about them and the way they run the game in Galway.

Some of the players have already looked into their souls and realised that they weren't properly mentally prepared to fight the dark demons that visit you in a championship battle. Acceptance isn't easy but introspection has hit Donoghue like Novocain; it has numbed the pain but it hasn't taken away that low feeling.

'Just imagine depression and then multiply it by about twenty,' he said. 'The last few days have been the most depressing of my life. When you get beaten like this, it just messes everything up. Everything you thought you believed in, everything you thought you knew, you just have complete doubts about. It still hasn't sunk in that we were beaten by twenty points. Nobody outside the players, management and your family realise what you put into it. I've spent my whole life trying to get into this position and it's just heartbreak. But if I asked myself in the morning would I do it again, I'd say: "Definitely."'

NO QUARTER GIVEN

It was 3am on Tuesday morning July 20th by the time Davy Fitzgerald left Kevin 'Trixie' Toomey's home in Hill Road, Bunratty. They had discussed every angle imaginable ahead of Sunday's All-Ireland quarter-final with Kilkenny and they arranged a training session in Clarecastle for Wednesday evening. They agreed to work on some of the specifics of Kilkenny's attacking game as well as to fine-tune Fitzgerald's goalkeeping even more. Practice doesn't make perfect. Perfect practice makes perfect.

The session Toomey had with Fitzgerald the week before Clare beat Offaly in the second round of the qualifiers was one of the best they'd ever done together. Colin Lynch and Brian Culbert nearly drilled holes in Fitzgerald with a relentless barrage of shots from fourteen metres but Toomey kept berating Fitzgerald and demanding perfection from the goalkeeper. By the end of the session in Sixmilebridge, Fitzgerald was like a man possessed.

He's been on edge ever since Clare drew Kilkenny. When Fitzgerald first heard the draw, he took off out the door and ran up and down the beach in Lahinch three times.

It looks like the draw from hell after Kilkenny's annihilation of Galway but Clare see this as a glorious opportunity for redemption. The squad got the 11.30am train from Limerick to Dublin on Tuesday and they trained in Croke Park at 3pm. The buzz was good and on the train back down that evening, word was filtering around that management was going to deliver a curveball from leftfield to try and throw Kilkenny.

The squad arrived back in Limerick just before 10pm and Fitzgerald was at home within the hour. He stayed up for a while and he wasn't long in bed when the phone rang in the house at 1am. He'd normally never answer the phone that late but he got up and took the call. It was

Dr Pádraig Quinn, the local GP and the Clare team doctor. Dr Quinn had bad news. 'Trixie' had just passed away.

Fitzgerald nearly collapsed on the spot. Quinn told him that some of Kevin Toomey's family had still to be informed but he still wanted him to know first. Fitzgerald couldn't take it in and his system was struggling to adjust to the shock. He sat down on the couch for about five minutes, before getting dressed and travelling down to the Toomey household in Bunratty at 2am.

Fitzgerald could often spend four nights a week with his friend but he never thought he'd see him like this. He stayed up with Trixie's wife Marie and their family all night Tuesday and Wednesday. He got a couple of hours sleep both mornings and at the funeral in Sixmilebridge on Thursday evening, Fitzgerald went into a mortuary for the first time in his life. He could never handle seeing somebody laid out before but he had to be there this time.

Fr Michael McNamara asked him on Thursday evening about delivering the graveside oration at the burial the following day. He talked to Marie about it and she told him it would be fitting if he did. Friday was a beautiful day and before a packed graveside in Bunratty graveyard, across from Bunratty Castle, Fitzgerald spoke passionately and affectionately about his friend.

'I'm sure that he is with us in spirit,' Fitzgerald concluded. 'And I'm sure that he'll be looking down on us on Sunday when we'll skin the cats.'

The former Kilkenny captain, Liam Fennelly just smiled and after the funeral party had reconvened to the Toomey household, Fitzgerald went to Marie.

'Listen Marie, I have to get my head back into this thing,' he said to her.

He went down to the gym in the Shannon Shamrock Hotel in Bunratty and went to work immediately with his personal trainer Darren Ward. He hammered on the punchbag for over fifteen minutes before nearly burning a hole in the ground from bouncing with a skipping rope. He worked on his feet for almost an hour and then went into the pool for another hour. After he had showered and changed, he sat into the car and headed straight for Clare training.

'I slaughtered myself,' said Fitzgerald. 'It was murder but I just had to torture myself and get my frame of mind back. I felt really down but I kept thinking about the match and I got myself back.'

The team was announced to the players in Cusack Park and then management informed the squad that they were lining out in an unorthodox formation. Alan Markham had already been spoken to about his role as a sweeper behind the half-back line and the gameplan was set down.

On Saturday, Fitzgerald's heart was still leaden and his head slightly cluttered but he was never as focussed and as determined to win a game. It was a high-stakes clash but it was different from any other match he'd ever played in. In his mind, he was playing for the pride of Clare and for the honour of his friend's memory.

'I had a lot of stuff to deal with and it's going to be hard to concentrate but I want to go out and play better than I ever did for him. I just want to. Even for him alone, I just want to do the business. I haven't spoken to anyone at all, I have my own ideas in my own head and I'm just trying to stay focussed. I'm ready for Kilkenny and I'm big-time up for it. The last few days have been terrible, but I'm ready for them.'

A few hours before Kevin Toomey passed away, Antrim had their press night in Casement Park ahead of their All-Ireland quarter-final against Cork. Last year's All-Star nominee, Ciaran Herron, was sitting at the top table in a small dimly lit room just down the corridor from the dressing rooms, talking quietly and politely about how he felt the team had improved. A minute later, Dinny Cahill sat down on top of the wooden table with a hurley in his hand.

Cahill told the gathered media to disregard Antrim's League form and he dismissed the idea that there will be any psychological baggage from Dunloy's All-Ireland club final hammering to Newtownshandrum. After claiming that Antrim's narrow defeat to Waterford in a challenge game the previous weekend was further validation of their conditioning programme over the winter, a journalist asked Cahill if he felt Antrim would benefit from next year's restructured championship, which would guarantee them at least three matches. Cahill, three years into a three-year term, shook his head and restated the goal he had made at the outset of his term.

'We're going to win the All-Ireland this year,' he claimed. 'That's what we're going to benefit from.'

The eight journalists gathered around Cahill started smiling but then they noticed Cahill hadn't. He was serious. Deadly serious. He was happy to look beyond Cork because Antrim could stop the O'Connors running with the ball, their centre-forward Niall McCarthy was 'dreadful', Cork's full-forward line had been 'dreadful' all year and that Brian Corcoran was 'finished'.

The journalists asked him was he not afraid that Donal O'Grady would pin his comments to the wall to motivate his players and Cahill just shrugged his shoulders. As far as he was concerned, the newspapers could publish what they liked and Cork could plaster the walls with whatever graffiti they wanted.

'I'm telling the truth. They're finished. Brian Corcoran was a great player but he's finished.'

When some of the Antrim players, who weren't at the press conference, opened the papers the following morning, their jaws nearly dropped.

'That's Dinny being Dinny but he shouldn't have gone running to the papers and said that,' said DD Quinn. 'We know rightly that it's going to spread and Cork will use it against us. Dinny has prepared us brilliantly and we're in great shape but I think this is going to put us under a bit more pressure. We'd be better off going into the game more low-key.'

Cahill was going on his instincts but his comments look like a misjudged call. Cork are driven enough and they don't need any extra motivation but Cahill's comments about Niall McCarthy and Brian Corcoran have stoked the fires even more.

'Donal O'Grady told us that this is personal now and that's the way we're taking it,' said Donal Óg Cusack. 'It has definitely focussed things for us but things have been personal for us for a long time. It's personal that we want to win this All-Ireland.'

Antrim are in good shape but it is difficult to tell if they are better than twelve months before when they should have beaten Wexford. The drawn Ulster final was a good match but it is easy to believe that it was a level below Croke Park standard. Even though their League form was terrible, their whole year was structured around peaking for high-summer hurling. Getting up to that level is always difficult but the stability in the side from the last three seasons gives them a decent chance and they feel in better shape than twelve months ago.

Under Cahill, Antrim have pulled themselves up by the bootstraps. They have always had to deal with their sense of isolation and the demoralisation it can engender but Cahill strengthened their minds and bodies and improved their hurling. Their All-Ireland quarter-final performances in the last two seasons have been Antrim's best championship displays in a decade. Making the next step though, is the key. The players' target is to get to an All-Ireland semi-final because under next year's Hurling Development Committee's format an Ulster title will not guarantee a straight passage into an All-Ireland quarter-final.

'We have to win this game because it's going to be set-up against us next year,' said Quinn. 'You hear these boys on the TV once the draw was made saying that Antrim are going to get stuffed by twenty points. But what did Clare lose to Waterford by? Kilkenny hammered Galway by twenty points and there's nothing ever said about that. If Antrim get well beaten, they'll say that we shouldn't be here and that's what pisses us off.

'We do as much work as anybody else but we get no respect for it. We get no credit and no boys get any recognition for what we do. We're training since last October but if things don't go well for us now, we'll be told that we shouldn't be here and we'll get the shit slated out of us. We're never going to get the same credit because we're too far away up here.

'It's all right for the boys down south. They can go an hour in any direction and they'll get a good game of hurling any night of the week. If we want a good challenge game, we have to go away for a weekend. We're just too far away and Cork wouldn't have any respect for us. We know that. But we'll have no respect for them when we go out on that field.'

Right from the throw-in on Sunday, the Cork tempo was furious. The effect of Cahill's criticism on Cork was obvious but Antrim were all over the place. Their touch and their striking was way off the pace and the game was effectively over after twenty two minutes when Brian Corcoran scored their first goal. He scored his second eight minutes later and Cork led at the break by sixteen points.

'Dinny didn't say a wild lot at half-time,' said Quinn. 'He just couldn't pinpoint how we could go out and play like that. We were thinking "where did this come from?" We were playing for a bit of pride. We knew there was no way back.'

Cork didn't let up after the break and Antrim continued to struggle with the intensity of the game. Their first real sign of any level of resistance came seven minutes into the half when Brian Murphy fouled Paddy Richmond twenty five metres out and as the ref was booking Murphy, Cusack switched the sliotar with one from his bag. Jim Connolly went back and penned Cusack into the back of the net to retrieve the original ball and a scuffle ensued.

'Here,' said Cusack, 'take what you want!'

Central Council formally approved new sliotars for the championship in May after a new ball had been developed from a winter of testing in Dublin City University. Croke Park settled on standard balls that are provided by ballboys behind the goal but a few keepers are still bringing their own sliotars. Cusack is one of them and it isn't going down well in Croke Park. Cork always used Cummins sliotars but they've changed to O'Neills and every Friday night before a big game, Cusack and Cork selector Seanie O'Leary go through a batch of new sliotars and select some for match day.

'They want us to use O'Neills balls and now we're using them and they're still on our case,' said Cusack. 'I always say to the young fellas beside the goals to give me a worn sliotar and not a new one because a new sliotar could go anywhere. The young fellas have copped onto it but I'll still be using the O'Neills balls out of my bag and that's it.'

Cusack wasn't really threatened in the second half but his striking and his handling was impeccable all through the match. At the other end of the field, DD Quinn was equally as impressive and Antrim would have been beaten by a lot more than twenty two points only for his display. At the outset of the season, Quinn's stated goals with Antrim were to win an All-Ireland quarter-final and to hopefully secure an All-Star nomination. Just a nomination would do. An All-Ireland semi-final never looked further away than it does now and even though he was Antrim's second-best player on the day, the thought of an All-Star nomination exists in a parallel universe.

'You don't really know what to think afterwards. It's another year gone and we achieved nothing really. We won Ulster and that's fair enough, but that's really nothing. We needed to be doing more this year in the All-Ireland series. All that work and then bang, bang and it's over. When we get hammered, they say we don't deserve to be here but that's one of those things in life when you're a hurler from Ulster. Croke Park is a lonely place when you're standing there and you're getting hammered. I know I trained hard all year and I wanted to be out there but you're just saying to yourself "blow that whistle up boy and get us out of here."'

Clare's normal routine over the years for matches in Dublin involved an early flight, breakfast, a lie-down in a hotel near the airport, a puckaround and stretch, refuelling the body with carbohydrates and fluid and then a police escort into Croke Park. They were forced to abandon that routine this time around because they couldn't get an early flight.

The squad met at 11.30am in the Great Southern Hotel at Shannon Airport and sat down to a light lunch. Their flight was scheduled for 1pm and they were on board a bus on the Dublin airport runway by 2pm. They took the short trip across to the airport recreational grounds at ALSA, and went for a puckaround and stretch before heading into Croke Park.

Kilkenny had already come up on the bus that morning but they went across town to base themselves in the Clontarf Castle Hotel because Cork and Antrim were in the Burlington Hotel. A couple of hours before the match, James McGarry and Martin Comerford went for a walk around the hotel and McGarry wasn't that happy with the vibe.

'I could hear a few lads laughing and joking inside in the room,' he said. 'If you're tuned in, you're not at that shit. Lads weren't laughing and joking before the Galway match. I just like to be on my own or to be with a few lads talking about what you're comfortable talking about. You know, about what might happen in the game. When you have lads laughing and joking, they're not thinking about the game.'

On the short bus journey into Croke Park, Noel Skehan turned around to McGarry with a stone-coloured face.

'No matter how good or how bad a Clare team is, they'll be savage hard to beat,' Skehan said to him.

Ever since Waterford annihilated them, Clare had come up with a motto and it was hammered off the walls once more before they took to the field. 'You have got to come to the battle ready to fight for your life. We are ready so let's go out and fight for our lives.'

Skehan was hanging around the tunnel when Clare came out and Seán McMahon nearly blew him out of his way as he clipped past him. Clare were really up for it and they made their intentions well known from the outset by playing Alan Markham as a sweeper, primarily to act as a screen to Henry Shefflin. They started well and Niall Gilligan scored the first three points of the match.

Kilkenny dug in as the game became an attritional battle of tactics and wits. Clare led by 0-4 to 0-1 at the quarter-hour mark when DJ Carey was fouled by Alan Markham thirty metres out. The referee Ger Harrington moved the ball into the 20-metre line for dissent and as Henry Shefflin stood over it, Fitzgerald was jumping on the line, banging his hurley furiously off the ground.

'Come on Shefflin, come on to fuck!' he roared at him.

After Shefflin drilled it over the bar, the goalkeeper ran out after him, waving his arms at his reluctance to test him.

The hurling was rugged and primal and raw and passionate. The sides were level at 0-5 each on thirty five minutes when Diarmuid McMahon soloed inside the right flank of the Kilkenny defence and shot across the goal. McGarry stopped it and the ball was flicked out for a 65 in the scramble. Seán McMahon pointed it to leave Clare a point ahead at the break.

Kilkenny shuffled their deck in the dressing room and sent Shefflin to full-forward, DJ Carey to centre-forward and John Hoyne came in as a sub. Immediately after the throw-in, Carey picked a ball outside the 45 and hared away from Markham before offloading a 25 metre pass into the path of John Hoyne. The forward had got inside McMahon and he fired the ball to the net after just twenty three seconds. Shefflin was standing on the edge of the square and he put his two hands up in the air and roared at Fitzgerald. The keeper got up off the ground and made for him. The Clare defence converged and a scuffle ensued.

'He was giving me shit and I made up my mind that I wasn't going to take any shit,' said Fitzgerald.

Shefflin got his own back by firing the next two points to push Kilkenny four up on forty nine minutes. Clare needed to keep the match to a football scoreline to have any chance but the game was slipping from them and they needed a big break. They got it a minute later when Gilligan caught a high Andrew Quinn delivery over Tommy Walsh's head and the defender dragged him down as he turned goalwards. Walsh had already been booked and he was marched as Fitzgerald came up to take the penalty.

Fitzgerald struck it well but it was high and was stopped by Noel Hickey.

'The feeling I felt inside was so bad,' said Fitzgerald. 'I wanted to do everything so right for him *(Toomey)* and for Clare.'

Clare needed a goal but they were coming more into the game and were generating more scoring chances. McGarry had previously called Cody to bring a man back down the field but before he took a puckout on forty eight minutes he marched out past the 20-metre line and began organising the defence.

'With two on two in the full-forward line, Clare were coming at us in waves. I don't think the lads were fully tuned in to what was happening. Three or four times, *(Peter)* Barry's man had got inside him and he never copped it. Another time there was three Claremen in front of me and if a ball had been hit in, it was a goal. We were losing our men big-time. I was shouting out at Peter and he couldn't hear me. I was shouting at *(Noel)* Hickey to shout out to him. Whatever way the breeze was blowing, he couldn't hear me. It was only when there was a break in the play that I got the word out to them.'

The chances were still opening up and on fifty three minutes, Tony Griffin got inside Noel Hickey. The full-back fouled Griffin but the ref waved on the play and the forward shot hard from fourteen metres. McGarry got his hurley to turn the ball out for a 65.

'I actually looked at the ref because I thought he was after blowing for a free,' said McGarry.' It was stupid. I thought I heard the whistle and I looked at the ref and then I looked at Griffin again as he was taking the shot. I just got the hurley to it but I was lucky I had my angles covered.'

McMahon pointed the 65 to reduce the deficit to three points and within ninety seconds, Clare had wiped it out. Jamesie O'Connor floated an inch-perfect pass into Griffin, who got inside Hickey and steered the ball past McGarry. He appeared to have taken too many steps but the full-back had hauled Griffin down and the referee Ger Harrington had already blown for a penalty. Gilligan stood over it and hammered it straight and low. McGarry got down but the ball went in past him and he held his head to the ground for a second. The game was deadlocked.

Meanwhile at that stage, the Cork squad had gathered in Heuston Station to get the 5pm train back home. The TV was on and the players were watching Clare pin Kilkenny back on the ropes. Seán Óg Ó hAilpín looked at Donal Óg Cusack.

'It has to be Kilkenny,' said Ó hAilpín. 'We want Kilkenny down the line.'

Diarmuid McMahon won McGarry's puckout and he soloed into the heart of the Kilkenny defence before landing the ball into Griffin's path. The forward turned Hickey again and offloaded a pass over JJ Delaney's head and into Tony Carmody's line of fire. The ball hopped up perfectly eleven metres from goal and Carmody met it sweetly. McGarry had no right to get near it but he stood big and the ball hit him on the forehead. A couple of inches lower and he could have lost an eye. It cannoned up in the air and Griffin doubled on the ball. It flew off the post and Hickey got a flick out on it.

'It hit me on the forehead and I knew nothing about it,' said McGarry. 'Not a thing. I was so focussed I never even felt it. I saw it coming but it was coming so fast I didn't see it.'

McGarry was single-handedly keeping Kilkenny in the match but the sides continued to trade punches and were still level with a minute remaining. David Hoey put Jamesie O'Connor in the clear with a through ball but McGarry came out and pushed it away to Seán Dowling. Ken Coogan picked up Dowling's clearance and drove it into Shefflin at full-forward. He caught it cleanly and was dragged down by Frank Lohan. Penalty.

Shefflin judiciously took the point and the game looked over for Clare. Kilkenny won the puckout but Paddy Mullally was blocked down by Jamesie O'Connor and the ball went wide to Carmody. He slipped the ball back to Gilligan, who in turn fed it inside to O'Connor. The forward got one split chance. Bang. He nailed it. Draw match.

Players were swapping jerseys when suddenly the PA crackled and it was announced that there would be twenty minutes of extra-time. Fitzgerald re-swapped with Shefflin and Clare gathered in a huddle beyond midfield. Kilkenny meanwhile were regrouping at the other side of midfield, twenty five metres in from the sideline of the Hogan Stand.

Brian Cody was frantically trying to find out if Tommy Walsh could come back on for extra-time but while he was waiting for confirmation, he gathered his troops around him and let fly.

'He was like a lunatic,' said McGarry. 'He started drilling it into us: "They're not going to fucking beat us now and get that into your heads."' Cody was waving his fist with froth foaming from his mouth. He kept jabbing his finger in the direction of certain players and then he began furiously pointing at Martin Comerford.

'Cody said earlier in the year that more than any other player, Martin Comerford lifted DJ up the steps of the Hogan Stand last September,' said McGarry. 'Martin was captain and Cody just kept roaring: "If we've to die on this field, we're going to get that man up those steps this year."'

Over in the Clare huddle, they were convinced the game was theirs. 'They're out on their feet,' said Fitzgerald. 'We're the team finishing stronger. They don't want extra-time. We do.'

On the sidelines, GAA officials were as busy as ants trying to sort out the confusion. Then the PA came back on and declared that there would be no extra-time after all, but a replay next Saturday. Both squads completed their warm-down but Kilkenny lingered a couple of minutes longer.

'Let them *(Clare)* off the field first!' Cody roared to his players.

The match was fixed the following day for Thurles on Saturday and the Clare squad travelled back to the beach in Spanish Point in Miltown-Malbay that evening to bathe their legs in the Atlantic Ocean. The players spoke afterwards and the mood was decidedly upbeat.

'I know we have to lift the intensity but I know we're going to beat them,' said Fitzgerald. 'They couldn't beat us and I'm convinced we're going to beat them now. Kilkenny are used to having too much respect paid to them but we will be up for it again.'

After Kilkenny trained on Wednesday night, the players held a meeting and McGarry spoke.

'I told the lads that I was talking to Brian McEvoy the other day,' said McGarry. 'He met Ger Loughnane in An Poitín Stil after the game and he said Loughnane was delighted with how Clare played and he thought that Kilkenny's legs were gone after being so long on the road. I said to them "let's go out and prove a point on Saturday that we're far from finished."'

Saturday was a scorcher and the crowds were streaming into the ground from early afternoon. Clare based themselves in Inch House, just outside the Ragg, and the team was only announced a couple of hours before throw-in. Brian Lohan was starting at full-back while Clare packed their half-forward line with three defenders: John Reddan, Gerry Quinn and Frank Lohan. The pack had been shuffled but Markham was still going to operate as a sweeper.

Kilkenny were ready for it this time around. 'We had a fair idea what they were going to try but the mood was right and Kilkenny were really up for it,' said McGarry. 'We had a lot of motivating factors from the first day but it was the whole physical nature of the drawn game that was the real incentive. The experienced lads would have expected that from Clare but we were still probably bullied around the place a bit and we were determined not to be a second time.'

Tactically, Kilkenny went like for like but they sent out a team set up for attrition. Martin Comerford nominally started at right corner forward but as soon as the ball was thrown in, he moved to a zone between centre-forward and full-forward and tried to attach himself to Markham. Comerford's marker, Gerry O'Grady, followed him out and with Kilkenny's two man full-forward line of Henry Shefflin and 'Cha' Fitzpatrick playing thirty five metres from goal, the space was congested even further so that Markham didn't have the space or the time he had enjoyed on the ball six days earlier.

Penned into their own half, Clare were struggling to stay alive. Kilkenny racked up 1-3 without registering a wide and while they were still on top throughout the second-quarter, their productivity and scoring rate dropped alarmingly. Clare kept shuffling their cards and looking for a good hand. Markham went from sweeper to left-half back to centre-forward while Clare had introduced three substitutes inside the opening thirty minutes.

'Their movement was unreal up front,' said Fitzgerald. 'We were expecting certain fellas to be on certain fellas and it didn't happen. We weren't ready for that.'

Kilkenny's five first half wides doubled to ten sixteen minutes into the second half and Clare were still hanging in the game. David Forde's successful introduction as the sweeper just before the break had settled them down and the changes at half-time were working as well. Niall Gilligan and Tony Griffin began playing deeper to try and find some space while Sean McMahon picked up Comerford and Clare were better able to control the spaces in their own defence. With just thirteen minutes to go, Griffin brought the margin back to a goal.

Kilkenny had just lost Henry Shefflin with a nasty eye injury but they found an extra gear. Martin Comerford fired over two points and they squandered a couple of more good chances to put real daylight between the sides. As the clock wound down, DJ Carey won a ball and landed it straight over the bar from in front of the stand to seal the win. He ran with his arms in the air in celebration after the score.

'There's an awful lot of pressure at this level and it's hard to enjoy it but when I saw DJ, I was thinking "Maybe he's right, maybe we should enjoy it more than we do",' said McGarry.

When the final whistle blew, Fitzgerald hunched down and put his hands over his face. A difficult two weeks had just got worse. McGarry meanwhile just sprinted like a hare for the dressing room. The Kilkenny players had still to complete their warm-down but he'd had enough.

Enough for one day anyway because Kilkenny aren't going to get much of a break. Waterford are coming down the tracks in eight days' time.

HARD LESSONS

Life hasn't been too easy for Stevie Brenner in the last few weeks. He's been injured, disillusioned, worried and no matter what he does, he is haunted by the bitter memory of the goal he conceded in the Munster final. People are beginning to question him now because his mistake was the only negative floating in a sea of positivity. The vibe that's been going around since the Munster final is that if Waterford had lost the game, Brenner would have been run out of the place.

That had even begun before some supporters left the ground. 'The two De La Salle boys did their best to throw the game anyway,' some people remarked. Everyone has known since the Munster final that the other De La Salle player, John Mullane, will miss the All-Ireland semi-final due to suspension so the focus has been on Brenner ever since. He's been under the spotlight for all the wrong reasons.

The morning after the match, Brenner opened his front door and was met with scowls and howls from a group of Wexford builders constructing houses across the road. 'What happened you?' they roared.

'We won, that's what happened!' he shouted back.

That night, he went into the city with Helena to celebrate with the rest of the players and afterwards they got a taxi home.

'Were ye at the match?' the taxi driver asked the young couple.

'We were,' responded Helena with a smile.

'Jaysus, 'twas great, but what the hell was that Brenner at? What in the name of Jaysus was going through his head for that goal?'

'I don't know,' said Helena. 'But why don't you ask him?'

'Whah...?'

'He's here beside me.'

The car took a little speed wobble and the driver gathered himself.

'Ah Jaysus, you were unlucky with that auld ball.'

'Sure who cares?' said Stevie. 'We won the match.'

He knows that it's not that simple though. He knows what is being said behind his back. Although the cup was put into cold storage after the match, the majority of the players still went out a couple of more evenings that week to celebrate. Brenner didn't.

'I didn't feel that I should. I know I contributed to the win but I could have contributed to us losing as well. I didn't want to take the plaudits for that. I just wanted to put my head down and put in the effort in to prove people wrong.'

He was always going to have to do a lot of convincing. The following Sunday, De La Salle played Ballybrown from Limerick in a Munster League game in Cleaboy in Waterford city. Brenner's back was still sore from the Munster final and he just played the first half. A few youngsters from Ballybrown were playing in the pitch beside the main field and as Brenner was making his way across to the dressing room, a re-enactment of Cork's goal was played out in front of him.

One of the youngsters sent a soft, dribbling ball towards the goal and the actor on the line opened his legs and let it trickle in under him. Their small audience couldn't contain their laughter at the mock-play and Brenner just looked at them. Although they were only young fellas, it hurt.

He let it go because he had other things on his mind. He had largely kept it quiet before the Munster final about his back injury and taking Nurofen painkillers for a week afterwards didn't soften the pain. When De La Salle played Ballyduff Upper in the Waterford championship two weeks after the Munster final, Brenner still wasn't sure if he'd be able to line out. He went out onto the pitch in Walsh Park half an hour before the game to go through a stretching routine. He couldn't run properly and as soon as he pucked a ball, he knew his back wasn't up to it.

The rumour mill went into overdrive around the county afterwards. Some were saying that he didn't have the confidence to play, while more said he didn't want to risk playing poorly again in case he'd completely jeopardise his chances of playing in an All-Ireland semi-final. When Waterford resumed full training a couple of nights later, Brenner didn't even tog out. He wasn't getting any relief from his back and on the Thursday night, Justin McCarthy approached him.

'Be honest with us now,' McCarthy said to him.

'I am being honest,' Brenner said. 'I'm just very sore.'

'We'll see how it goes, get it sorted and we'll take it from there,' replied McCarthy.

Doctor Tom Higgins examined Brenner in the dressing room afterwards and put him on a high dosage of anti-inflammatory tablets; three tablets a day for seven days and then one a day for a straight week. They kicked in almost immediately and Brenner was able to resume training that weekend.

He'd missed nearly three weeks and it was always going to take him time to readjust and prosper in the crucible of training again. As well as trying to get his touch right, his handling perfect and his eye back in, he had to banish the demons from inside his head. No matter how mentally strong a player is, a public humiliation is always going to burn a hole in your confidence.

'My confidence did take a small bit of a knock. I was even struggling to control balls like the goal in the Munster final. All that mattered was we'd won the game and I kept saying to myself that I'd never make that mistake again and that there was no point in letting it get to me. I knew what some people were thinking but I was trying not to let it affect me. I was very down for a while after it. I was saying "Just my luck now." I had visions that I wasn't going to be able to play in the All-Ireland semi-final because of that one mistake. I did feel under pressure. I was even saying to Helena "Jesus, I think I could be gone for the next game." She was telling me not to be stupid.'

With the threat of exclusion hanging over him, Brenner began to feel the strain. A couple of nights later, the squad were playing a training match when Dan Shanahan came through with a ball one-on-one with Brenner. The goalkeeper held his ground and the ball hammered off his knee and rebounded out.

Almost in the next sequence of action and in an almost identical simulation of the previous incident, Shanahan broke through again and let fly. Brenner moved to one side and tried to stop the ball with his hurley. 'I'm not getting another slap of this thing,' Brenner thought to himself. 'I felt that my confidence was low enough and the last thing I needed was a couple of slaps.'

Ken McGrath interpreted the whole episode differently and he snapped.

'For God's sake, don't be moving off the goal!' roared the captain.

'I didn't fucking move!' Brenner barked back.

It was all said in the heat of the moment but it left an empty feeling in Brenner's stomach. He could feel the walls closing in around him.

'I was saying to myself "am I wasting my time here? Is my body crying out for mercy or what?" I really felt that there was a chance that I mightn't make it. Jesus, it's depressing. Nightmare stuff.'

Brenner didn't hang around too long after training and all kinds of negative thoughts floated in his head on the way home. Then at 11pm, the phone rang. It was Andy Maloney.

'Jesus, are you alright? You seemed a bit down at training,' said Maloney.

'I'm grand, Andy,' said Brenner.

'Don't worry about what happened in the Munster final, you know you're good enough,' Maloney reassured him. 'Go up training and show them that your hunger is back and you want to be in there.'

It was just the reassurance Brenner needed. Someone to believe in him and to snap him out of his well of self-pity. The next night at training, Justin McCarthy took him aside and peppered him with sliotars for half an hour. He was wrecked afterwards but he felt good, happy that his form and confidence were returning at the right time.

'I was flying around the place. I felt a lot better. I just said that it was time to get back on this horse now and get back into it.'

That weekend, the squad travelled up to Antrim for a training spin. They left Waterford at 10.30am on Friday morning and didn't arrive in Ballycastle in North Antrim until 11pm. It was a hellish journey and

Brenner's back had tightened up from being static for so long. When the majority of the squad went sightseeing and browsing around the following day, Brenner sat it out.

He stayed watching the British Open all morning and early afternoon in his hotel room in Ballycastle. The event itself was taking place just thirteen miles across the Irish Sea on the Ayrshire coast at the Royal Troon Golf and he was glued to it. But in between, he was stretching and trying to free up his back because Waterford were playing Antrim in a challenge game that evening in Loughgeil.

Waterford carried an extended squad and had the numbers to make up a second team to play against a selection of Antrim panellists combined with members of their Intermediate side. Waterford had brought up a third goalkeeper as well, Clinton Hennessy, from Ardmore.

Beforehand, Justin McCarthy went to Brenner and told him that they didn't want to risk him in the senior match with his back and that they were going to play him in the first match. Brenner played most of that match while Ian O'Regan lined out for the seniors. On the journey back home the following day, Brenner knew for real that the heat was coming around the corner faster than he'd anticipated.

He just put his head down and kept working hard. He didn't go on a specific diet but he cut out bread and junk food and starting loading water into himself. He wanted more of an edge and he lost half a stone in weight in the space of two weeks. Paul Flynn lost over a half stone before the Munster final and Brenner had seen the benefits.

Two weeks before the All-Ireland semi-final, the squad travelled to Croke Park to watch the All-Ireland quarter-finals and they had a training session on the field afterwards. Justin McCarthy told Brenner in the middle of the session to practise puckouts and to land most of them in the training game down on top of Dan Shanahan.

'That's a good sign anyway,' he said to himself.

Brenner felt good in the training match and was happy that his hurling was getting sharper and his injury was clearing up. When he switched on his phone afterwards however, he got a phone call immediately from

Helena. She was crying and was distressed with pain. He told her that he would be home as soon as he could and when he got back home at 11.30pm, Helena's father was asleep on the couch and she was upstairs.

She couldn't sleep with it on Sunday night and Stevie brought her into Ardkeen hospital first thing on Monday morning. She underwent an operation on Tuesday.

The following evening, Waterford took on Wexford in a challenge game in Wexford Park and Brenner was selected to play the first two twenty-minute quarters of the match. He played well and although Ian O'Regan made a couple of good stops, Brenner was confident as he headed back in to see Helena afterwards that he had cemented his position on the team.

After her operation though, Helena picked up pneumonia and an infection, which meant she wasn't going to be released for at least another week. When Waterford trained on Friday night, Brenner showed up for just half an hour and then went back out to Ardkeen to see his wife. His priority was her welfare and Helena knew her husband had a lot on his mind. She told him to stay positive and to think of the All-Ireland semi-final. When he went back home that night, his mind was buzzing with anticipation again.

'There is a lot of weight on my shoulders since the Munster final but I thrive on the extra bit of pressure,' said Brenner. 'I can't wait to run out on the field and get into it to prove a point. I know that there's going to be a lot more focus on me this time around but I don't mind that. The Waterford supporters are after coming on an awful lot anyway. They can sense the success there now and they know that the team are doing their best and that we're all putting in a massive effort. Whereas before, there could be one or two championship games and we'd be gone and they'd be saying that we were only a shower of ghoulers that were down town drinking and doing this and that. Now they know. They don't see us anywhere.

'The All-Ireland semi-final is a massive game for us but to be honest, the whole year is going to be a failure if we don't win the All-Ireland. There are fellas like myself that are coming to the end of our careers.

There aren't going to be too many more chances for me to play in an All-Ireland semi-final and to get to an All-Ireland final.'

The following Tuesday night before the match, Justin McCarthy picked an A and B team for a training match. When Brenner heard Ian O'Regan's name called out first on the A list, his heart sank on the spot.

'I'm gone,' Brenner said to himself.

He dejectedly strolled up to the top goals. He was playing OK in the training game but he was facing Waterford's starting six forwards and before he knew it six goals had gone past him. He lost the rag with himself. He fired his hurley into the net after a couple of the goals and his temper was at fever pitch. After training, he ran straight into the showers, didn't talk to anyone and was gone before any of the other players knew where he was. He went straight out to Ardkeen to see Helena.

'I think I'm gone,' he told his wife.

'Don't be stupid, the team hasn't been picked yet,' she said.

He hardly said a word because a thousand thoughts were circling in his head. Even though his wife was still very uncomfortable with pain, Brenner's mood was turning sourer by the minute

'Look,' Helena said, 'if you're going to be like this, go home. You don't know yet and things could be worse. You could be inside here.'

He went off for a long walk down the hospital corridors. He got a drink from a vending machine before heading back to his wife. There wasn't another word about hurling spoken until he left the hospital after 12am. When he got into bed, Brenner couldn't switch off. He was staring at the ceiling until after 2am so he got up and took a sleeping tablet to knock himself out. He knew what was coming and he was bracing himself for it.

'Wednesday was a nightmare,' he said. 'I was just waiting for bad news.'

Things didn't get any better on Thursday. He woke up in the morning with a stiff back and before training that evening, he bought more anti-inflammatory tablets. He couldn't get the ones that Dr Higgins had prescribed so he picked up the highest dosage possible over the counter. He popped two of them and headed down to Walsh Park feeling like a man awaiting a death sentence.

When he arrived into the dressing room, there were drug-testers from the Sports Council present to take urine samples from four players ahead of Sunday's game. When Brenner was one of the players selected for a drug test, conspiracy theories started formulating in his head. He didn't know if the anti-inflammatory tablets he'd just taken contained any traces of a banned substance on the Sport's Council's Anti-Doping list.

'I just said to myself "What the hell is going on here, is someone out to get me?" I knew I wasn't going to fail the test but Jesus Christ I wasn't fully sure either.'

During training, James Murray and Andy Maloney asked Brenner twice if McCarthy had said anything to him but the goalkeeper hadn't given him a chance. Anytime the manager came near him, Brenner dodged him. He didn't want to hear what he feared was coming. When the session ended, all the players went into one of the dressing rooms to pick up their new gear for Sunday and when Brenner walked out the door, he passed McCarthy. The manager called him back.

'I've bad news for you Stevie,' he said.

'I know,' Brenner responded.

'You can't know, nobody knows,' said the manager.

'Look Justin, I just know. I could feel it coming.'

'But you'll be behind us.'

'Jesus, of course I'm behind us, I'm 100% behind this team.'

He put on a brave face and walked away but it felt like his insides had been ripped apart.

'It was hard. I was absolutely devastated.'

The Waterford squad was scheduled to fly to Dublin at 10.30am on Sunday but torrential rain led to the decision to cancel all flights out of Waterford airport that morning. Management was only informed just before 8am and a mad scramble ensued to ensure they were on board the 10am Dublin train.

An extra carriage was added onto the main train. The other carriages were full of Waterford supporters and when the train stopped in Thomastown, a crew of Kilkenny fans joined them. Some of them strolled through the carriage where the Waterford players were based and the wisecracks were rebounding off the walls.

'We're in the wrong carriage,' one supporter remarked.

'Yeah,' replied Brenner, 'the back door is down that way.'

When they arrived in Connolly Station, a police escort ferried them out to the Holiday Inn near the airport and they had their pre-match meal a little later than planned. Their schedule was more condensed than they'd expected and the team bus pulled into Croke Park just before 3pm.

Ken McGrath led Waterford out onto the field just after 3.13pm and his clubmate Ian O'Regan was right behind him. Brenner was one of the first substitutes out. He was carrying O'Regan's and the full-back line's hurleys and he jogged up to the 20-metre line at the Canal End goal and dropped the sticks on the turf. Then he made his way over for the team photo. He edged his way into the back-row and extended both of his arms around Tony Browne and Shane O'Sullivan.

Brenner zipped back on his tracksuit top and went back down to the Canal End goal. Three other substitutes were taking shots at O'Regan and he went in behind the goal to gather loose sliotars. He took a few shots and after a minute, he walked up to the young goalkeeper.

'Keep the full-back line on their toes and make sure Ken isn't wandering away from centre-back,' he told him. 'Keep roaring and shouting at them and make sure they can hear you.'

Meanwhile at the other end of the pitch, James McGarry and Noel Skehan were surveying the pitch, the bounce of the ball and discussing the greasy wet conditions.

'It's going to be a different type of game for you today,' Skehan said to McGarry. 'You're not going to get too many shots. It will be more breaking balls and you might have to be playing off your line a bit.'

When the teams joined the parade, Brenner carried all the hurleys in from the 20-metre line and placed them meticulously into the back of the goal. He lined O'Regan's hurleys out in a line and put the full-back line's sticks just beside them, making sure the names were visible on each one. Brenner then packed his bag with sliotars and made sure that O'Regan's towel wasn't getting wet from the rain.

As the teams were marching in front of the goalmouth, Brenner hunched down on the endline beside one of the umpires, looking out like a sentinel with his arms folded. Then like a shot, he bolted for the sideline. He'd forgotten to put a waterbottle in O'Regan's bag.

By the time he was back on the pitch again, the Waterford players were just about to gather into a huddle before the national anthem finished. Brenner handed the waterbottle to Ken McGrath, Paul Flynn and then Dan Shanahan. He was in the middle of them all but when McGrath convened the huddle and they all gathered around him, Brenner just walked a few yards away. And stood. Alone.

As O'Regan made his way down to take his place, Brenner handed him the water-bottle and patted him on the back.

'Best of luck,' he said to the young keeper. 'You'll be back here for the final in five weeks.'

Then he ran up to take his place in the stand.

Kilkenny went for the jugular early. They knew O'Regan was inexperienced and untested at this level and the wet conditions were making it a nightmare for keepers. After just four minutes Henry Shefflin breached the Waterford rearguard and was coming in near the endline. O'Regan came out but he left his near post slightly exposed and Shefflin drove the sliotar in past him.

Kilkenny adapted better to the conditions and their defence was strangling Waterford's attack. On twenty four minutes, Eddie Brennan got loose fourteen metres from goal and fired a rocket goalwards. O'Regan blocked it but Declan Prendergast slipped when he'd a chance to clear and Brennan whipped the loose ball to the net.

Goals in such difficult conditions were always going to surpass their three-point value and Kilkenny cashed in again just before the break when John Hoyne lofted a ball goalwards from near the sideline. O'Regan went to claim it but James Murray momentarily lost his footing and Shefflin got in ahead of the keeper and defender and knocked the ball to the net. Kilkenny led by 3-6 to 0-11 at the break.

Brenner went down to the Canal End goal and gathered up all the hurleys in the goalmouth. He carried them down to the Hill 16 goal and after he'd laid them out, he plucked a ball from O'Regan's bag and started hammering it off the wall in front of the Hill. He looked up the pitch on his way back to the dugout and just silently shook his head. In such difficult conditions, his physical presence had been missed.

Skehan's prophecy to McGarry before the game, meanwhile, had come through. Kilkenny enjoyed 57% possession and McGarry hadn't touched the ball in the first half. The keeper knew if they could keep a clean sheet, the game was Kilkenny's.

'If we scrub out their main men, where are they going to get the scores from?' McGarry asked his team-mates in the dressing room.

He was right because Paul Flynn was the only Waterford forward causing any damage. Kilkenny stretched their lead to six points by the forty seventh minute and while Waterford pulled it back to three, they failed to capitalise during a critical seven-minute scoreless period midway through the half. Kilkenny's scoring rate had dropped but Waterford couldn't penetrate their defence to get the goal they needed to save the game. Finally with three minutes remaining, a chance fell to Paul O'Brien. One chance.

He got inside the Kilkenny full-back line but he slipped at the critical moment and JJ Delaney got the flick and Tommy Walsh drove the sliotar down the field. Waterford kept coming back and with a minute to go, McGarry scrambled a ball away from Jack Kennedy in the square by just letting fly on it.

'I never felt they were going to score a goal,' said McGarry. 'Even with all their pressure. The time your man O'Brien missed the ball I looked up at the referee because he did handle it on the ground. It was that split second and then I couldn't see it because there was a group of players coming in but JJ got the flick. I should have been concentrating on the ball.'

When the referee finally blew the whistle, McGarry sank to his knees and looked up to the heavens. He shook his fist out at Michael Kavanagh and the corner-back reciprocated the same gesture. They were there. At last.

Brenner meanwhile ambled out onto the pitch to console some of his team-mates and as he was heading for the dressing room, he walked over to Justin McCarthy and shook his hand.

'You played a big part in getting us here,' McCarthy said to him.

He togged in quickly and before the players went upstairs for a drink, he rang his wife.

'I was devastated but all I really wanted to hear was that Helena was OK.'

The squad got back to Waterford at 9pm and Brenner just picked up his car and drove straight out to Ardkeen and stayed there until after midnight.

Brenner had taken the Monday off after the game to go on the beer but he couldn't face the post-mortem. He went out to the hospital again at 10.30am and spent the whole day with his wife. They went for a walk and discussed the game and both agreed that matters could be a lot worse. And then Stevie casually brought up retirement.

'Cop yourself on, will you?' Helena said to her husband. 'Go back there next year and prove a point.'

It was all he needed to hear.

'I wanted to go back straightaway then,' he said. 'I want to go back and prove a point but I don't know really if I will be proving a point. I don't know if I was dropped because Helena was in hospital or because of the Munster final, I don't know. I'll probably never know.

'I was in and out of Ardkeen so often that a lot of people thought there was all sorts wrong with me. My brother-in-law heard in a garage in Kildare before the game that I was after having a nervous breakdown. Then they were talking about Helena, saying that she had this sickness and that illness. Someone sympathised with me over it. That's fairly severe shit to have to take.'

Success is like anything worthwhile. It has a price. Once a goalkeeper agrees upon the price he and his family have to pay for success, it enables him to ignore the minor hurts and risks of playing on the edge at the highest level. But sometimes that price can be too high.

Hurling is a lot like life in that it teaches that work, sacrifice, competitive drive and ambition is what you have to pay to achieve any goal that is worthwhile. But it can also teach you harsher lessons. That you are public property and people can say what they want about you and your family, in a way that is completely outside of your control. Brenner has really learned those lessons over the last six weeks but absorbing the most important one will decide his future. It's not whether you get knocked down. It's whether you get up again.

He has to be honest with himself as well. Really honest. When he was dropped earlier in the year, he would have done anything to get his place back. When he did get back, he took his foot off the gas. Being an inter-county goalkeeper at the highest level is not about doing things right 95% of the time; it's about doing things right all the time. Certain things were out of his control but Brenner is honest enough to realise you always have be 100% prepared and focussed. He has accepted that reality the hard way.

'Getting dropped was devastating but I have to be honest with myself as well. I know I let myself down this year by easing back and I know exactly when it happened. After the Clare game, cockiness crept into me. After we beat Clare so much, I thought we were all invincible. You think you can do nothing wrong and your normal lifestyle comes back into it and you start eating things you shouldn't and you don't push yourself as hard as you should in training.

'I don't know though. Helena started getting sick around that time and maybe that was subconsciously on my mind. Maybe I was a different person at training. The way I got nervous before the Tipperary game wasn't normal and maybe that was the start of it. But I was playing a lot better earlier in the year and it's amazing how well you play when you're under pressure and you think you're going to be dropped.

'I had to go through a lot of shit both on and off the field but I think I've learned a lot from it. I'm pissed off and I could pack it all in now but I don't want to go out like this. I've made my mind up that I'm going back there next year and a lot of fuel has been added to my fire. I want to try and take it on another level. But I'm going back because it would be hard to imagine my life without hurling for Waterford.'

The harder you try and the more you want something, the harder it is to surrender. No matter what is fired at you.

THE GREATEST CRAIC
OF ALL TIME

On the week of the All-Ireland semi-final, Donal Óg Cusack followed his normal ritual of taking the Wednesday and Thursday off work to train and rest before a big championship match. On Wednesday though, Cusack got up out of his bed at 5.30am. Cloyne were training at 6am and it was basically a sweat session of punishment. Some of the fitter players who didn't need the slog stayed in the hall lifting weights but the crew who needed the work had to grind their teeth through a three-mile run. Especially with Cusack there: he was acting as the pacemaker and they all completed the route in twenty minutes and seventeen seconds.

Cusack had his day mapped out beforehand in his diary. After training he went back to bed until 11am before driving up to a summer camp in Grenagh that Tom Kenny was working at. He spent an hour and a half there with the kids before heading back down to Cloyne and jumping back into bed to store up on his sleep. He was up again at 5pm and on the road to Cork shortly afterwards for county training at 7pm.

Cork had trained the previous night and Cunningham had put him through a wringer of a session. The last thing Cusack wanted now was to appear tired because Cunningham would cop it. For the last couple of months, Donal O'Grady and the former keeper were onto Cusack about applying the brakes on the extra training, particularly the morning gym sessions. Even though Cusack was only running and stretching in the gym coming up to big matches, Cunningham was worried that he was burning too much fuel and that he'd eventually run out of gas.

Finally, a couple of weeks back, Cunningham lost it with Cusack. He was out on his feet one night at training before the Antrim game and

Cunningham did some investigative work. He found out that Cusack had been training with Cloyne that morning and he wasn't happy about it. He prescribed a high dosage of rest coming up to that match and Cunningham felt he was a different keeper during that game. Cusack had agreed to put a halt to the daybreak sessions and that's why he doesn't want anyone to know about this morning.

'If Grady knew about it he'd go off his game,' said Cusack. 'Cunningham would do the same and they'd be dead right. I know it wasn't the right thing to do but anyway, I did it.'

At training tonight, the squad primarily went through their organisation for puckouts, particularly short ones. They've had their signals worked out for months now but they were just fine-tuning them. By the time the session was over, they were content that everyone would be fully tuned into the goalkeeper's frequency on Sunday.

Cusack took Thursday off from work as well. He got up at 11am, did his stretching routine, had some food and then went to a dental appointment. That evening he took the training session with Cloyne. The club trained again the following morning at 6am and although Cusack didn't train, he was there. That evening, he was back in Cork again for county training.

After he'd finished his dinner in the canteen in Páirc Uí Rinn, Donal O'Grady showed Cusack clips of the Wexford forwards from the Leinster final on his laptop. He studied their technique and how they had a tendency to drive the ball across the goalkeeper's body. Then they spoke more about puckouts before they were all given their arrangements for the following day.

The Cork team left Kent Station at 1.30pm on Saturday. After they were settled in at the Burlington Hotel, they had mass at 5.30pm before sitting down to their evening meal. Afterwards Cusack took off on a walk with Tom Kenny, Sean Óg Ó hAilpín and the masseur Jim McEvoy. They took their hurleys with them, headed out towards Ballsbridge and happened upon Raglan Road. Cusack stopped a passing woman and asked her if that was the road that Luke Kelly sang about. She told him it was before telling the group another story about Patrick Kavanagh. Before they left, she asked them if they'd win tomorrow. She said she hoped they would because she was a Corkwoman; she was a sister of Denis Walsh who had won an All-Ireland with Cork in 1990.

The four strolled into Herbert Park and as they neared the lake, they spotted two men walking towards them. They noticed that the younger man of the two had large scars on the side of his head and the two stopped up and asked the players about their chances against Wexford. They began chatting and the older man introduced his son who was recovering from a brain tumour operation he'd had the previous week.

They ambled down the path and veered right towards the huge oak trees and began pucking around for thirty minutes. It wasn't a leisurely few pucks with the four lads standing and striking. Not with Ó hAilpín around. His attitude insists that everything is done at pace and with perfection. He was in good company because Tom Kenny is one of Ó hAilpín's disciples.

When they got back to the hotel, Ó hAilpín put on an Australian Rules Football video and then Cusack went off up to bed. He was rooming with Wayne Sherlock and Cusack went through his normal routine of putting new grips on all of his hurleys. Although he'd only used his fifth-choice hurley once that week, he still changed the grip on it. Just for peace of mind's sake. Before he went to bed, he spoke with Sherlock of the collective spirit and will in the camp and the importance of winning the next day.

'There's an aggression and a determination that's after being taken onto a new level now,' he said. 'Maybe we needed that *(Munster final)* defeat to remember the bad days again because that feeling afterwards was heartbreak. It's total and absolute that we have to win. One game and we're back to where we want to be. Then it will be like as if we closed our eyes, then opened them and said "right, let's go again."'

And then it was time to close his eyes and prepare for the following day's battle.

At around 2.45pm on Sunday, Cusack went to selector Seanie O'Leary in the Cork dressing room. He told O'Leary that he wanted to go out on the pitch beforehand to try out the boots he was wearing. He had worn boots with steel blades against Antrim but he found them hard on his feet and had decided to change to rubber blades for the semi-final. Only he wasn't 100% sure how the boots would feel on the Croke Park sod.

O'Leary gave him the green light so Cusack, Paul Morrissey and Martin Coleman put on their training tops and spent the last five minutes of the minor match stretching inside the line in front of the Hogan Stand. As the minor match edged closer to its conclusion, they made their way up along the endline. The second the minor match was over, the three tore onto the field.

Mark Herlihy, the Galway minor keeper, was celebrating his side's win over Cork with his full-back line and by the time he went back into the goalmouth to retrieve his hurleys, Cusack was shuffling along the line in sharp footwork bursts. He stopped momentarily and shook hands with Herlihy and when the young keeper had gathered his sticks, Coleman and Morrissey began launching high balls in on top of him.

The boots felt fine and his handling felt good but Cusack didn't want to leave anything to chance. After five minutes the three made their way up through the centre of the pitch and Cusack ran towards the Canal End to check the footing in the goalmouth.

At 3.04pm, Cusack jogged back into the dressing room and the team emerged out onto the field at 3.09pm. The roar that greeted them was loud but nothing as thunderous as that which met Wexford when they ran onto the field at 3.11pm. Damien Fitzhenry was the third-last man out and after the team photograph, he ambled down to the Hill 16 goal and rolled a sliotar into his hand. As he casually began warming up with the subkeeper Matty White, he looked completely detached from the tension that was simmering on the pitch. When his name was announced over the public address as the goalkeeper on the Wexford team, the decibel levels nearly went through the roof. Fitzhenry smiled.

'I get a great oul laugh out of that,' he said.

As well as being their most experienced player, Fitzhenry is the

Wexford supporters' favourite. For the first couple of minutes on the field, he will often hear his name carrying in the breeze from the shouts around the ground. But after two minutes the barriers go up and the noise bleeds into a drone. He's trained that into his mind over the years and if he hears anything after the two-minute cut-off point, he knows he's not tuned in.

He'll allow himself a little escape valve in the parade, where he'll look around and drink in the atmosphere. The serious stuff will begin again as the match is about to start but his mind is always clear, he's never bedevilled by doubts and his body is certainly never wracked with tension. When he says he's easygoing and he takes it all in his stride, it's easy to believe it by his body language on the pitch.

He has a healthy perspective on life and hurling anyway. The previous week Fitzhenry travelled to Adamstown to visit eleven-year-old Brendan Furlong, whose father and brother were killed in a car accident when travelling to the Wexford/Derry All-Ireland football qualifier in July. Brendan was in the same car and was lucky to be alive. His whole back was in a cast but he had his Wexford jersey on over it. One of his hands was also in a cast but a big smile came to his face when Fitzhenry put a hurley and sliotar into his other hand. Fitzhenry had in some small way helped bring some light into the darkness but Brendan Furlong had also discreetly reinforced the goalkeeper's whole belief system about hurling.

'That brought it all home to me and why would you be nervous? At the end of the day, you're going out to play in a game of hurling, that you're meant to go out and enjoy. If you're nerved up to the last, you won't enjoy it. I try to go into every game chilled out and just head out and hurl. There's enough lads going up there wasting their own energy on nerves. It kills some lads but this is the greatest craic of all time.

'People ask me do I enjoy it and by Jaysus, for sure I enjoy it. Dead right I do. Listen, in five years time where will I be? There's no point saying that you don't put things on the back burner for the length of time that you're hurling inter-county. You do and why put everything on the back-burner for twelve years and not enjoy it? Sure that would be like cutting off your nose to spite your face. And I'm being 100% honest with you there.'

He's not superstitious but he has two rituals before big games. Like Cusack, he always puts new grips on his hurleys. Unlike Cusack, he doesn't shave for three days beforehand. On match days he never has George Michael designer stubble, just a raggedy look that he's content with. When the match is over, he shaves himself immediately in the dressing room.

'I've no idea why I do it. I just do. It's a strange one now. I wouldn't be happy now going in if I did shave. And if I did, everyone would be on to me. "You're after shaving." Then that would make you worse.'

Unlike the damp conditions for the previous week's semi-final, the day was warm and the pitch was a kiln of tension and heat. The ground was crackling but when the parade began, Fitzhenry looked like he was walking down the street in Enniscorthy. The former Cork trainer Teddy Owens told Cusack years ago to never look at the crowd during the parade and he never does. Fitzhenry wouldn't be able to translate that language.

'I'd always take an odd look up in the stand to see if I can spot somebody I might know,' he said. 'I wouldn't be glued to the crowd but I'd take a good look around now all the same.'

Fitzhenry though, always backs up his laid-back approach with his goalkeeping and he was mentally bracing himself for a mammoth battle. Wexford knew what to expect from Cork and they had decided to adopt a mobile marking system instead of a zonal defensive system to deal with Cork's possession game. The latter was probably a better strategy given Cork's pace but Wexford decided that if a Cork player took off on a solo-run, it was up to his marker to chase him and try and tip the ball away if possible. Fitzhenry re-echoed the gameplan and what was at stake but he also laid down the law.

'We have to stop the runners and keep one man on one man,' he said to his team-mates before the game. 'Lads ye know what ye have to do, individually and collectively. And I don't want to be hearing it on

Monday in Enniscorthy, saying we should have done this or we should have done that. We fucking do it now.'

The match began at a ferocious intensity and all the early indications were that it was going to be a repeat of the previous year's classic drawn All-Ireland semi-final. Nine minutes in, the game was still tied at 0-2 each and Fitzhenry had a similar vision from last season.

'I said to myself this is going to be an absolute humdinger. The ball was just flying up and down the field.'

A minute later though, Timmy McCarthy ran onto a crossfield pass right in front of the goal inside the 20-metre line. When he secured possession, he was right through but Fitzhenry dashed off his line and spread himself. He got his body in the way and the ball cannoned over the bar. A minute later, the keeper had to be alert to tip a forceful shot from Ben O'Connor over the bar.

Gradually, the game was starting to drift in Cork's favour. Their play was more controlled, their forwards were sharper to the breaking ball and the red lights were beginning to flash for Wexford. The cracks that appeared in the Leinster final resurfaced except Cork were coming with a bigger wrecking ball than Offaly came with.

Cork kept hammering away with points and then on the twenty ninth minute Tom Kenny pushed the lever and blew a huge hole through Wexford's foundations. Kenny ran all the way from midfield and an off-the-ball run from Niall McCarthy completely opened up the centre. Kenny kept going, Fitzhenry had him in his sights but just as he was about to let fly, Doc O'Connor came across the goalkeeper's line of vision on the 20-metre line. O'Connor was hoping to try and take another couple of steps forward to get a block in but he completely unsighted his goalkeeper. Fitzhenry never saw the ball and he just felt it clipping the sleeve of his jersey at the elbow on the way past him.

'I only saw it when I was picking it out of the net. If I'd been another half-step to my left it would have hit me on the arm. But it would have broken my arm. When the goal went in though, I just said to myself "this is going to be a total onslaught."'

In the twenty five minutes before the break, Cork outscored their opponents by 1-11 to 0-2. This game was over.

'When we went in at half-time, I knew we'd be doing well to come out of the game half-respectful,' said Fitzhenry. 'Lads were shell-shocked, wondering what in the name of Jaysus had happened. I said "we're winning no puckouts, we're winning no breaking ball, what's the story? We can blame whoever the hell we like but we only have ourselves to blame." I was just trying to get across to them how bad the display was. But what do you do?'

Although they had played near perfect hurling, the Cork dressing room wasn't exactly brimming with satisfaction. Donal O'Grady certainly wasn't handing out plaudits because he hadn't witnessed total perfection.

'Donal cut loose at half-time,' said Cusack. 'He told us we were a shame with the way we were after playing in the last ten minutes. A bit of messing had gone on with the ball and we probably weren't as professional as we should have been. I just detached myself from it. I know it probably annoys him because I'd be very vocal at training and I'd be one of the two fellas that always speak. But the day of a match I wouldn't even get involved in huddles or anything. When he's speaking I'd nearly be in the toilet.

'When he was roaring at us I was saying to myself "this is only an act now to make sure we don't back off." Even though you'd know it, it would still hit you somewhere and you'd drive on. But in goals, even if you're twenty five points up, if you make one mistake, you'll be thinking about that going down in the train.'

Cork put their foot on the gas again at the start of the second half. Wexford couldn't make any inroads and Cusack's puckouts were helping twist the screw. The margin was up to seventeen points by the forty seventh minute but Cork kept going for the kill. Diarmuid O'Sullivan made his way up the field and floated a delivery goalwards that Joe Deane got his stick to. Fitzhenry reacted sharply to touch it away but he was under pressure to clear it and he overflicked the pass away to

Malachy Travers. The ball made its way back to Deane and he drove it over the bar.

From the puckout, Wexford had a chance to shave three points off the deficit when Mitch Jordan pulled on a cross from eight metres. Cusack got down low with his body and the ball ricocheted off him for a '65. It was a smart stop. Just a minute later Deane careered through the centre and let fly from the 20-metre line. Fitzhenry dived to his right to parry the shot and just as Brian Corcoran was about to pounce on it, the keeper flicked it out for a '65. Corcoran nearly decapitated him with the swing but when the keeper got to his feet, Corcoran patted him on the back of the head.

Cork relaxed and Wexford tried to salvage some pride. They hit six points in eleven minutes but the mass exodus from the ground had long begun before the game reached its conclusion. Just as the ref was about to blow the final whistle, Fitzhenry had the ball in his hand and he just tapped it out the field and turned to gather his sticks. He shook hands with a couple of the Cork forwards before he made straight for Cusack.

Cusack doesn't believe in swapping jerseys after games. Firstly because he doesn't like giving away Cork jerseys and secondly because he has a list of people looking for them. But when Fitzhenry approached, Cusack whipped the shirt off his back before words had even been exchanged.

'Fair play to you Damien,' he said. 'You played well as usual.'

'Good man Donal,' responded Fitzhenry, 'you played well yourself.'

Cusack and Cork were back to where they wanted to be but it was Fitzhenry's fourth All-Ireland semi-final defeat in eight seasons. When he looked at it in cold blood afterwards, he thought about the motivational speech the Irish rugby player, Gordon Darcy had given Wexford two weeks earlier. Darcy had told them about how Ireland had fully believed in their ability to beat England in the Six Nations Championship in February and that the parallels were the same now.

Fitzhenry believed beforehand that they could pull it off but when he cast his eyes back on their application, he wasn't sure if the environment had been totally conducive to foster that belief. After the Leinster final, the squad took a two and a half week break to allow the players to go back to their clubs for the domestic championships.

The goalkeeper had no great problem with that set-up but he felt that there should have been some form of continuity with county training. When they returned, they had lost some of their momentum and bloodymindedness and Fitzhenry picked up on it. Just a few weeks before, he and the other members of the players' committee called a meeting with the management to try and address the problem.

'I honestly thought myself that the boys *(management)* were coming to training and they were happy with their lot after the Leinster final,' said Fitzhenry. 'I think everybody, including players, took a step back and thought it was great, when that was the time to be pushing on. We tried to get it across to management that if the team were happy with their lot, well and good and we'd jack it in to fuck and wouldn't bother training. But I thought they were coming in laughing and joking and they were happy. For a shit start to the year, we were Leinster champions. But Jaysus, we wanted more than that.'

Jerry O'Connor was man-of-the-match after scoring six points from play but Fitzhenry had distinguished himself once more on the big stage. He has been the best goalkeeper in the country this season and Wexford's eighteen point humiliation would have been a lot worse only for his four excellent saves. Even the Cork crowd acknowledged that.

Immediately after the match, an RTE reporter and a cameraman positioned themselves outside the ground to canvas opinion from the crowds spilling from the stadium. The images were shown on *The Sunday Game* that evening.

'The best man on the pitch was Damien Fitzhenry,' said one Cork supporter. 'And if we had him for the last few years, we'd have won a lot more than we have.'

Two clean sheets in-a-row, a class save and an exhibition of pinpoint distribution from Cusack? Loyalty, respect and understanding from some Cork supporters? It's easy to see who are the guys Cusack would die for. And who are the people he doesn't give a damn about.

THE SILENT WARRIOR

On a lovely balmy day a couple of weeks before the All-Ireland final, James McGarry was staring out over the white fence at the bottom of St James' Park on the outskirts of Kilkenny City. Two young hurlers were up at the other end of the field practising their shooting but McGarry's eyes were trained on the sloping piece of ground along the right side of the vast park. The strip along by the stone wall and the beat-up sheds, with the undulating contours and the railing fences halfway up the deceptive sloping field.

The glitz and glamour of the All-Ireland final is looming on the horizon but McGarry shakes his head when he thinks back to the starting point on the road the previous winter. It began here in the torture chamber during the dark evenings. St James' Park was their visit to purgatory in January after returning home from their lavish team holiday.

Kilkenny were never slaves to the culture of penal suffering on the training field but after Limerick, Clare and Wexford raised the bar in the 1990s, they were challenged to change or be eaten alive. Their trainer Mick O'Flynn didn't panic and he blended the team's training over the years with his own fitness templates. The players were never flogged over the winter but a certain amount of penance and hardship still had to be endured to sustain their fitness base.

St James' Park is bleak in the winter and the ground is lit from street lamps along the road outside the bottom wall and from floodlights behind the goal. The players begin their stamina-run in the bottom corner of the field, heading up outside the railing before turning at the dip in the far corner. They make their way back down the field before turning through the last gap in the railing and then up the sharp incline and back around a series of stakes. It is only times like this that McGarry can look back and smile at the memory of it.

It's been a long road back for Kilkenny this season. In the previous two years, it took them three games to reach an All-Ireland final. This time around they've had to play six matches to get back on the grand stage and have no Leinster title either to show for their efforts. Setting out to win the three-in-a-row at the outset of the campaign, the last thing Kilkenny needed was to lose to Wexford and be forced to take the scenic route.

'If you'd said after the Wexford game, or the following day that we'd be back in an All-Ireland final, you'd have thought "no way",' said McGarry.

That they are is testament to the massive drive in this squad. Kilkenny achieved three-in-a-row once before, between 1911 and 1913, but one of those titles was granted in the committee room and Kilkenny people don't boast about that feat. For this Kilkenny team, the match in two weeks' time is their shot at immortality. For McGarry, it could be his last chance to win another All-Ireland medal.

'In a lot of ways I'm glad that I've had success late in my career,' he said. 'I think I appreciate it more and I reckon it helped a lot of us because we had the experience. I often think of the Clare boys winning their All-Irelands at a young age. You have to admire them coming in so young and doing it so young but I bet that if they won another one now, they'd find it nearly sweeter than the other two.'

No one in Kilkenny could have predicted five years before that McGarry would go on to become the goalkeeper he has. At that time he had made a name as a keeper with the Kilkenny Juniors but he played a lot of his hurling out the field with his club Bennetsbridge. When the county went through a mini-goalkeeping crisis in the middle of the 1997 championship, McGarry wasn't even in the picture. When he finally edged his way into the frame a year later, he was twenty seven.

He was the subkeeper as Kilkenny lost the 1998 All-Ireland final to Offaly and the enthusiasm was slowly beginning to seep out of him like a sieve. In his mind's eye, all that was stretching out in front of him was a position on the bench. When Kilkenny played their first match after that All-Ireland (a SouthEast Tournament game in October), McGarry went out drinking the night beforehand. Kilkenny didn't have a manager at the time and McGarry was only a sub so he didn't see the need for restraint.

Before the match, however, Joe Dermody cried off with an injury and McGarry was picked to play. He wasn't mentally or physically ready for it, he didn't command his goal-area and conceded three goals in the process, two of which were his fault. Just before the throw-in, he noticed Brian Cody walking into the ground. When Cody was installed as the new manager a week later, McGarry thought it was curtains.

It was when he returned home in January from the team holiday in Tenerife. He received a letter from the new management informing him that he was no longer on the Kilkenny panel but that they would be monitoring his form in the local championship. With Martin Carey called into the squad, McGarry was effectively over the cliff edge with no rope to pull him back up.

Just nine days later though, he was thrown a lifeline. Kilkenny were due to play Tipperary in another south-east league match when Joe Dermody was forced to pull out of the squad with another injury. Carey, DJ's brother, was installed as number one but Cody rang McGarry to ask him to return to the panel. In a discreet manner, McGarry let Cody know he was annoyed at being dropped but his tone was still laced with diplomacy and he said that he'd go back.

When McGarry arrived for training the following evening, Cody never saw him coming into the gym just behind him. Willie O'Connor was kicking a soccer ball around the hall and he spotted the new arrival. 'Ah McGarry, welcome back,' said O'Connor. 'The best goalkeeper in the county.'

Cody just glanced over his shoulder. 'I could see him blushing,' said McGarry. 'Next thing he turned around and welcomed me into the panel.'

McGarry got a couple of runs in the SouthEast League but Martin Carey was still first-choice for the League matches. Dermody was expected back from injury and McGarry wasn't sure if he was going to hold onto his place in the panel. Even though Carey was getting married in March, McGarry never saw his enforced absence for a couple of weeks as an opportunity. Although Kilkenny were down to play Dublin in a challenge game the day after Carey got married, McGarry cut loose at his first-cousin's wedding.

'I drank all day at the wedding,' said McGarry. 'I was after writing off my chances at that stage. I knew I was going to be playing against Dublin but I didn't give a shit. I went in and Jaysus who was doing umpire only *(Noel)* Skehan. Didn't balls hit off me the same day. I can still see one ball that your man pulled on. It hit me and it looped back in over me. I said "fuck it, I won't even go back for it." What did it do, it hit the inside of the post and came back and I got a flick out on it. It looked brilliant. Then Skehan was beside me: "Go!", "Stay!", "Go!", telling me when to go and stay and to stand up. Jaysus if you tried to play better, you couldn't. It was just one of those days but it couldn't have happened at a better time for me.'

By the time McGarry had togged in afterwards, nearly everyone else had gone. He was walking out by the corridor and was gone past Cody when he heard the manager calling him back.

'He said "Jaysus James, that was a great performance",' said McGarry. '"Listen here I couldn't give a damn if Katie Barry played in goal for Kilkenny but if you keep that up, you'll be there. You're in possession of the jersey now." Ever since then, it's just happened for me. I've played in four All-Irelands since and now this is going to be my fifth.'

After Kilkenny had beaten Waterford to secure their passage back to this final, McGarry ran into Willie O'Connor in the players' lounge in Croke Park. A minute later Cody walked in. 'Ah Jaysus Cody, I always told you that McGarry was the best keeper in the county,' said O'Connor.

The manager laughed. After they'd won the 2000 All-Ireland, Cody told O'Connor on the team holiday in Thailand that he'd rarely felt as small as he felt that night when O' Connor made the comment about McGarry in his presence. Four years later, Cody still remembers that time. But so does McGarry.

He still has Cody's letter at home from the time he dropped him.

Over the last six seasons, McGarry has been the safest goalkeeper in the game. He has conceded just fifteen goals in twenty four championship matches and has kept twelve clean sheets in the process. The only goal he was ever culpable for with Kilkenny was a long-range Eugene Cloonan free in the 2001 All-Ireland semi-final but he hasn't made a mistake since. If he doesn't concede a goal against Cork in two weeks' time, he will become the first keeper in the history of the game to keep three clean sheets in All-Ireland finals.

He plays behind an excellent defence. But McGarry is a paragon of consistency, who merges perfectly the simplistic and fundamental aspects of goalkeeping. Some of the most important saves he has made over the previous couple of years have involved using his body and standing up to the ball. In the 2002 All-Ireland semi-final he stood his ground to an Eoin Kelly rocket which hit him on the shoulder and rebounded onto the crossbar. In the first half of the 2003 All-Ireland final, he rushed Setanta Ó hAilpín and forced him to flash his shot wide. Simple but effective.

'A lot of my saves are not spectacular but I'm not into that,' he said. 'I'm definitely not spectacular anyway. I'd be more safety first and I play for the team first. I think the way the game has gone, if you have your backs organised, you should have very few shots to stop. The one thing Skehan drilled into me early on was to keep the backs on their toes. I feel my strongest point is reading a game. Being sharp off the line and as Skehan says, nipping things in the bud.'

McGarry grew up just eight doors down from Noel Skehan in the Woodlawn estate in Bennetsbridge. He lived in the corner house opposite a little green with two trees that used to act as goalposts. The Bennetsbridge pitch was just to the left behind the estate but McGarry and his friends would always play in the green because they wanted Skehan to notice them.

Skehan was a legend. The record holder of nine All-Ireland medals won between 1963 and 1983, McGarry modelled his game on Skehan's and the old master coached him about the specifics and technicalities of goalkeeping long before he ever made it with Kilkenny. He always made McGarry feel important because he knew what it felt like to be on the outside looking in. Skehan won three of his All-Ireland medals as sub to Ollie Walsh.

'Father Maher *(former Kilkenny coach)* had an absolutely huge effect on me when I was the subkeeper,' said Skehan. 'I couldn't put into words what he did for me. He worked very hard with me but he always made me feel very important and that is something that managers have to be very aware of. He made me as important as Ollie and it made it a lot easier for me when I came into the position. If he was disregarding me, maybe I would have felt differently about it all then. I don't know. Maybe I would have given it all up. It's quite possible that I would have.'

Skehan has been a selector with Kilkenny for the last number of years and he has been an invaluable mentor to McGarry. In an era of high-tech coaching culture, Skehan has never gone for rocket science. He religiously preaches the Old Testament verses of safety, handling, feet movement, first-touch and covering angles to McGarry and the subkeeper PJ Ryan. He regards the New Testament soccer-type, hurling goalkeeping as heresy.

'To me goalkeeping is all about safety,' said Skehan. 'When I see goalkeepers diving, it vexes me. I don't care how fast a ball is travelling, if you can take one step, you can cut off a lot of that angle. I never even put a single thought into diving. I'm not into that at all and you won't see James at it. If he does, I'll be asking him the next night at training why he was.

'I'm always telling him to try and get himself in front of those balls and in fairness to him he works fierce hard at that part of his game. He is a great keeper but he's a real winner. Most of the keepers now are all top class, make no mistake about it. They're as good as ever anyone was and I'd have no qualms saying that. There's no point saying they weren't. They are and James is one of them.'

Most nights at training, McGarry will do all the outfield drills. Any goalkeeping drills he does are based primarily on handling and feet movement. He will stand in the middle of the goal, catch or control the ball, move with it to the left or right and return it to the striker before repositioning himself for the next shot. Continuously.

'I never do any shot-stopping in training,' said McGarry. 'Hardly ever. I just never do it. I do all the outfield stuff. But moving to the ball the whole time. That's the one thing Skehan always stresses, move to the ball. He reckoned that if Brenner moved in the Munster final, he wouldn't have conceded that goal because he'd have had a chance of getting back to it.

'It's all about the basics and concentration. No matter how well you're playing, a simple ball can do you. That goal in 2001, I still use that as a motivation. You can always get nailed and you have to be aware of that. I look on the seventy minutes as a day's work; you can either do it right or do it wrong so you get tuned in and have no regrets coming off that field. It's tough going and the only time you can enjoy a match is when it's over and you win. I can't understand these lads who say they enjoy county hurling. You can't enjoy county hurling.'

McGarry keeps his head down, does his job and leaves it at that. He doesn't do interviews and never seeks out the limelight. His personality doesn't lend itself to that part of the game.

'I keep myself to myself and I don't want to be known as a big player. Even going to club matches you'd have lads saying "oh, there's your man." You'd know yourself what they'd be saying and you'd be thinking "would you ever just look at the match and never mind me?" Even young lads coming up looking for autographs, I will always sign them but I wouldn't be into that at all.'

Then in December 2003 he was cast into the spotlight through none of his own doing. In his speech to the Kilkenny GAA convention, Pat Dunphy, the secretary, described how it appeared incumbent on a goalkeeper to spend the summer 'diving all around your goal area and letting in plenty of goals' to make the All-Star team. Dunphy was castigating the All-Star selectors for omitting McGarry once more. But it was an apparent reference to Brendan Cummins' more flamboyant style and a crass characterisation, which denigrated the excellence of

Cummins' work as a shot stopper.

'I was disgusted with the whole thing,' said McGarry. 'Skehan was disgusted over it as well and there was no need for it at all.'

Before Brian Cody departed for Phoenix, Arizona in January with the All-Stars touring party, McGarry approached him with a message for Cummins. He wanted the Tipperary man to know how he felt about the whole episode and Cody relayed his sentiments to Cummins as they were getting on the plane in Dublin. Cummins appreciated them.

McGarry has been a consistent All-Star nominee since he started with Kilkenny but he has still to win an award. He was extremely annoyed not to get one in 2002 and he let a few people know about it on the night of the event. He is disappointed he doesn't have one but introspection has measured his tone and altered his outlook in the meantime.

'The fact that I'm not spectacular has probably gone against me,' said McGarry. 'Another thing that has gone against me is that I don't talk to the media but it doesn't bother me anymore. It used to but it bothered me more in the sense that Kilkenny lads were getting on to me. They were nearly on about the All-Star more than winning the All-Ireland. But I'd rather have the All-Irelands in my back pocket.'

Winning a fourth medal now would be the sweetest of all. If they do, he will pack it all in. If they don't, he'll weigh up his options and decide what path he's going to pursue over the next couple of months. That thought has been banished from his mind for now but whenever he does decide to walk away from Kilkenny, it won't be an easy parting.

'I know lads can go off the rails a bit at times but hurling is all of our lives on this team,' said the keeper. 'When Henry *(Shefflin)* wasn't going as well as he can early in the summer, he was coming in early to training for two weeks, belting balls over the bar. When *(Michael)* Kavanagh was dropped, he was fierce disappointed but he worked hard to get back into the team. All the lads on this team are fanatics and I'm lucky that I came along with a group like them. Jaysus, I take hurling fierce serious but I'm just blessed to come at the time I did and to play in all these All-Ireland finals at the end of my career.'

He'll cocoon himself now for the next two weeks. He'll go to the handball alleys in St Kieran's College to keep his touch sharp and his eye in and he'll avoid any contact with hurling talk. On some occasions if there are members of his family in the kitchen and living room, he'll head to his room for the evening and watch TV on his own. He'll ease up on his work and concentrate on getting into a positive frame of mind about the match.

Kilkenny are entitled to be favourites in two weeks' time but their case is not as convincing as it was in 2002 or as persuasive as it was in 2003. Cork had them on the ropes in that game and they couldn't drop them. In the meantime, Wexford and Clare have proved they're not untouchable and Waterford nearly beat them with only one forward functioning properly. They haven't hurled with easy fluency in their last three games but their defence has been the difference between survival and drowning. On paper, their attack is potentially lethal, but that's not the way they've been playing.

'In 2000 we were playing like Cork now,' said McGarry. 'Then in 2002 we got more physical and this year it's kind of a combination of both. We just know how to win matches but I'd be worried that we're not scoring enough. We got three goals against Waterford in the first half but we didn't create any more goal chances after that.'

In the end it might come down to more powerful things than mere strategy. Kilkenny have a raw desire and an ability to peak but McGarry remembers the feeling of desolation after losing the 1999 All-Ireland final to Cork and how it drove them on to slay all before them a year later. Twelve months previously after the final whistle, the Cork players gathered in a circle in the middle of Croke Park and swore retribution. Kilkenny know the high-powered fuel that can come from defeat so they are going to have to tank up to stay the distance.

'When a Kilkenny team is determined and focussed, it will take a savage team to beat them,' said McGarry. 'Our intensity hasn't been what I would have liked it to be all year but we'll have to be savage hungry to beat Cork. That's where '98 and '99 stands to some of us. We learned an awful lot from those defeats and that's why you'd have to be worried about Cork. They went into a huddle after that defeat last year and swore that they'd be back to win it.

'It is a bit of a worry going in that a lot of our younger lads don't know what it's like to lose an All-Ireland final. When you have something in life, even your health, you don't really appreciate it. Then when something goes wrong, you do appreciate it. It's the same in hurling. We have the McCarthy Cup for the last two years but earlier on in the year, you could be bringing it to some function and you wouldn't even look at it. When it was gone from us in 2001, we would have gone through a wall to get it back. It's the same with Cork now. That's the hunger that we're going to have to match.'

They're going to have to go through a wall to hold on to what they have.

REBEL YELL

On the Monday evening before the All-Ireland final, the Cork squad watched the horror show that was the first half of the 2003 All-Ireland final. On Wednesday evening, they watched the nightmare sequel that was the second half of the same game. Just to refresh their memories and revisit the hurt. Cork don't use a sports psychologist but management have grasped a practical knowledge of sports psychology and its importance and the message in the recording was clear. It's been crystal clear ever since they beat Wexford.

For the last two years, the walls of the dressing room and meeting room in the hotel before matches, have been host to a gallery of pictures communicating subliminal messages and catchphrases designed to create an environment of heightened awareness and passion. Before the All-Ireland semi-final there was a clipping from an article with Denis Byrne, the former Kilkenny hurler who transferred to Tipperary, which implied that Cork didn't have the bottle to win last year's All-Ireland final.

In the three weeks after the Wexford match, the walls were plastered with negative images from that All-Ireland final: Setanta Ó hAilpín crying disconsolately, Joe Deane with his hands over his head and John Gardiner down on his knees. Before they trained last Friday, Donal O'Grady opened up his laptop and brought up the image of the whole squad gathered in a huddle after last year's final. 'Do ye want to be in that position again?' he asked them. They went on to have one of the best sessions of the season.

Ever since then, the images have been positive. On Monday night, a picture of Christy Ring was hanging above Cusack's seat in the dressing room. There was another motto in Irish which translates into: 'We are Cork, we are REBELS and we are proud.' Cusack's favourite saying wasn't posted up but it has been encrypted it into his mind for a long time. It's from Terence MacSwiney, the former Lord Mayor of Cork who died in a British prison in October 1920 after seventy four days on hunger-strike. 'It is not those who are willing to inflict the most, but those who can endure the most, who will eventually triumph.' O'Grady often uses that quote to the players.

When Cusack turned up on Wednesday evening, there was a newspaper report from the 2002 League final pinned above his spot in the dressing room. It contained harmless quotes from Peter Barry, but management knew it would keep Cusack stimulated and focussed. Although Kilkenny narrowly beat Cork in that match, the game was largely remembered for a number of Cork players staging a protest in the parade beforehand. They marched with socks down and jerseys out as a token gesture of solidarity with the Gaelic Players' Association (GPA), which is not recognised by Croke Park as a representative body.

A plan to make that gesture was drawn up at the GPA's EGM in Portlaoise eight days earlier but whereas the majority of the Cork team was committed to the protest, Kilkenny captain Andy Comerford was the only one to publicly make a show of support on his team. The fall-out from their protest had a seismic effect on Cork hurling that summer and the players have never forgotten Kilkenny for it. Especially Cusack.

'That went against everything we stand for,' he said. 'We stood up for all the players in Ireland and they didn't. Comerford was the only Kilkenny fella that did. That was their choice but we'll never forget the way Peter Barry spoke after that game. We were after hanging ourselves out to dry in the protest and we knew that beforehand as well because we're not fools. We knew that it was serious dodgy territory and he came out afterwards and said that all he cared about was wearing the jersey. The media in Cork and the people who were on our case had a field day with that statement. He should have realised that if they didn't want to support us, don't support us but don't stick the fucking knife in our backs when we're on the ground.

'All the boys remember that and Kilkenny are the team we've wanted all along. Seán Óg said to me before that if it's not Kilkenny, it's not going to be the same. We want them, big-time. They are perceived as the best and we want to beat the best. They've beaten us twice in the last three years but we were also hurt by the way they spoke after last year's game about us being lucky in 1999.

'Even though they are our enemies because of what happened in 2002 and last year, I respect them. They have some great players and even though they are our enemies on the field, you know that if a lot of those guys were on your side, including *(Brian)* Cody, you would have great time for them. I know Cody was definitely not on our side back in 2002 but I still shook his hand after the All-Ireland final last year. I said to him "we will meet again." Now we are. And I know that he won't forget that.'

After training Wednesday evening, Dr Con Murphy told the Cork squad a story about Christy Ring and his views on proper preparation. Murphy told them all that they were in the shape of their lives and that they were the best-prepared Cork team he had ever seen. Management wasn't present during his speech and his words meant a lot to the players because they knew Murphy had seen a lot of great Cork teams over the years.

Cork are the most meticulously prepared hurling team in the country and, without doubt, the most scientific and professional outfit to ever play the game. Their training methods and beliefs are fostered in a completely professional culture, which had never before framed the preparation of a Cork hurling team. They are a group of elite athletes who are treated as professional sportspeople and who behave in turn as if they have that status. All of that was completely new to Cork.

Donal O'Grady has built the ingenious structures and framework of the system. The players are treated as professionals but the standards, which are set, imply responsibility on the players to act and train in that manner. It isn't enough to be on time for training; players have to leave enough time to prepare themselves to train. If a player has an issue to iron out with the County Board liaison officer, Mick Dolan, he is expected to have cleared it up long before training began. If the session begins at seven, the masseurs are ready to give rubs from half five onwards.

The players have personalised training gear with their names stitched onto the back of their training tops. Some of their gear is prepared for them when they arrive and is taken away and laundered after each session and laid out in their place when they arrive for the next session. After training, a banana and an isotonic drink are waiting for each player before they jump into an ice bath. Logistics with all the training gear that makes up the apparatus of their sessions is never a problem: at the beginning of the season, O'Grady secured a sponsored van from Ford, with Cork crests on it, to transport all the necessary requirements.

The fine detail of their training and gameplan is prepared with forensic attention. Individual performances are constantly analysed by O'Grady and stored on his laptop computer for one-on-one tutorials. Training is heavily planned and even the warm-up that Cork do with the ball before every match was devised in consultation with the players. The sixty touches of the ball that each player is guaranteed has all been worked out.

Everything is planned minutely. Last week they practised shaking hands with the president before the match, with O'Grady in the title role. Even the tomato sauce for the pre-match pasta lunch is taken care of and O'Grady told the players that it would be arranged if any of them wanted to have their own pillows brought up for their beds in the Burlington Hotel the night before the match.

Before Cork played Wexford under lights in March, Cusack was provided with a thermal vest to protect him from the cold and everything is done with the greater good in mind. Off the field, that language continually translates into discussions between the players and the County Board. Progress meetings are constantly called by the Players Committee to seek whatever they're looking for. A copy of all the players' accounts is sent to the captain on a term basis, or monthly if the players wish. If they want more tickets or new gear, there isn't a problem and lines of communication are always open on both sides.

The players have a very healthy and open relationship with Mick

Dolan and County Board Chairman, Jim Forbes. When the board complained to the players after the Limerick match that they didn't agree with them walking through the hotel lobby with bottles of beer while kids were present, the players assured them it would never be repeated. It hasn't been since.

'Before, you wouldn't get a banana in Cork for nothing,' said Cusack. 'We have a professional set-up now but it has also forced us to take on more responsibility. Everything is done right and that's why you create such a positive attitude.'

The new regime under Donal O'Grady in the last two years has been a revolution in Cork. But nobody is more responsible for that than Donal Óg Cusack.

Cusack fired the first shots of the revolution on Friday August 16 2002 on Cork's 96FM. He was asked on a morning talk show to discuss the GPA along with Dessie Farrell and Pat Spillane. He knew in a way that he was being set up by the station but he was happy to play the game.

His comments amounted to a stunning dismemberment of the County Board's poor treatment of the players and of how younger panel members were told that their county careers would be in jeopardy if they involved themselves with the GPA. In a thinly veiled reference to Frank Murphy, the County GAA Secretary, Cusack said 'one man is running the show in Cork'.

Not every media organ picked up his comments that day and it was only when the interview was replayed on Saturday night that the heat began to rise. On Monday, the County Board rejected Cusack's comments and the team manager Bertie Óg Murphy denied that the players were told that their position would be jeopardised if they joined the GPA.

At a County Board meeting on Tuesday night, the wagons were circled. One delegate who criticised players for looking for two sets of boots said they'd get the second if they won the All-Ireland. Another said the players should 'put up or shut up'. In the following day's *Irish Examiner*, seven players rowed in behind Cusack and openly criticised the treatment of Cork hurlers by the County Board. That number soon swelled to twelve.

During that week, some players called for a revamp of the selection committee, shrinking it to three, and a clear-out of the current selectors, with the exception of the coach. Frank Murphy was a selector in 2002 but the selection panel was a serious issue. Five days before the League final, one selector, John Meyler, sidled up to Mark Landers, a leading GPA member and told him to take a good look around Páirc Uí Chaoimh because 'you'll never see it again'. That evening a group of players rounded on Meyler and demanded an apology. They didn't get it.

Tensions had reached a volcanic boiling point by the time Cusack opened the lid but they had been smouldering beneath the surface for quite a while. The previous year, a garda escort to take the players from Páirc Uí Rinn to Páirc Uí Chaoimh for their championship match with Limerick never arrived and they had to make their way through the thronged crowds in packed cars to get to the ground. When they arrived, they didn't have enough space for their warm-up because the adjoining dressing room was being used by the Cork Intermediates. They warmed up in the gym but there were no toilets in the gym and some players were forced to urinate on damp towels.

The following March, the squad made a farcical bus trip to Derry for a League match. There was no team doctor present and Niall McCarthy was treated by the Derry team doctor after sustaining a nasty head wound. He bled the whole way home and was only treated after his parents took him to hospital when he returned to Cork.

They had plenty of other grievances too. The squad's winter gear only arrived in April along with their summer gear. Then there was a subsequent retraction of gym privileges in a city hotel and the players never felt the meals were up to standard either. By the time Galway wiped them out in the qualifiers, team morale was on the floor and Cork hurling was at an all-time low. Something had to give and Cusack made up his mind that he was going to set the ball rolling.

'The reason I did it was because there was something seriously wrong.

You had fellas going out playing in front of 60,000 people under serious pressure, dedicating most of their lives to hurling and putting their names on the line for the good of Cork hurling. Lads loved playing for Cork but the back-up wasn't at the same level as they were at. Even when I was a minor, it never made sense to me. Players had been talking about it for a long time but there was never really anything done about it. Teddy Owens was a brilliant trainer but I said to him that summer that I was going to do something about our back-up.

'I didn't really have a problem with Frank *(Murphy)*. I had, and still do have good time for him, but I was totally against the way players were treated and he was at the head of the organisation that was responsible for that. It wasn't Frank the person but what his rule stood for towards players; I was going to fight tooth and nail against that.'

In Murphy, Cusack knew he was dealing with one of the most powerful figures in the history of Cork GAA and one of the most skilful politicians in the GAA's history. He knew that if the players were going to mobilise a campaign to improve their basic welfare rights, they were going to have to do everything by the letter of the law to get around the intransigence of Murphy and the board. At the end of August, Cusack and Mark Landers went to one of Cusack's best friends, Diarmuid Falvey, a solicitor based in the South Mall in the city.

'I thought you'd be into me alright, Donal Óg,' Falvey said to Cusack the second he walked in the door.

Falvey had played for Cloyne for years so he understood where Cusack was coming from and they drew up a strategy immediately. Cusack organised a meeting of all the players and they all decided that whatever they would go for, every player would have to agree to it. Then they made up their minds that they were going to see it through to the bitter end.

'We were only young fellas and it was upsetting us all,' said Cusack. 'We weren't sure of our future but we had to make a stand for future generations of Cork players.'

They organised a committee, where each person on the committee had to keep a certain group of players briefed and updated on their actions. Everyone was contacted on a regular basis and no decision would be reached, or press statement released, without everyone's consent. Even John Browne in England was kept up to date.

All of their meetings were held in Falvey's office and any information that players had were documented and recorded. A plethora of statements were released to counter and reply to certain comments made in the press and they drew up a list of demands which they delivered to the board.

When the County Board eventually agreed to a meeting, the players went into preparatory overdrive. Every player in the committee was given a brief and they were expected to acquire an expertise in that area to plug any loopholes. They even had test-runs to prepare for the negotiating table. They met regularly, sometimes daily, and with the many forms of outside support they received they had soon turned into a well-oiled machine.

In early November twelve players finally sat down with the County Board. An equivalent number of board officials were present and over twenty people assembled in a room in Páirc Uí Chaoimh. Shortly after the meeting began, the players were given a typed handout, which outlined the board's response to all their demands. The players left the room to consider the details and then returned for a meeting that lasted almost four hours.

Certain players were designated to handle individual issues: ticket allocation, gear, gym facilities, a holiday fund and the issue of the selectors. The debate became heated but there was no tone of settlement from the board and they refused to budge on certain demands. Central to any resolution was a new selection committee and a new manager but the players were told that a new manager would be appointed within seven days.

That target was missed a week later and the players subsequently wrote to the board on November 21, expressing their disappointment with the reaction to their demands but offering the possibility of another meeting.

In response, Murphy suggested that a meeting might be arranged with smaller representations from both sides but he also said that his hands were tied by Central Council on many of the players' demands.

However, the players were told at the last meeting that the County Board was already in breach of Central Council guidelines by supplying them with their current gear allocation. The players felt that the board was happy to break guidelines as long as the cost to them was minimal. That response was unacceptable to the players and a heightened degree of militancy set in amongst them. A week later, they made up their minds to go for broke.

On Thursday November 28, the whole squad met in a corner of a function room in the John Barleycorn Hotel, five miles from Cork City. The meeting was only convened earlier that day but thirty players were present. Once more they examined their position and how they could go about improving it. They evaluated the potential consequences of their actions but after 9pm, every player present signed the notice to strike.

It was decided that Cusack, Seán Óg Ó hAilpín, Fergal Ryan, Joe Deane, Diarmuid O'Sullivan, Mark Landers and Alan Browne would make up the top table for the press conference which was arranged for the following day at 5pm. They gathered at mid-morning to prepare themselves for whatever questions might be thrown at them. In the Deane Room in the Imperial Hotel later that afternoon, they announced that they were withdrawing their services.

The County Board was caught completely off guard because they believed all along that the players would crack. The strike was a huge GAA issue but it had deeply wounded the GAA establishment in Cork. After the convictions expressed in their press conference, most pubic sympathy was directed towards the players. All the board could say was that they would be making no comment until after Tuesday's board meeting.

The heat on the board grew more intense over the weekend but from the outset of their meeting on Tuesday evening, the executive of the board set out to convey an attitude that a resolution was imminent. They insisted that certain issues were being addressed but they had no concrete evidence to back up their claims. They needed to be seen to be moving forward but the players weren't buying any of it. In their view, too many key issues remained unresolved.

The board still refused to bend on serious issues. They refused to guarantee that a doctor would be present at every match, including challenge games, which the players had requested. The players' request that members of the executive would never again be team selectors was completely dismissed. On other issues such as compensation for loss of earnings, mileage rates and ticket allocations, the board said their hands were tied by Central Council policy.

They knew the players couldn't work with the present selection committee yet the board still did nothing to defuse the situation. PJ Murphy had indicated his intention to step down as a selector days before the strike but that was never conveyed to the players. Frank Murphy knew that if the selection committee remained, it would create a war he couldn't win but he still had another battle on his hands. It was only 5.30pm on Tuesday that John Meyler agreed to resign.

The players' committee met in Falvey's office at 6.30pm the following evening to discuss their options. They were happy with the issue that the new coach would be allowed pick his own selectors but they were still looking at the bigger picture. They wanted to see other concessions written down in black and white that were binding for the future. A statement was prepared and every other player on the panel was contacted before the go-ahead was given to release it. They were prepared to go into negotiations but they were still on strike.

With the County Convention taking place on Sunday, the players were happy to let the board stew in the meantime and draw further wrath from the grassroots at the convention. The players had established their own network of intelligence which had allowed them to keep a step ahead of the board but events spiralled further out of the board's control on Wednesday night when the Cork footballers announced that they were joining the hurlers on strike. The last opinion poll taken in *The Evening Echo* that week was 86% in favour of the players and the board knew that they would have to cut their losses and concede.

On Friday night December 13, a meeting was arranged at the Silver Springs Hotel between representatives of the players and the board. The whole mood from the board was conciliatory from the outset and they had clearly come to broker a peace deal with a settlement package sufficient to meet the players' demands. The board went far beyond what they had already declared and the package, which the negotiating team brought back to their players in the hotel, was unanimously accepted. The players had won.

The issues ranging from transport, meals at training, gym membership, team doctors present at matches and the availability of masseurs and physios were all addressed to the players' requirements. A liaison committee between the teams and the board and a Support Fund were also established. The Cork Team's Support Fund would stage fundraising initiatives to reap the largely untapped goodwill of the corporate sector in Cork. The fund would provide for Cork teams at all levels and would be separate from the players' fund and holiday fund.

The concessions continued into the fine detail but on the thorny issues of mileage and ticket allowances, the board said that they would advocate for change at central level to meet their demands. On the issue of compensation for loss of earnings, the board said they would convey the players' views to Croke Park.

Diarmuid Falvey was present with the players at the meeting and his secretary documented extensive notes, as had been done through the whole campaign. In the end there was no binding agreement signed, just a final pact between the players and the board.

It was a quantum leap forward for the future of Cork GAA but the strike had far wider-ranging implications. In terms of players' welfare, the Cork strike was a watershed in the history of the GAA.

The revolution had been won but not without some collateral damage for Cusack. He knew he was going to create hurt by his actions. Bertie Óg Murphy had given him a huge break with the Under-21s in 1996 and all the players had great time for him. Cusack had just as much respect for Teddy Owens and he always believed he was ahead of his time with Cork. Dr Con Murphy meanwhile, had meticulously looked after Cork players over the years. When Cusack was a minor, Murphy diagnosed him with an overactive thyroid gland and arranged the best of treatment for him immediately. If it hadn't been diagnosed, Cusack might never have hurled for Cork.

The only way Cusack could justify the wounding of those three friends was the knowledge that they were setting a precedent for the GAA's welfare state. Not just in Cork, but around the country.

The players put the responsibility on themselves to prepare properly and to earn back respect for Cork hurling. One of the main points that was overlooked was that most of the players were from hurling strongholds and from families that were immersed in Cork hurling. Diarmuid O'Sullivan's father, Gerry, was an officer of the County Board at the time and he was sitting across the negotiating table from his militant son. The strike was one of the biggest issues to ever hit the GAA and yet all the players were willing to make a stand.

They were under huge pressure and they had to place a lot of trust in each other. A lot of what they achieved depended on taking a chance and on everyone sticking together. A single player breaking ranks could have finished them but it brought them all closer together and that responsibility has been reflected on the field ever since. After the strike, they had nothing to fear from adversity ever again.

Although Cusack faded into the background after firing the first shots, he was the main general directing the campaign behind the scenes.

'Other players were publicly driving it forward,' said Ger Cunningham. 'But Ogie was the guy at the gear-stick. He was controlling where they were going.'

Cusack's decision to get Diarmuid Falvey on board though, was ultimately the real difference between the strike being a success and a failure.

'Diarmuid is a special man,' said Cusack. 'Without him, we would have been fighting in the dark. He has everything you would want in a person: intelligent, honest, loyal and genuine. The amount of time he put into it all was frightening. I can remember him being sick and he still turned up for meetings. If you ever want to achieve anything of significance, you have to go beyond the call of duty. And he went beyond the call of duty. Diarmuid has had more to do with the success of this team over the last two years than people will ever know. The only thing he kept reminding us during it all was that there would have to be a payback. But that payback was never financial.'

At the height of the strike, Falvey's whole office was working on the case and his final legal fees totalled €55, 000. The players had the money to pay him but he waived his entire fee.

'The only payment I want back lads is for ye to win the All-Ireland next September,' he told them the night the strike finished.

They didn't make that payment to Falvey last September. But they hope to close the deal on Sunday.

TRY WALKING IN MY SHOES

At 2.57pm on All-Ireland final day, September 12, the Kilkenny 1979 Jubilee panel was introduced to the crowd by Marty Morrissey. They were guests of the Irish Nationwide Building Society and the GAA, and they had just come from a celebration lunch where they were presented with a Jubilee award. It was to commemorate their All-Ireland victory of twenty five years ago when Kilkenny defeated Galway by 2-12 to 1-8.

The 1979 All-Ireland final was a poor final, one of the least memorable in the last twenty five years. The attendance was the lowest since 1958, primarily because of the bad conditions and an unofficial train drivers' action that prevented scheduled excursion trains leaving Galway. It secured Kilkenny their twenty-first All-Ireland title but, outside of the county, the match is primarily linked to one character: Seamus Shinnors.

Shinnors was a Tipperary man from Newport in north Tipperary. He won a Dr Harty Cup medal with Limerick CBS in 1964 and was a member of the Tipperary Under-21 squads that reached three consecutive All-Ireland finals between 1964 and 1966. Immediately after he won an All-Ireland Intermediate medal the following season, he joined the senior squad.

He appeared to be signing up at the right time. Shinnors was subkeeper to John O'Donoghue in 1967 and 1968 as Tipp reached the All-Ireland final in both years. They lost both games to Kilkenny and Wexford, however, and after the 1970 championship O'Donoghue retired. The door was wide open for Shinnors but before the 1971 championship, he was cut from the squad and Tipp went on to win the All-Ireland.

When his chance did come with Tipp, it arrived too late. He was the first-choice keeper in 1974, 1975 and 1976 but Tipp never won a single championship game in the three years.

Shinnors had moved to Ballinasloe in Galway in 1975 so the extra travel and the increasing disillusionment saw him pack it in with Tipp after 1976. In his own mind his inter-county days were over until Michael 'Babs' Keating approached him in November 1978 with a view to transferring to Galway. Keating had coached Galway in 1977 and although Joe McGrath had taken over as coach a year later, Keating returned after that year's championship.

Keating and Shinnors had played on the same Tipperary Under-21 team that lost the 1965 All-Ireland final so Shinnors agreed to join but he trained in secret on his own until May 1979. At that stage Michael Conneely and Frank Larkin had been vying for the number one spot but neither was going that well and Shinnors was drafted in at the beginning of the summer. After waiting seven years for the chance to play for Tipp, he only had to wait over seven months for the same chance to fall into his lap with Galway.

Initially it looked like an inspired move. When Galway halted Cork's bid for four All-Irelands in-a-row that August in the All-Ireland semi-final, Shinnors was excellent, making a series of fine saves in the process. It was over a decade since he sat on the bench for two All-Ireland finals and now the dice seemed to be rolling towards a windfall. Galway had beaten one of the best teams of all time and were just one good roll away from striking the jackpot.

All-Ireland final day on September 2, 1979 was a dog of a day, especially for a goalkeeper. A heavy drizzle had preceded the match all morning and it carried on into the first half of the game. The pitch was greasy but conditions were made more treacherous by a deceptive gusting breeze.

Although Galway were playing with the aid of the breeze in the first half, their profligacy was killing them and they couldn't shake Kilkenny. The conditions made striking extremely difficult and when Liam 'Chunky' O'Brien struck a '65 just four minutes before half-time, he never caught it the way he intended to.

It seemed that the ball would be gobbled up in a packed defence as it came through a cluster of players but it carried through and Shinnors only saw it at the last second. He was anticipating the hop and went to gather it into his chest, but the ball kicked off the wet surface and spun higher than he expected. It hit him on the shoulder and bounced up and into the net. If he'd taken one more half step out, the ball would have gone over the bar.

Even though Galway had played with the wind, they had shot eleven wides and were generating sufficient possession. The game was still there for them. A Noel Lane goal early in the half put them back in the driving seat but Kilkenny clawed their way back. Galway couldn't reel them in but they had a great chance to go ahead with seven minutes remaining when they won a penalty. They were only two points down but when John Connolly's shot was blocked, Galway's chance went up in smoke.

Shinnors knew it. He knew too that the All-Ireland flame that had been burning inside him for over a decade was being extinguished. With three minutes remaining, he was standing inside the 14-metre line in a near daze when Mick Brennan hit in a high ball from outside the '45. The keeper back-pedalled furiously to try and catch the ball and then launched himself backwards in an attempt to snap it.

If he'd used his hurley he would have stopped it but the ball arced over his hand and went beyond his reach. He banged his head and his back when he crashed against the post and then the roar from the crowd told him where the ball had ended up. The All-Ireland was gone but now this was humiliation at its most extreme. Picture your worst nightmare and multiply it by a thousand. You're not even close to how Shinnors felt afterwards.

'It's an awful, awful experience and terribly difficult to put into words how hard it was,' said Shinnors. 'You just feel terrible for your family and your friends. Nobody wanted to win an All-Ireland medal more than I did and it was a chance that came my way out of the blue after I had given up hope. When I was growing up I sacrificed everything else in life to try and win an All-Ireland medal. I was so desperate, and I suppose I was more desperate than anybody to make that happen. I wanted it so badly that it hurt.

'I couldn't get out of Croke Park quick enough and I was just totally numb for the rest of that day and that night. We went out to the Green Isle Hotel and I will never know how I kept together to get that function over and get to bed. And then having to face the morning and to get up. I don't know how I got the strength to get over it because it was just a terrible, terrible time.'

And then the rumours and the innuendo started which rubbed more salt into the wound. The Galway hurling public was sore after the defeat and some of them were out to get Shinnors. It went around that he had thrown the game on purpose and was playing a sick joke on Galway in the process.

On the Friday night before the final, the former Clare goalkeeper Seamus Durack and his wife Anne had travelled down to Ballinasloe to offer Shinnors their support and best wishes. Both men had worked together in Scarriff and Durack presented Shinnors with one of his Clare caps for luck. When the sun briefly came out in the second half of that final, Shinnors put on the cap. The line afterwards was that he was wearing the Tipperary colours while dancing on Galway's grave.

That was the toughest week of his life but he somehow summoned the steel and the resolve inside him to travel to Kilkenny to play Wexford the following Sunday for an Oireachtas game. He played well and when the League began a month later, he took up his position between the posts and kept working hard. Galway weren't that far away from an All-Ireland but at that stage, the quest for the Holy Grail had been replaced by a manic desire to get back to the big stage and exorcise the black spirits that were haunting his soul.

Everything was going to plan. He played all the opening League games and on St Patrick's Day in 1980, he was on the Connacht team that won the Railway Cup for only the second time - and the first in thirty three years. He continued in goal for the League and all the signs were that he would remain as first-choice keeper for the championship.

Just a few weeks before Galway were due to play Kildare in the All-Ireland quarter-final in July though, Shinnors was in Galway working for the day and he had his gear with him for training that evening in Athenry. His wife Chrissie had been trying to contact him all day and eventually she managed to track him down in a hotel in the city centre where he was having his tea before departing for training.

She got him just in time because a letter had arrived home that morning informing Shinnors that his services were no longer required with Galway. He'd spent almost a year trying to rebuild his confidence and now this. The 1979 final had lanced his heart, but this was a rapier thrust to his spirit.

'I couldn't do anything about 1979 but all I wanted was a chance to redeem myself. That's what was really driving me on. You're always judged on your last game. Other fellas got the chance to go back and do something about it but I never got that chance.'

When Galway drafted Michael King into the panel, Michael Conneely was convinced the new keeper would take over but management reinstated Conneely as first-choice for the first time in two seasons. Initially it looked like the move had backfired when Conneely had a nightmare in the All-Ireland semi-final against Offaly and nearly cost them the game.

When Galway won their first All-Ireland title in fifty seven years on September 7 1980, Michael Conneely got man-of-the-match. When he played what he thought was his second-last game of hurling for the Sarsfields juniors in 1974, a day like this was on the far side of the abyss and wasn't even a fantasy.

Conneely only started playing in goal for Galway in 1974 by accident. He was playing junior hurling with Sarsfields at the time but football was his first love and he had his mind made up to pack in hurling at the age of twenty four. He decided to finish out the couple of games Sarsfields had left that season before hanging up his hurley. But in his expected second-last game, he played really well and suddenly a call came from nowhere to join the Galway squad the night before a tournament game against Dublin in Tuam.

Galway hurling was on the floor at the time and Conneely's only desire was to get one run-out in Croke Park and then call it a day. In 1975 though, he went on to play in an All-Ireland final against Kilkenny. Although he hung in on the panel for the next five years, he was dropped more times than he was picked. His career was a constant struggle but his life changed within the space of an hour and a half in September 1980. He will always be remembered as the man-of-the-match on that historic day. Seamus Shinnors, meanwhile will always be remembered for dropping two balls into the net for Galway in their 1979 defeat to Kilkenny.

'Seamus was a brilliant goalkeeper,' said Conneely. 'Galway could still have won that 1979 final despite Seamus making those mistakes. Our forwards had plenty of chances to score and they didn't but because he was from Tipp, a lot of what was said afterwards was down to absolute meanness and begrudgery. It could just as well have turned out for Seamus as it did for me. I had plenty of bad days and I could have been dropped in 1980 just as easily as he was.'

After Galway won the All-Ireland in 1980, the Ballinasloe club saved up the money to buy a ticket for Shinnors to go to the US when Galway were playing the All-Stars later that year. Shinnors wasn't that keen on going but he couldn't refuse when the club had shown him such support. The trip was very uncomfortable for him.

'I would have felt awkward at the time and I still do feel awkward in the presence of Galway hurlers,' Shinnors admitted. 'I still feel awkward because I let them down and because I'm from Tipperary as well.'

Shinnors never played as a goalkeeper again after he was dropped in 1980. He continued to hurl out the field for Ballinasloe but the innuendo and the spite trailed him anytime he ever went out on a hurling field again. If he didn't hear the comments, he felt them smouldering beneath the surface waiting to ignite. When he won his last hurling medal when lining out at full-forward for Ballinasloe in the 1986 Galway junior final, he walked away. Some of the Abbey-Duniry supporters kept calling him a traitor that day in over the wire. One of them never stopped telling Shinnors to give back the £10,000 he was supposed to have received for throwing the 1979 All-Ireland final.

Shinnors just accepted afterwards that that was the perception some people were always going to have of him, no matter what he did. He had enough on his plate anyway with building up his own business and creating jobs for the Ballinasloe area. Western Postform Ltd employs forty five people today and is one of the most successful furniture manufacturing businesses in the west of Ireland.

If the dice had rolled differently for him, Shinnors could have ended up with four, possibly five All-Ireland medals between his involvement with Tipperary and Galway. His one and only playing experience in an All-Ireland senior final though, made the fact that he never won a medal even harder to deal with.

He just got on with it because he had to. Hurling was important, but family, work and future were way more important. The type of person he was and became mattered more than any medals he might have won. Life lessons. Shinnors understood that but a part of him still died that day on September 2 1979.

'In many ways I came out of it a way better person. I was gutted and there's a part of me still gutted and always will be gutted over it. I certainly feel a lesser person in many ways in my life because I failed that day. But the way it has been directed towards me, I have taken full responsibility for it. I don't drink and I never resorted to drink after that even though I felt so ashamed that I let my wife and my family down. There would have been a great temptation there for me to take the easy way out but I got on with it and my family and good friends kept me going.

'I would have given anything to have won that All-Ireland for Galway and my friends and family, but the way I look at it all now is that it has been balanced out. I have been lucky in my career outside of hurling. I have made it happen. I see a lot of fellas who have All-Ireland medals but who have been unlucky in life and maybe the man above has balanced it out for me. If I can avoid it, I never try and look back at it but I suppose that memory will always be there no matter what I do.

'I still have nightmares about it and it will never leave me. Never, never, absolutely. I thought about it every single day for fifteen years afterwards and it would always flash through my mind at some stage during the day. I suppose in the last ten years I would have thought about it every second day or sometimes I might not think of it for a week. But when the hurling season starts, it all comes back to me again.

'As far as I'm concerned that is the only game of hurling that I ever played in my life. That's the only game that I remember because of the prize that was at stake and how it all worked out. It's now 2004 and that happened in 1979 and I still haven't got over it. I never will. Never, ever will.'

That's what is potentially at stake for a goalkeeper on All-Ireland final day. That's the risk that James McGarry and Donal Óg Cusack have to take in half an hour's time.

ALL OR NOTHING

Donal Óg Cusack awoke at 9am in the Burlington Hotel on September 12. He would have been up earlier only Wayne Sherlock likes to lie on and he didn't want to disturb his room-mate. Sherlock was still asleep but Cusack quietly shuffled out of the bed and as he was heading for the bathroom, he noticed a sheet of paper that had been slipped under the door. He picked it up and looked at it. It was a plain white sheet with just four words written on it. Intensity. Concentration. Composure. Quality.

Sherlock got up about fifteen minutes later and the two strolled downstairs for breakfast. Cusack had porridge that he sprinkled with Cloyne honey, which he had brought with him in a jar and the two spoke fondly about the previous evening. They were in their room watching TV along with Niall McCarthy, Diarmuid O'Sullivan and Ronan Curran when there was a knock on the door. It was Setanta Ó hAilpín and they all welcomed him like a lost brother. He stayed for half an hour and they spoke with such ease that it was like he had never been away.

After breakfast, Cusack and Sherlock went for a walk around the block to stretch their legs before heading back to their room to watch *Cribs* on MTV. After an hour of lying down, Cusack headed down to the hotel car-park with his hurley and a sliotar. He began his ritual of pucking the ball off the same curved wall he has been using on the morning of a big game since he was a minor. The ball never comes back straight at him so it's perfect for judging his first touch.

When he went back to the room, Diarmuid O'Sullivan was there but Cusack went for another lie-down before the whole squad met at the side of the hotel. Players and management used the staff elevator and went out back exits to avoid the packed lobby. They all went for a walk around the block and on the way back, Donal O'Grady stopped them and they had a meeting on the side of the road. They went through their tactics again and then one of the team's trainers, Seanie McGrath, spoke about the importance of composure.

Before last year's final, management felt that the players were in the wrong state of agitation before leaving the dressing room. They were psyched beyond optimum levels and so pumped up that the two trainers Jerry Wallis and Seanie McGrath couldn't get their attention on the field to sit down for the official team photograph. As the players wandered over, Kilkenny emerged from the tunnel and took their place on the bench in front of the photographers. First blood to Kilkenny. They decided this time that they weren't going to tear out on the field, except Cusack wanted to go a step further. He told McGrath that they should just walk out onto the pitch.

The squad had their pre-match meal in a corner of the hotel restaurant upstairs when they returned and then Cusack got a rub on his back from Jim McEvoy. All rubs had to be completed at a given time before they all met in the team room. The room was plastered with positive messages and images and the squad's CD was playing in the background. The players were quiet and the tension was evident in the air as the clock ticked closer to game-time. Dr Con Murphy sensed it and began cracking jokes to try and soften the mood.

Still, Cusack could feel the resolute sense of purpose in the room. He was sitting on the floor as O'Grady spoke to each member of the team individually. He was visualising what lay ahead. The night before, he met Ger Cunningham and the two talked for nearly an hour in a quiet corner of the hotel. They spoke about dealing with every type of match situation and when O'Grady approached Cusack, the two debated about dealing with one-on-one situations with a Kilkenny forward.

'If they're one-on-one with me, what do you think?' the goalkeeper asked. 'Will I go or will I stay?'

'Do you remember the time with Eddie Brennan?' responded O'Grady in reference to an incident in a League game sixteen months earlier when Cusack ran out and tried to take the forward out. 'If you go, the two of ye will be travelling so fast that it won't happen and he'll go past you. Just stand and make yourself as big as you can.'

Cusack had no problem standing big. Last year O'Grady had him padded out like an ice-hockey keeper with the subkeepers lacing balls at him from seven metres. It was to train Cusack to get his body behind the ball. When O'Grady had finished his individual tutorials, he gathered the squad closely around him to watch clips of Kilkenny on his laptop. When O'Grady had finished speaking about the gameplan, he stood at the top of the room and delivered an oration designed to strike deep at the heart of every player.

'It was a brilliant speech and he finished it with a great line,' said Cusack. 'He said that if you get a gift from God, like we have been given, the greatest way of giving back to God is by making full use of that gift.'

Cusack grabbed his gear and jumped on the bus, sitting down beside Mickey O'Connell. The famous 'game of inches' speech taken from the American football film *Any Given Sunday* was playing loudly on the bus CD player as they pulled off behind the garda escort. There was no going back now. They were on their way to the battlefield. Ready with their swords and shields. Prepared and willing to fight for everything they believed in. Pride. Respect. Honour. And, ultimately, victory.

'I remembered reading an interview with Neil Back *(England rugby player)* and he said that before the World Cup final against Australia, he felt like a suicide bomber,' said Cusack. 'I don't agree with that stuff but that's honestly the way I felt. That whatever I needed to do to win, I was going to do it.

'You know that you're heading into a battle. You know that there's a war ahead of you but we just look after each other. There's nothing else on your mind and your life is ending as far as everything else is concerned. There's no other thought in your head. It's a war of everything. A war of attrition, a physical battle and a skilful battle. And a battle inside your head.

'We know that it's going to be a ferocious battle and they're going to come at us with everything they have. Because they know that we'll be coming with everything right back at them. But this is it. As Seán Óg said to me "the day will always come, Judgement Day will always come. Whether it's two days, five years or twenty years, it's always going to come." For us, Judgement Day is here.'

At roughly the same time, the Kilkenny players had just finished their warm-up in Parnell Park. Even though there was a black cloud lingering over the panel, the mood was still very positive and the squad felt very confident. It had been a difficult journey to Dublin. Just before they departed Kilkenny City by bus at 9.30am, Brian Cody's wife, Elsie, approached James McGarry.

'I knew by the way she was coming across to me that it was bad news,' said McGarry.

She told him that Richard Mullally, father of Richie and Paddy who were on the panel, had passed away just that morning. The news hit McGarry like a steam-train.

'I was thinking of the two lads straightaway. But I was also asking myself, is this going to be our day?'

They drove straight up to their base in the Clontarf Castle Hotel, before having their pre-match meal and then a team meeting. They emphasised the importance of getting quick ball into the full-forward line. They had played a game in training last Saturday evening and the forwards were on fire. It was the best McGarry had seen them play all year and they appeared to be coming good at the right time. There was an edgy tension in the air but the mood was still confident.

'We felt good. There was a lot of pressure on the players and you could see the tenseness but that can often be an advantage. It was no different because before a big game, everyone is trying to get their heads right. But a lot of fellas knew that the two lads (*the Mullally brothers*) were coming and they were wondering what time they were arriving at and what way they would react.'

After the bus had travelled the short distance across to Parnell Park, the Mullally brothers arrived by car. Some players were getting rubbed and

302

strapped in a couple of the other rooms but each player went to them at different times to sympathise.

As the squad warmed up on the pitch, McGarry was working on his own at the side of the field. He was hitting balls off the side of the stand wall behind the goals, running towards them and controlling them first time. After a while he began striking balls across the pitch to PJ Ryan to get comfortable with his handling.

McGarry sat beside Martin Comerford on the bus journey into Croke Park. He had his hurley beside him and a sliotar in his pocket. Every so often he would grab the hurley and take the sliotar out to get a feel of both in his hands. He was already togged off so he stripped off his tracksuit the minute he went into the dressing room. He went straight into the warm-up area and as he was lacing balls off the wall, Noel Skehan approached him.

'The match doesn't start until 3.30pm,' he told him. 'The only time they can score in you is between 3.30pm and 5.00pm. So don't be worrying.'

McGarry's head was clear. He knew exactly what lay ahead of him.

'At this stage, it's dog-eat-dog. And win at all costs.'

McGarry was the seventh Kilkenny player out of the tunnel at 3.07pm as the squad was met with a wall of noise. Cork had been out on the pitch nearly five minutes earlier, while Cusack had been out earlier again after checking his footing with Paul Morrissey and Martin Coleman. They weren't supposed to be on the field during the introduction of the Jubilee team and at one stage a steward confiscated one of their sliotars.

Noel Skehan was standing to McGarry's right on the goal-line during his warm-up while PJ Ryan was taking every range of shot at McGarry, even kicking some balls at him. McGarry's touch was impeccable but after a brief discussion with Skehan, the former keeper instructed Ryan to go out about thirty five yards and drill balls in along the ground to see if they were going to skid off the turf.

'Be careful,' Skehan said to McGarry. 'Those balls are going to bounce up, they're not going to skid.'

Just before the players made their way over to meet the dignitaries, Morrissey and Coleman hugged Cusack and he went back into the goal for a water bottle before he joined the huddle. They got the formalities out of the way and after the parade, Cusack darted straight across the field. It appeared for a second that he was going to shake hands with McGarry but he sped past him and went straight for the referee Aodán MacSuibhne in the middle of the field.

'Aodán, if I'm going to play the lines today and keep inside my square, you have to play the lines and watch Kilkenny fellas in the square,' Cusack said to him. 'If I have to play it, I want every other fella to have to play it as well.'

As the Kilkenny players gathered in their huddle before the national anthem and a minute's silence for the murdered children of Beslan and for Richard Mullally, McGarry blessed himself.

'I was thinking about the boys' father.'

When the national anthem was over, Cusack ran into the Canal End goal and began re-echoing to the umpires what he had just said to MacSuibhne.

'If I'm going to play by the rules, I want something back as well. If there's a line there for me, there's a line there for forwards as well.'

Kilkenny were playing with the breeze and they came out blowing up a storm from the throw-in. The ball was shunted forward to John Hoyne who whipped on it first time. Wayne Sherlock slipped and Eddie Brennan was right in behind him. DJ Carey was also coming at speed onto the loose ball but Brennan picked it up just outside the 14-metre line. He shot hard but the ball went to the right and wide.

'It would have been a great start,' said McGarry. 'If DJ had got it and stuck it in the net, it would have been like two goals to us.'

Kilkenny had three wides inside the opening two minutes before Cork had the opening score of the game through a Joe Deane free. Just three minutes later, Henry Shefflin was pulled for overcarrying near the endline and Cusack hit the deck feigning a leg injury. Wayne Sherlock had slipped twice in the opening period and he had just given Cusack a message that he wasn't going to be given time to change his boots. Cusack was buying him the time to make the change and he made that clear to Declan O'Sullivan after the physio had come to check on him. He radioed back to the line to clear it up but then Dr Con Murphy arrived and started sticking his finger into Cusack's eye because he thought he'd lost a contact lens.

Shefflin equalised on nine minutes and from the puckout, Cusack tried to pick out Seán Óg Ó hAilpín. The ball skidded off the turf and went between Ó hAilpín's legs. Shefflin picked it up and short-passed it to 'Cha' Fitzpatrick who drove it back over the bar. After the puckout, Cusack called out to Ó hAilpín and he beat his chest in a signal to his team-mate to drive on.

Joe Deane levelled it up with a free on twelve minutes and he had a chance to put real daylight between the sides two minutes later when he got inside Michael Kavanagh and was right through on goal. McGarry came out to cut down the angle and Deane's shot from eight metres flew past him and crashed off the crossbar. Ben O'Connor was charging in for the rebound but his ground shot flew into the side netting.

'If I stayed it was a definite goal but I knew I had a chance if I put a bit of pressure on him,' said McGarry. 'It was more a miss on his behalf than having anything to do with me. It was a great chance for them but I still felt we were on top and we had them rattled.'

Kilkenny counter-attacked from McGarry's puckout and Martin Comerford put them back in front. JJ Delaney had won Cusack's previous long puckout so he went short to Niall McCarthy this time and Peter Barry won it. Cork knew that Kilkenny were going to crowd the corridors of space in Cusack's line of vision and force him to puck the ball long. Cork had gone through it on a chart after mass the previous evening so the keeper called Kevin O'Grady, Donal's son, who was acting as a runner.

'Tell Donal they've set it up exactly the way we thought they would,'

Cusack told him. 'And ask him how things are going.'

A Shefflin free stretched Kilkenny's lead to two at the quarter-hour mark but there was a break in the play before the free was taken and Donal O'Grady arrived into Cusack.

'Stick to the plan, don't puck the ball long for the sake of it,' O'Grady said to him. 'Just because things aren't going well, keep pucking where you're trying to hit.'

Cusack was urging Brian Murphy to spread out as a potential receiver because Fitzpatrick was pulling deep down the field but the corner-back had just picked up a bad leg injury and Cusack couldn't risk hitting him. He had no option but to drive it long and Delaney caught it over Ben O'Connor's head. After a Martin Comerford point on nineteen minutes, Cusack drove the puckout down the field again and Tommy Walsh caught it over Timmy McCarthy. After the wing-back almost sent it back over the bar, Cusack ran out the field and lost it with McCarthy. A minute later, O'Grady arrived back into him.

'You're better off hitting it into space, even if we're only winning the breaking ball,' the manager told Cusack.

Delaney and Walsh won two of Cusack's next three puckouts but he still had the courage to pick out Timmy McCarthy with a lovely ball on thirty one minutes. McCarthy was fouled, Ben O'Connor pointed and two minutes later Brian Corcoran had their first score from play. Kilkenny had dominated possession but Cork had toughed it out and they were just a point behind.

Shefflin and Jerry O'Connor traded scores just before the break but two minutes into injury time, John Gardiner won a ball near the sideline and drove it long and into space in front of the goal. It carried through to McGarry but its bounce wasn't true and he tried to control it low down. His first touch wasn't perfect and Joe Deane arrived ahead of Michael Kavanagh and got his foot to it. The ball flew two feet wide of McGarry's right post.

'Kavanagh was going for it and then he kind of stopped and left it to me,' said McGarry. 'I thought he had it cut out but he didn't and I kind of went and stopped and then went again. It was just luck that it went wide.'

McGarry just put his hand up to acknowledge the mistake and went back in and dried his hands and his hurley. When the half-time whistle blew two minutes later, he gathered up all his stuff and headed into the dressing room. Both sides had created fifteen scoring chances but Kilkenny had enjoyed a greater ratio of possession.

'The feeling amongst a lot of lads was disappointment that we were only a point up,' said McGarry. 'But more lads were saying that we weren't hurling well and we were still a point up and that there was a lot more in us. I was just trying to sort my own head because I wouldn't be the type of player that would feel confident at half-time, even if we were ten points up. I just wanted to keep the foot to the pedal and keep driving on. You can't be thinking any other way, especially as a goalie.'

The Cork players, meanwhile, were all in the warm-up area, except Cusack who was still in the dressing room. He asked selector Seanie O'Leary if he needed to know anything and then he changed the grip on his hurley, checked his boots and his gear and made sure he had enough sliotars in his bag for the second half. He could hear his team-mates roaring in the next room but as always he detached himself to keep his head clear.

They eventually called for Cusack and he took his time before going into the warm-up area. The mood was a bit calmer then but the volume was turned up through the roof when they gathered in a huddle four minutes later before they went back onto the field.

'There's no way,' roared Brian Corcoran 'that we're coming back in this door a beaten team!'

It only took Cork two minutes to get level after the break when Niall McCarthy fired over a point from close range. At that stage, Cusack was trying to keep himself warm in the goal and he picked a sliotar out of his bag and hammered it into the side netting. Then he broke into his sharp feet movement drill to keep his legs warm and his toes sharp.

Shefflin and Kieran Murphy traded scores before Tommy Walsh won a Cusack puckout and fed the ball to John Hoyne, who was dragged down by John Gardiner for a free 25 metres from goal. Diarmuid O'Sullivan picked up the sliotar and threw it back in to Cusack to check if it was a brand new sliotar. The goalkeeper looked at it and threw it back out to Shefflin.

After the pointed free, Cusack arrowed the puckout straight out to Niall McCarthy who darted up the sideline and struck the ball off his hurley and straight over the bar to level the scores for the fifth time in the match. As McGarry pucked out, Cusack was lacing sliotars against the side netting to keep himself warm and his striking fluent.

On fifty four minutes he picked out Tom Kenny with another beautiful puckout and the midfielder offloaded it to Niall McCarthy for another fine score. The second the ball went over the bar, Cusack ran from his line and punched the air three times. That was what they had planned. He wasn't putting the ball at risk inside his own '65 but the space had finally opened up and his potential targets were making themselves more available. Their strategy was working.

Kilkenny came back at them from McGarry's puckout but they were struggling to find their scoring range. They dropped two balls short within the space of forty five seconds and Cusack dealt with them smartly. After he fielded the second one, he got out past Shefflin and picked out Kieran Murphy. The corner-forward was fouled and Ben O'Connor converted the free to send Cork three in front. Cusack just went back in and clanked his studs off the butt of the right post.

By that stage Cork had created five more scoring chances and the game was slipping from Kilkenny. They needed to make something happen fast to arrest the trend. They hadn't scored for twelve minutes when McGarry pucked out on fifty eight minutes and the ball travelled over Ronan Curran and John Hoyne and into the path of DJ Carey. He lost his hurley and was bottled up by Diarmuid O'Sullivan outside the 45 metre line but he got off a reverse hand-pass that flew nearly thirty yards into John Hoyne's hand. Carey had completely split open the Cork defence and now Kilkenny were two on one with the goalkeeper.

Wayne Sherlock had to leave Henry Shefflin in front of goal and go to the man in possession.

'Shefflin's in,' Cusack thought to himself.

Hoyne slipped the ball into Shefflin.

'Stand up,' Cusack said to himself.

Shefflin didn't try to catch the ball and he doubled on it just eight metres from goal. As soon as he wound up, a vision of the net rattling was forming in the collective mind's eye of the crowd.

Cusack stood tall, held his ground and tried to make the target as small as possible. Shefflin connected well on the sliotar but Cusack got his body behind the ball and stopped it.

'If he'd mishit it, the ball would probably have gone past me.'

He went to ground but he didn't know where the ball had gone and he turned around frantically searching for it. It was lying underneath him but he coolly roll-lifted it, got up, took his four steps, drew Shefflin in for the block and slipped the ball to Wayne Sherlock five metres away. The corner-back handpassed it to Jerry O'Connor, the midfielder picked out Niall McCarthy with a 35 metre pass and McCarthy drove it into Joe Deane who had peeled off his marker. When James Ryall upended Deane for a free outside the 20-metre line, Sherlock ran in towards Cusack and the goalkeeper just edged out past him. He clenched his fist and pumped it forward.

Deliverance was close at hand but Cusack couldn't sanction any thoughts on the outcome. After Deane pointed the free, the keeper walked out towards the 20-metre line.

'Remember all the long nights now Sull,' he said to O'Sullivan. 'Remember all the bad nights. Keep thinking, keep concentrating, keep going.'

Another Deane free pushed Cork further ahead and when a Hoyne pull across Kieran Murphy set up Ben O'Connor with another scoreable free on sixty six minutes, McGarry just put his hands on his hips and shook his head. It was his fifth All-Ireland and he'd never been in a position where the game was gone from them with five minutes left.

'The second half flew but that happens when you're behind. After Henry had the chance, I just thought "that was the one". You're hoping you might get back into the match after that but the game is over before you realise it.'

Kilkenny failed to score in the last twenty five minutes and after Brian Corcoran scored Cork's seventeenth point a minute into injury time, MacSuibhne blew the final whistle. McGarry just turned and picked up his gear and headed for the tunnel. At the other end of the field, Cusack just stood still before Jim McEvoy grabbed him and hugged him. For a couple of seconds, it appeared that he was frozen to the spot. Then it finally hit him.

The whole full-back line were about thirty yards from goal but each one of them instinctively turned and ran towards Cusack. John Browne ran to the keeper and Cusack dodged him with a body swerve. Wayne Sherlock took off after him and Diarmuid O'Sullivan just flung himself down on the ground in front of his lifelong friend. Cusack ran towards the Cusack Stand, roared to release his pent-up emotion, and then went down on one knee and just slapped his hurley into the turf. It was like as if all the pain and mental suffering had passed from his body to his stick and he was finally burying the hurt in the only place he could.

Twelve months ago to the day, he had spoken to his team-mates through the coma of defeat and asked them to make a promise to do whatever it took to get back and heal the hurt. That was what had driven Cusack all year and they had finally delivered on their promise. The bad memory of last year's final had just been exorcised from his brain. All the inner pain and longing had been washed away. He'd finally found what he'd been looking for. Finally.

'The way the other players ran to Ogie summed it all up,' said Ger Cunningham. 'He is their real leader. He was the main man during the strike and he is the guy they all look up to. He is the main man in this team.'

Cusack was swallowed up in the crowd as all the other Cork players had made it to steps of the Hogan Stand. McGarry was trying to come to terms with the defeat but he was one of a cluster of Kilkenny players who had stayed out in the tunnel and he was making it his business to shake hands with as many Cork players as possible.

He embraced Joe Deane and when he grabbed Wayne Sherlock by the hand, the corner-back was in a daze and it never registered. It did with Diarmuid O'Sullivan and when McGarry spotted Seán Óg Ó hAilpín, the Cork man clasped the Kilkenny man's hand in a massive exchange of respect. McGarry, though, was still visibly looking around for one man in particular.

'Donal Óg made it his business to come to me last year and I wanted to congratulate him.'

Eventually McGarry spotted him. Cusack caught his eye and although there were people jumping on top of him, they shook hands with the warmth of that special goalkeeping bond. Respect. Absolute and total.

McGarry lay up against the wall of the tunnel alongside the devastated Martin Comerford. The steps up the right-hand side to the presentation area were blocked and Cusack wanted to be at the top so he walked over and made his way up the steps on the left side. When he reached the podium, he stood in front of the cup and just raised his two arms in delight. The crowd responded with a huge acknowledgement and Cusack caught his jersey at the crest with his left hand and pulled it out towards the crowd.

He had no sooner turned around when Donal O'Grady had come across the podium. He shouted at Cusack before cupping the keeper's face in his hands and planting a kiss on his cheek. The two men embraced before Cusack wrapped his arms tightly around Tom Kenny. When Ben O'Connor raised the Liam McCarthy Cup over his head, the goalkeeper shut his eyes, raised his head and roared to the heavens.

Deliverance.

At last.

EPILOGUE:
RESPECT AND HONOUR

The long journey had finally ended for Donal Óg Cusack. He had experienced the explosion of emotion on the field but the dressing room was just a deep inhalation of satisfaction. He took deep breaths and savoured the sweet sensation. There was no shouting or roaring. Just peace and satisfaction in Cusack's heart and mind. And deep in his soul.

He sat down quietly in his cubicle in the dressing room, just enjoying the feeling of having played and won together with his team-mates. At this particular time in their lives, this All-Ireland had mattered most to them. They had fulfilled their promise and now Cusack and all his friends could live the realistic dream that he spoke about the Friday night before the Munster final. They wouldn't have that pain deep inside their guts anymore. His head would be clear over the winter. No matter where they all were.

After a few minutes of quietly basking in the warm afterglow, Cusack went to each member of the squad and either embraced them or shook their hand. He remembered talking to John Browne at Wayne Sherlock's wedding last year and Browne telling him of the dream he had that they would both play together in this year's All-Ireland final. Browne wasn't on the panel last year but his dream had come through. So had the goalkeeper's.

Cusack had come up through the ranks together with most of his team-mates and their brotherhood had been cast in blood after the strike two years before. He had come to know and trust the new panel members and to totally respect their dedication to the cause. Cusack was sitting beside Paul Tierney and he caught him by the hand and told him it was an honour to train with him. He was a peripheral, almost unknown member of the squad, but Tierney's sacrifice and application made Cusack look up to him nearly more than any other member of the set-up.

That was the real satisfaction for Cusack. The dressing room was a priceless memory but it was just part of a beautiful collage. As Muhammad Ali once famously noted, the fight is won or lost far away from witnesses, behind the lines, in the gym and out on the road, long before it's time to dance under the lights. The really memorable moments were the private ones away from the bright lights, when all they had was grit in their hands and they panned it into gold.

The three-mile training run under the searing sun on the sand in China Beach that nearly killed Mickey O'Connell. The day they spent in Killaloe Adventure Centre in Clare when Brian Corcoran was in great form and they all knew he was really back. The brilliant training session the Wednesday night after the Munster final when their world looked to be caving in. And the night before the League game in Galway when Cusack, Tierney, Adrian Coughlan, John Gardiner and Sean Óg Ó hAilpín spent hours playing a ferociously competitive game up against a wall under a dimly lit streetlamp. Just a few lads having fun.

Brian Cody came into the Cork dressing room and made a fine, sporting speech to the players and Cusack went up and shook his hand afterwards. Outside the ground, all Cusack's family and friends were walking tall, happy and content after enduring all the criticism and bad days with their son, brother and friend. It was nearly as sweet for them as it was for the goalkeeper.

Over half an hour later, Cusack and Sean Óg Ó hAilpín were the last two to leave the dressing room. The two sat there momentarily, content that all their hard work and training had paid off. The 7am training sessions they did in Vietnam had served their purpose. It was a special moment.

James McGarry was long gone at that stage. He was devastated but he was coping fine. The moment he entered the dressing room after the match, he spotted the pain and the hurt and the deep sense of loss on the faces of Richie and Paddy Mullally. Kilkenny had lost an All-Ireland but the two lads had just lost their father. It put everything into perspective.

At the end of any year, only two goalkeepers get the opportunity to play in an All-Ireland final. Cusack and McGarry are the lucky ones. Cusack has played in three finals and McGarry has featured in five but they have earned their right and their place in history. Along with Tom Mulcahy and Dave Creedon from Cork and John Commins from Galway, Cusack had just become the fourth keeper in the history of hurling to keep two clean sheets in All-Ireland finals. McGarry meanwhile had just quietly walked into folklore, without any fanfare or acknowledgement of his achievement. He is the first hurling goalkeeper to keep three clean sheets in All-Ireland finals.

Goalkeepers never attract those laurels but they don't expect them. Cusack and McGarry have shown what it takes to survive at the top level but they have also shown the character that is required to be a goalkeeper of this standard. As have all the hurling goalkeepers that play at this level. Keepers tend to be lone minded because they have to be but they'll only survive through a rigorously policed policy of self-discipline and brutal honesty. It's the same with any serious athlete, but goalkeepers have long accepted a much more savage equation.

Very few team players in any sport and certainly no other GAA players, in hurling or football, live and die as treacherously by the sword in the way that the hurling goalkeeper does. Football goalkeepers have to deal with the same mental anguish and pressures but they can get their two hands behind a much bigger ball that is travelling a lot slower than a rocket of a sliotar.

Outfield, where perfection is unasked for and often deemed unexpected, mistakes are passed over in silence or lost in the fluid instability of the match. But for a goalkeeper, reputation, pride, confidence and ultimately the ability to perform the most basic hurling skills are exposed and open to be destroyed every single time a goalkeeper goes out on the field. At any level, but particularly inter-county level. The bad one can always be the next one. And if it comes, there is no redemption from the past. Hero for a day. Villain for life.

Hurling, like a lot of team sports, often finds it hard to look goalkeeping in the face. Even though they are loved, goalkeepers are too often inherently distrusted. Although hurling goalkeepers show the greatest bravery imaginable and perform some of the most artistic skills and acts possible on a sporting stage, scepticism largely trails them. Unfairly so.

They are routinely blamed for faults, which are clearly not theirs and they carry a disproportionate level of blame, which they're entitled to. Three missed scoreable frees never equals the concession of a poor goal. They're expected to be supermen who possess the reflexes of Spiderman and who can stop bullets like Batman. Because some shots really travel like bullets.

They're not padded up like ice-hockey or hockey keepers and yet they're expected to stop shots with their body if they can't get there with their hurley. They have to catch a small ball while looking into a blazing sun and deal with spinning, looping, deceptive shots that are kicking and skidding on the turf while forwards are converging. They can place pinpoint puckouts into a team-mate's hand forty five metres away and are still hammered for not driving the ball further.

They have to perform against the wide assumption that goalkeeping is easy and any fool could do it but only the bravest ever will put their neck on the line. Only the bravest will bite the bullet and run the risk of the humiliation and mental torture that Stevie Brenner suffered in the Munster final. Or risk the pain that Seamus Shinnors will carry with him for the rest of his life. Or the stigma that Eoin McMahon has been unfairly labelled with. Or risk losing an eye like Tommy Coen, or a testicle like Joe Quaid. Or the verbal abuse that Davy Fitzgerald has to put up with.

Yet like Timmy Houlihan, they all keep coming back for more because it is in their blood. It is who they are. Goalkeeping is precariously balanced between failure and triumph and in lots of ways, it mirrors real life. Except it is a life on the edge and perhaps that is the real attraction to it. Because a hurling goalkeeper will only survive by being honourable and true to himself.

Donal Óg Cusack has a tattoo on his back, just under his right shoulder. He got it in Spain four years ago while the Cork squad was on holidays. It's a Japanese symbol that stands for two words. Respect and Honour.

It's a perfect code for hurling warriors. And particularly for the last warrior. The true, sole warrior at the last line of defence.

Respect and Honour to the Last Man Standing.

MORE BEST-SELLING GAA SPORTS BOOKS FROM THE O'BRIEN PRESS

Munster Hurling Legends

Eamonn Sweeney

In Munster, hurling is a religion. This superbly illustrated book is a unique record and celebration of the star players, the incredible games and the legends and lore that surround this, the fastest field game in the world.

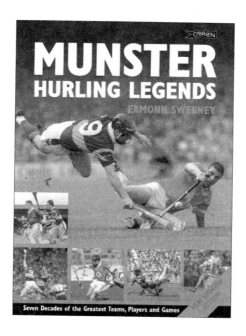

'Sweeney has a wonderful ability to merge the art of storytelling into the provision of a history lesson ... this effort is a joy as he weaves the reader through the ages.'
The Irish Examiner

'A zestfully written, hugely entertaining account by a top-class ink slinger.'
The Irish Independent

O'Brien Pocket History of Gaelic Sport

Eamonn Sweeney

A concise introduction to Gaelic sport, covering football, hurling, camogie and handball. This book deals with the origins of these games and their revival, the history of the championships and the GAA, the rules and scoring systems, famous teams and players, great GAA grounds, All-Star awards and tours, the gear and the trophies, as well as compromise games with Aussie rules.

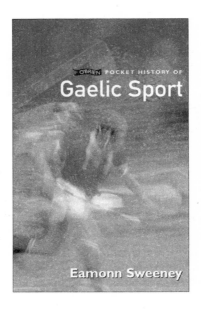